JavaScript®
Weekend Crash Course™

JavaScript®
Weekend Crash Course™

Steven W. Disbrow

Hungry Minds™

Hungry Minds, Inc.
New York, NY • Cleveland, OH • Indianapolis, IN

JavaScript® Weekend Crash Course™
Published by
Hungry Minds, Inc.
909 Third Avenue
New York, NY 10022
www.hungryminds.com

Library of Congress Control Number: 2001016760

ISBN: 0-7645-4804-2

Printed in the United States of America

10 9 8 7 6 5 4 3 2 1

1B/SV/QU/QR/IN

Distributed in the United States by Hungry Minds, Inc.

Distributed by CDG Books Canada Inc. for Canada; by Transworld Publishers Limited in the United Kingdom; by IDG Norge Books for Norway; by IDG Sweden Books for Sweden; by IDG Books Australia Publishing Corporation Pty. Ltd. for Australia and New Zealand; by TransQuest Publishers Pte Ltd. for Singapore, Malaysia, Thailand, Indonesia, and Hong Kong; by Gotop Information Inc. for Taiwan; by ICG Muse, Inc. for Japan; by Intersoft for South Africa; by Eyrolles for France; by International Thomson Publishing for Germany, Austria, and Switzerland; by Distribuidora Cuspide for Argentina; by LR International for Brazil; by Galileo Libros for Chile; by Ediciones ZETA S.C.R. Ltda. for Peru; by WS Computer Publishing Corporation, Inc., for the Philippines; by Contemporanea de Ediciones for Venezuela; by Express Computer Distributors for the Caribbean and West Indies; by Micronesia Media Distributor, Inc. for Micronesia; by Chips Computadoras S.A. de C.V. for Mexico; by Editorial Norma de Panama S.A. for Panama; by American Bookshops for Finland.

For general information on Hungry Minds' products and services please contact our Customer Care department within the U.S. at 800-762-2974, outside the U.S. at 317-572-3993 or fax 317-572-4002.

For sales inquiries and reseller information, including discounts, premium and bulk quantity sales, and foreign-language translations, please contact our Customer Care department at 800-434-3422, fax 317-572-4002 or write to Hungry Minds, Inc., Attn: Customer Care Department, 10475 Crosspoint Boulevard, Indianapolis, IN 46256.

For information on licensing foreign or domestic rights, please contact our Sub-Rights Customer Care department at 212-884-5000.

For information on using Hungry Minds' products and services in the classroom or for ordering examination copies, please contact our Educational Sales department at 800-434-2086 or fax 317-572-4005.

For press review copies, author interviews, or other publicity information, please contact our Public Relations department at 317-572-3168 or fax 317-572-4168.

For authorization to photocopy items for corporate, personal, or educational use, please contact Copyright Clearance Center, 222 Rosewood Drive, Danvers, MA 01923, or fax 978-750-4470.

About the Author

Steven W. Disbrow (a.k.a. "Diz") is a freelance writer, technical instructor, and programmer. He was the publisher of *GS+ Magazine* from 1989 to 1995. Since then, he's been writing articles for various technical publications and is the current "JavaScripting" columnist for *Java Report* magazine. He also creates and delivers courseware for most Web-based technologies including JavaScript, HTML, and XML. This is his first book.

Credits

Acquisitions Editor
Debra Williams Cauley

Project Editors
Barbra Guerra
Neil Romanosky

Technical Editor
Galen Mayfield

Copy Editor
Maarten Reilingh

Project Coordinator
Dale White

Graphics and Production Specialists
Joe Bucki
Sean Decker

Quality Control Technicians
Laura Albert
Andy Hollandbeck

Permissions Editor
Laura Moss

Media Development Specialist
Travis Silvers

Media Development Coordinator
Marisa Pearman

Proofreading and Indexing
York Production Services, Inc.

This book is dedicated to everyone who supported **GS+** *Magazine, my parents, and Robin and Maia.*

Preface

This book is for anyone who needs to learn how to create a JavaScript-based Web site. If you have no programming experience, you'll find a complete introduction to the JavaScript language along with examples of how to carry out common Web-programming tasks. If you already know about "JavaScript the language," you'll find a ton of tips and techniques that you can use to enhance your existing Web sites.

Who Should Read this Book

If you need to put together a Web site that does something more than just sit there, this book is for you. Over the course of one weekend, you'll learn about the JavaScript language and how it fits into the scheme of Web page creation. Along the way, you'll learn about lots of other Web-based technologies and how JavaScript can work with them to create interactive and interesting Web sites.

It's important to note that this is *not* a JavaScript reference book! If you are looking for table after table of JavaScript language minutiae, you won't find it here. Instead, you'll find examples of how JavaScript can be used to solve real Web-programming challenges.

What's in this Book

This book is divided into 30 sessions, each addressing one aspect of the JavaScript language or some technique for which JavaScript can be used. Each of these sessions should take you about 30 minutes to get through, although you can expect to spend more time with each session if you examine the source code on the accompanying CD-ROM. Because the goal of this book is to teach you the basics of JavaScript in a weekend, it's been broken into six parts:

- Part I contains four lessons (which should take about two hours to complete) that will teach you the basics of the JavaScript language and how JavaScript fits into a Web page.

- Part II is six sessions long (and should take about three hours to complete). It will introduce you to some of JavaScript's built-in objects, the Browser Object Model, and the concept of browser events.

- Part III is also six sessions in length. The focus of this part of the book is on how JavaScript can be used to dynamically create HTML and manipulate the various controls that are found in an HTML form.

- Part IV is just four sessions long, but that's just enough time to give you an understanding of how you can create your own objects with JavaScript and use them to enhance your Web pages. The last session in this part also tells you how you can dynamically build and execute JavaScript statements *after* your Web page has been loaded.

- Part V is six sessions long. The sessions in this part focus on identifying different browsers, using Dynamic HTML and Cascading Style Sheets, and working with windows and frames.

- Part VI is four sessions long and focuses on how JavaScript can be used to communicate with other processes. These include server-side CGI processes, browser plug-ins, and Java applets.

At the end of each session, you'll find a short summary and a set of questions, both designed to remind you of what you've learned in that session. At the end of each part, you'll find twenty questions that will test how much you actually remember from the previous sessions. Some of these will be simple short-answer questions, but many are actual programming puzzles. You are encouraged to try and solve these on your own, but, if you need the answers right away, you'll find them on your CD-ROM. Once you've finished the entire book, you'll probably want to try the self-assessment test on the CD-ROM. This is a simple multiple-choice test that will give you a good idea of how much you've actually learned.

In keeping with the title *Weekend Crash Course,* you'll find that this book is about learning how to *get things done* with JavaScript. Because of that, this book is a bit different from most of the other JavaScript books out there. Whereas most books start off by telling you how fragmented the JavaScript "standard" is (each version of each browser has its own flavor of JavaScript) and then spend a tremendous amount of time teaching you how to work around all the differences, you'll be learning techniques that should work in *all* of the various browsers. Of course, you *will* learn how to work around browser differences, but you'll find that it isn't that hard or even all that necessary when using the latest browsers.

The text itself is adorned with icons designed to catch your attention.

**30 Min.
To Go**

The "minutes to go" icons mark your progress in the session.

The Tip icon offers information that can save you time and effort.

The Note icons highlight incidental or technical information that clarifies and expands the discussion.

The CD-ROM icon refers to material furnished on the book's CD. Use it to find electronic versions of programs and software elements mentioned in the text.

Acknowledgments

Of course, I have to thank Neil Romanosky, Barbra Guerra, Galen Mayfield, Maarten Reilingh, Dale White, Debra Williams Cauley, and all the other great folks at Hungry Minds. I had always feared that writing a book would be hard, but these guys made it seem like a piece of cake.

I'd also like to thank Lisa Swayne and everyone at the Swayne Agency for taking a chance on me and looking out for me.

Finally, I need to thank Zack Czengöldi, Jami Lowery, and Jeff Berger for donating their time and effort to "reality check" the book as I wrote it. Thanks, guys!

Contents at a Glance

Contents

Contents

☑ **Friday**

☐ Saturday

☐ Sunday

Part I — Friday Evening

Session 1
Getting to Know JavaScript

Session 2
Statements and Operators

Session 3
Flow of Control Statements

Session 4
How to Write JavaScript Functions

PART

I

Friday
Evening

Getting to Know JavaScript

Session Checklist

✔ Learning a bit of JavaScript's history

✔ Understanding what JavaScript can and can't do

✔ Understanding how JavaScript fits into a Web page

✔ Creating your first JavaScript-based Web page

**30 Min.
To Go**

In the beginning, the Web was void and without form... Well, OK. It wasn't really "void," but boy was it dull! Oh sure, you could find lots of technical papers and Web sites with information about various hobbies and such, but it was all very static and very, very dull. Then the folks at Netscape (makers of the Netscape Navigator Web browser) decided that the Web would be much more interesting if users could actually interact with the contents of Web pages. So, they created a scripting language called "LiveScript."

The idea was that Web page authors would place small blocks of LiveScript code into their Web pages. These "scripts," as they were called, could interact directly with the elements of the Web page (for example, by inserting a string into a text box or popping up an alert window to give the user a message of some sort), creating a more interesting experience for the end user.

What's that? You've never heard of LiveScript? That's not too surprising, actually, since LiveScript never made it out of the lab... at least not under that name.
You see, at about the same time that Netscape was set to release LiveScript, Sun
Microsystems announced the imminent release of a new programming language
called Java.

Java appeared to have a lot going for it: Sun claimed that it was small (so you
could use it in a lot of different places, including the Web), familiar (it was based
on the C programming language, with which *millions* of programmers were familiar)
and it would, eventually, run everywhere. For these reasons, and many more, Java
became the hottest buzzword in the computing industry. Java's sudden popularity
got the attention of the folks at Netscape, so they looked at it and noticed something very interesting: LiveScript and Java *looked* a lot like each other. The reason
for this was that LiveScript, like Java, was based on the C programming language.
In fact, the two were so similar in appearance, that if you simply glanced at a
block of LiveScript or Java code, you might not be able to tell them apart!

With all the "buzz" surrounding Java, Netscape decided to change the name of
LiveScript to JavaScript. This was an excellent move on Netscape's part. The name
change got people to notice and try JavaScript, and the fact that it was actually a
powerful language that could do amazing things got them to create Web pages that
relied on it. So it wasn't long before JavaScript-enhanced Web pages began popping up all over the Web.

Eventually, JavaScript found its way into *millions* of Web pages. In fact,
JavaScript became *so* popular that Microsoft decided to create its own version
(cleverly named JScript) for use in their Internet Explorer Web browser.
Unfortunately, JScript was just different enough that lots of programs written for
it wouldn't work in Netscape Navigator (and vice versa). This cost a lot of programmers a lot of time as they struggled to create programs that worked in both
browsers.

After a few years of this, everyone involved decided that a standardized version
of JavaScript would be a good idea, so they called upon the European Computer
Manufacturer's Association (an independent standards organization) to help create
one. The result was called *ECMAScript*, though most folks still just call it
"JavaScript." ECMAScript is the version of JavaScript that you'll find in the most
modern browsers, and it's the one that I'll be focusing on in this book.

**Throughout the book, I'll be using the terms "program" and
"script" to refer to blocks of JavaScript code. While JavaScript is
technically "just a scripting language," it has all the computa-
tional power of a "real" programming language. Besides, saying
"JavaScript script" sounds silly when compared to "JavaScript
program."**

So, What Can JavaScript Do?

In today's world, *everything* is hyped to the point that no matter how good something actually is, once you get your hands on it, you can't help but be disappointed. Fortunately, like this book, JavaScript is one of the rare exceptions that probably *won't* leave you feeling let down! Among other things, JavaScript can:

- Generate custom Web pages and dynamically alter the appearance of a Web page
- Validate the contents of a form on a Web page
- Communicate with Java "applets" in a Web page
- Create custom animations on a Web page
- Perform traditional programming language tasks

You might have noticed that most of the entries in this list involve Web pages. However, JavaScript isn't just restricted to Web browsers. Netscape has a server-side version of JavaScript (called LiveWire or simply Server-Side JavaScript), and Microsoft has included server-side JScript support in their Web server as well. Both of these allow you to write server-side JavaScript programs that can perform all kinds of cool and useful tasks. For example, you could pull data out of a database and present it on your Web pages, if you had the urge! Microsoft has even integrated JScript support into the Window's Scripting Host (WSH). This means that you can write JavaScript programs to automate tasks in Windows 95 and later. In this book, however, we'll be concentrating on JavaScript as it is used inside your favorite Web browser. The main reason for this is that once you learn JavaScript for the Web, you can easily take that knowledge and apply it to any of these other environments.

So, in order to complete the exercises in this book, you *must* use a JavaScript-capable Web browser. Fortunately, both of the "big-name" Web browsers (Netscape Navigator and Internet Explorer) support JavaScript. If you don't have one of these browsers, you'll find them, along with all of the source code from the book, on the enclosed CD-ROM. Unless otherwise noted, all of the code in this book is "browser-agnostic" and should work with the latest version of either browser. (At the time of publication, that's version 6 of Netscape Navigator and version 5.5 of Internet Explorer.) If you want to write browser-specific code, we'll be covering that in Session 26 on Sunday.

What JavaScript Can't Do

Of course, JavaScript isn't perfect. While JavaScript is very powerful, it's also had some pretty severe restrictions placed upon it. (Note that these restrictions are mostly found in the JavaScript that runs inside your Web browser. Other JavaScript environments are a bit less restrictive.)

- JavaScript can't read, write, create, or delete disk files. This is strictly a security issue. After all, you wouldn't want to open a Web page that trashed all the files on your hard disk, would you? (JavaScript *can* create and manipulate cookies (which we will discuss tomorrow afternoon in Session 16), but this ability is tightly controlled by the Web browser itself.)

- JavaScript can't perform operations over the network. (An exception to this rule is that JavaScript can force the Web browser to open a different Web page, which can be anywhere on the Web.)

- JavaScript can't create stand-alone software. Remember, JavaScript began life as a way to add interactivity to otherwise static Web pages. So, JavaScript always has been (and probably always will be) a scripting language. All that means is that it's intended to control (or "script") the operation of another program — in this case, a Web browser. If you want to write a stand-alone piece of software, you'll need to use a more traditional language like Java, C, or C++.

- While JavaScript *looks* like Java, the two aren't the same. Due to the similar names and appearance, a lot of people are under the impression that JavaScript is just a "slimmed-down" version of Java. This simply isn't true. Java and JavaScript are two separate technologies that happen to have similar names and a similar heritage. The biggest difference between the two is that Java can create stand-alone software. While JavaScript is a powerful language in it's own right, this is something that it just can't do.

**20 Min.
To Go**

How JavaScript Fits into a Web Page

As mentioned earlier, JavaScript's main purpose is to make Web pages more interesting and/or useful. To achieve this goal, the folks that invented it decided that JavaScript programs should be embedded directly inside the Web page itself, so they invented a new HyperText Markup Language (HTML) tag that could be used to enclose JavaScript code inside a Web page. This tag is called simply the "script" tag and it looks like this:

```
<script language="javascript">
...your JavaScript code would go here...
</script>
```

As you can see, the script tag looks pretty much like every other HTML tag. There are a few differences to note though:

- It has a "language" attribute that lets you specify which programming language is used in this script block. Depending on which browser you are using, you could also specify either VBScript or PerlScript. All the major browsers, however, support JavaScript, and, since it came first, it's the default language. If you are only working with JavaScript, you don't *have* to specify a language, but you should, just so someone looking at your code will know for sure which language you are using.

- Unlike some HTML tags, you can't put other HTML inside a set of script tags. JavaScript code is the only thing you should put inside a set of script tags!

- Like most other HTML tags, a Web page can contain as many sets of script tags as you like, and you can place them just about anywhere you like inside the HTML document. However, a convention has emerged where most, if not all, of your JavaScript will probably be contained at the top of your Web page, between the <head> and </head> tags. There are, of course, exceptions to this rule, as we'll see over the next few days.

- In addition to the script tag, you can also embed JavaScript statements inside other HTML tags. These embedded JavaScript statements usually take the form of tag attributes and they are usually executed when a particular condition arises in the Web browser. (These "conditions" are called "events" and we'll be discussing them throughout the remainder of the book.)

- By this point, you are probably wondering what this looks like in a real Web page. So, here's a simple HTML file with a simple block of JavaScript code in it:

```
<html>
<body>
<script language="javascript">
document.write("Hello World!")
</script>
</body>
</html>
```

If you load this into your Web browser, you should see a page with the simple message "Hello World!" on it. Here's how the script works: First, you should notice that this is just a simple HTML file. As with every other simple HTML file you've seen, every bit of it is pure, human-readable, ASCII text. There aren't any "binaries" or "plug-ins" or anything else to worry about. This is a very important point: Like every other part of your HTML file, your JavaScript code is just plain-old ASCII text!

Since this is just a simple HTML file, it is processed like every other HTML file: from the top to the bottom. So, first the `<html>` tag is processed (which tells the Web browser to turn on its HTML parser), then the `<body>` tag and then the `<script>` tag. When the browser reaches the `<script>` tag however, it does something a little different: It turns over processing to the JavaScript interpreter that is built into the browser. The JavaScript interpreter looks at each line of JavaScript and runs it immediately. In this case, the single line of JavaScript tells the interpreter to `document.write("Hello World!")`. Without getting into too much detail, "document" is an object that represents the HTML document that's currently loaded into the Web browser. The "write" part of the statement tells the `document` object that you want to display a string in that HTML document. Finally, "Hello World!" is the string that you want to display. (We'll be looking at the `document` object in Session 9, tomorrow morning.) When the interpreter reaches the end of the script block (signified by the `</script>` tag), it turns control back over to the HTML parser. The HTML parser then finishes up by parsing the ending `</body>` and `</html>` tags and displaying the page in the browser.

The fact that JavaScript code is just simple ASCII text means that you can create your JavaScript-based HTML files using *any* editor that can save text files. For example, on the Macintosh, you can use SimpleText. If you are using Windows, you can use WordPad or even Notepad. If you are using Linux, you can use vi or any other editor that came with your distribution! Of course, you can also use a specialized editor that's intended for creating Web pages. The point however, is that you don't have to! I've built complex Web sites that were full of JavaScript using nothing more than Notepad. For this book, I'll assume that you are using HTML Kit (on Windows) or BBEdit Lite (for the Macintosh). These are freeware editors with extensions to make creating Web pages much easier.

**10 Min.
To Go**

Creating Your First JavaScript Program

I've always been of the opinion that the best way to learn a new programming language is to define a small project and then use that language to complete it. So, over the course of this weekend, that's exactly what we'll be doing. In particular, what we are going to do is create a JavaScript-based shopping cart application. Shopping carts are fairly simple, but building one will allow us to exercise almost every aspect of the JavaScript language. All we have to decide now is what we'll be putting into our shopping cart. Since everyone loves babies, our shopping cart will be for the fictional baby supply store, baby-palooza.com. Since we've already seen how to output a string in our obligatory "Hello World!" script, let's rework it a bit to create an initial welcome page for our storefront.

```html
<html>
<head><title>Welcome to Baby-Palooza!</title></head>
<body bgcolor="white">
<center><h1>
<script language="javascript">
document.write("Welcome to Baby-Palooza!")
</script>
</h1></center>
</body>
</html>
```

This is almost exactly the same as the example we looked at earlier. The main difference is that we've placed our JavaScript code smack in the middle of some HTML markup tags. The end result is, when you load this page, you get a centered heading welcoming you to the baby-palooza.com site, as shown in Figure 1-1.

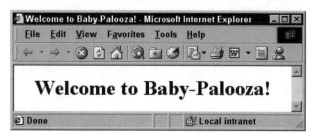

Figure 1-1
The output of the code

If you are wondering why it works this way, remember that HTML files are processed top to bottom. When the HTML parser reaches the opening `<script>` tag, it's already processed the opening `<center>` and `<h1>` tags and put them into the stream of output that will eventually end up going to the browser window. So, when the `document.write()` statement executes, its output (which is the string "Welcome to Baby-Palooza!") is sent to this output stream as well. In fact, as far as the browser is concerned, the code you just saw might as well have looked exactly like this:

```
<html>
<head><title>Welcome to Baby-Palooza!</title></head>
<body bgcolor="white">
<center><h1>Welcome to Baby-Palooza!</h1></center>
</body>
</html>
```

Done!

Being able to mix HTML tags with the output of JavaScript statements is one of the most powerful features of a JavaScript-capable browser. In fact, this ability is the heart and soul of the dynamic, interactive Web that we've come to know and love!

REVIEW

In this session, you learned about the history of JavaScript. More importantly, you learned how JavaScript fits into a Web page. We also briefly touched on how HTML pages are parsed and the fact that you can mix the output of JavaScript with HTML tags. Everything else that we discuss this weekend is built on these concepts, so be sure you've got a good handle on them before proceeding!

QUIZ YOURSELF

1. Is JavaScript just a "slimmed-down" version of Java? (See "What JavaScript Can't Do.")

2. What are some of the things JavaScript can do? (See "So, What Can JavaScript Do?")

3. What are some things JavaScript *can't* do? (See "What JavaScript Can't Do.")

4. What is the purpose of the `<script></script>` tags? (See "How JavaScript Fits into a Web Page.")

5. What kind of editor must you use to create Web pages with JavaScript in them? (See "How JavaScript Fits into a Web Page.")

Statements and Operators

Session Checklist

✔ Writing assignment statements

✔ Creating and using variables

✔ Understanding JavaScript data types and variable naming
  conventions

✔ Becoming familiar with all assignment and mathematical operators

✔ Putting comments in your JavaScript

**30 Min.
To Go**

Being a descendant of the C language, JavaScript comes with a wide variety
of statement types and operators. These can seem baffling at first, but
you'll find that for the most common programming tasks (like assigning a
value to something or comparing things), you only need to be familiar with a
handful of them.

Assignment Statements

The most basic of JavaScript statements is the assignment statement. As the name implies, the purpose of an assignment statement is to assign a value to a variable. Here are some examples:

```
fName = "Maia";
lName = 'Disbrow';
count = 10
pi = 3.14159;
```

As with most other languages, the structure of these statements is quite simple: A variable on the left-hand side of the equal sign takes on the value that is on the right-hand side of the equal sign. Even though these are simple statements, they actually demonstrate a couple of important rules of JavaScript programming:

- You can enclose strings in either single-quotes (' ') or double-quotes (" "). The quotes you use are really just a matter of your preference. Also, a string enclosed in one type of quote can contain the other type of quote. However, if you are going to nest quotes, you can only do so up to one level deep. For example, the string "Brian O'Toole" is enclosed in double-quotes and contains a single-quote. This is perfectly legal. However, the string "Brian O'Toole says, "Top 'o the morning!"" would be illegal, because you can't have double-quotes inside double-quotes. (There is a way around this limitation, which we'll discuss in Session 5.)

- JavaScript statements must end with a semicolon... or not! In JavaScript, a semicolon marks the end of a statement. However, the end of a line also marks the end of a statement. So, if you place only one statement on each line, you do not have to use semicolons at all. However, if you want (or need) to place more than one statement on a single line, you can do so simply by placing a semicolon at the end of each one. For example, our example statements could have been written on a single line, like so:

```
fName = "Maia"; lName = "Disbrow"; count = 10;
```

JavaScript Variables

In some other programming languages, you have to declare your variables before you use them. Not only that, when you declare a variable, you have to specify what kind of data it will hold (an integer, a string, and so on). JavaScript does things a bit differently: In JavaScript, you create a variable simply by assigning a value to it. At that point, your variable is ready to use. If you are used to declaring your variables before using them, this shortened process can take a bit of getting used to. But once you've worked with it a while, you'll find it to be quite a bit easier.

Data types

Something that's a bit harder to deal with is the fact that JavaScript variables are *loosely typed*. This means that when you create a variable, the value you assign to it determines its type. So, if you assign a string to a variable, it's a string variable. To complicate matters further, you can actually assign *any* type of value to *any* variable; regardless of what type of value it currently holds! Consider the following code:

```
myVar = "Hello";
document.write( myVar);
myVar = 100;
document.write( myVar);
myVar = "Goodbye!";
document.write( myVar);
```

Here, we create the variable myVar and assign a string to it. After displaying this string, we assign it an integer and display that. Then, to bring things full circle, we assign another string to myVar and display it. As you might imagine, loose data typing is a *very* powerful feature of JavaScript that allows you to write some very flexible code. However, if you abuse this feature, it can lead to problems that are difficult to track down and fix. My advice is to assign only one type of data to any given variable and use this feature only when absolutely necessary.

At this point, you might be wondering what basic data types are actually available to JavaScript programs. At the lowest level, there are really only four JavaScript data types: integers, floating point numbers, characters, and Booleans (true or false). All of the other types you'll encounter in JavaScript are *objects* that combine these basic data types in some way. Strings, for example, are objects that represent collections of characters. We'll discuss these other data types as we encounter them and we'll discuss the topic of objects in great detail on Saturday evening.

JavaScript actually allows you to specify your numbers in four different formats: floating point, integers, octal, and hexadecimal. You are probably already familiar with floating point and integer numbers, but octal and hexadecimal might be new to you. Basically, octal and hexadecimal numbers are integers that are expressed in a different numerical *base*. Normal integers are base 10 (also known as decimal) while octal numbers are base 8 and hexadecimal numbers are base 16. In JavaScript, you can specify that a number is octal by starting it with a zero (0). For example, the statement x = 077; would assign the octal value 77 (which is 63 in decimal) to x. Similarly, hexadecimal numbers are preceded by the characters "0x". So, the statement x = 0x3F; would assign the hexadecimal value 3F (which is also 63 in decimal) to x. If this is a bit confusing, don't worry! There are only a few instances in JavaScript programming where you have to know anything about octal or hexadecimal numbers. The point of this note is just to let you know what they are so that you'll recognize them when they pop-up.

Variable names

When you create and name a variable, there are a few rules that you have to follow:

- Variable names are case sensitive. That means that myVar and myvar are two completely different variables. (Actually, every aspect of JavaScript is case-sensitive, not just variable names. This means that if you want to write an "if" statement, you must use lowercase "if"; "IF" won't work.)

- Variable names must start with an alphabetic character, a dollar sign, or an underscore and can contain letters (a to z or A to Z), digits (0 to 9), the dollar sign ($), or the underscore character (_). No spaces or other special characters are allowed.

- For all practical purposes, variable names can be as many characters long as you want. However, to keep things manageable, you should probably keep them under 50 characters long.

To help put all of this into perspective, Table 2-1 contains examples of several valid, and invalid, JavaScript variable names.

Table 2-1
Examples of Variable Names

Valid Names	Invalid Names	Why It's Invalid
numBottles	99bottles_of_beer	Starts with a digit
_systemName	name of system	Includes spaces
$charVar	char-var	Hyphen not allowed
_99FlagVal	o'toole'sbar&grill	Apostrophe not allowed

**20 Min.
To Go**

Assignment Operators

At the beginning of this lesson, I said that the equal sign represents a "simple" assignment statement. JavaScript features a host of other assignment operators that, while not really complex, certainly aren't simple, either. These operators allow you to perform operations in a single JavaScript statement that would take two or more statements in some other languages.

The += operator

Perhaps the most useful of these other operators is the "addition with assignment" operator (+=). What does this operator do? Well, consider the following code:

```
x = 10; y = 5;
x = x + y;
```

It turns out that the operation shown here (adding two variables together and putting the result back in one of them) is so common that folks could save a lot of time if there were a shorthand operator for it. That's exactly what the += operator is. So, assuming that x and y are defined as shown in the preceding code, the following lines of code have exactly the same effect:

```
x = x + y;
x += y;
```

So, that saves us about four keystrokes, right? That might not sound like a lot, but if you multiply that over a lifetime's programming, you've seriously reduced your chances for a repetitive stress injury!

Other assignment operators

So, what are the other assignment operators? Table 2-2 has the answers.

Table 2-2
JavaScript Assignment Operators

Operator	Operation	Sample Code	Equivalent To
=	Simple assignment	x = y;	N/A
+=	Assignment with addition	x += y;	x = x + y;
-=	Assignment with subtraction	x -= y;	x = x - y;
*=	Assignment with multiplication	x *= y;	x = x * y;
/=	Assignment with division	x /= y;	x = x / y;
%=	Assignment with modulo	x %= y;	x = x % y;
&=	Assignment with bitwise AND	x &= y;	x = x & y;
|=	Assignment with bitwise OR	x |= y;	x = x | y;
^=	Assignment with bitwise XOR	x ^= y;	x = x ^ y;

Hopefully, most of the operators in this table will seem straightforward to you. The last four however, involve mathematical operations that you might not be familiar with. So, let's talk about mathematical operators.

Mathematical Operators

Thus far, all we've looked at are simple assignments: copying one variable to another or setting a variable to some simple value. In the real world, most assignment statements involve some sort of calculation. So, JavaScript is equipped with several different mathematical operators to make those operations as easy as possible. These are shown in Table 2-3.

Table 2-3
JavaScript Mathematical Operators[1]

Operator	Operation	Sample Code	Result	Equivalent To
++	Increment by 1	x++	11	x = x + 1;
- -	Decrement by 1	x- -	9	x = x - 1;
+	Addition	z = x + y	13	N/A
-	Subtraction	z = x - y	7	N/A
*	Multiplication	z = x * y	30	N/A
/	Division	z = x / y	3	N/A
%	Modulus	z = x % y	1	N/A
&	Bitwise AND	z = x & y	2	N/A
|	Bitwise OR	z = x | y	11	N/A
^	Bitwise XOR	z = x ^ y	9	N/A

[1] *For all examples, assume x is 10, y is 3, and z is 0.*

Since you are almost certainly aware of the four basic math operations of addition, subtraction, multiplication, and division, let's look at the other operators.

The increment and decrement operators

When programming, it's often necessary to increment the value of a variable by one. For example, the following code might look *very* familiar: x = x + 1

The increment operator allows us to replace this code with the following: x++

This is *exactly* the same as the statement x = x + 1. More importantly, by having this functionality in an *operator* we can perform increment operations inside other statements! (We'll see this in Session 3, when we discuss flow of control statements.)

Another important aspect of the increment operator is that it can be used in either *prefix* or *postfix* form. In other words, you can put the operator before or after the variable you want to increment. Like so:

```
++x
x++
```

In these simple statements, the position of the increment operator doesn't really matter. However, in a more complex statement, the position of the increment operator *is* important. In prefix form (++x), the increment operation takes place *before* the value of x is used in the surrounding statement. In postfix form (x++), the increment operation takes place *after* the value of x is used in the surrounding statement. Consider this code:

```
x = 10; y = 0; z = 5;
y = z * x++;
y = z * ++x;
```

After we execute the statement, y = z * x++, the variable y will contain the value 50 and the variable x will contain the value 11. Because we used the postfix form of the increment operator, the initial value of x, 10, is used for the multiplication and the incrementing of x does not take place until after the multiplication is complete.

When we execute the next statement, y = z * ++x, the variable y will contain the value 60 and the variable x will contain the value 12. This is because, by using the prefix form of the increment operator, the value of x was increased from 11 to 12 before the multiplication occurred.

If there's an increment operator, there should be a decrement operator, right? Right! The decrement operator is represented by two minus signs, and it works just like the increment operator, except it *subtracts* one instead of adding one. For example, these two lines are equivalent:

```
x = x - 1
x--
```

Modulus operator

**10 Min.
To Go**

The increment and decrement operators are actually pretty simple once you know what they do. The modulus operator (%) however, can take some explaining. You can think of the modulus operation as a cousin of division. The difference is that a modulus operation divides its two operands and then returns the *remainder* of that division. So, going back to the example in Table 2-3, we divide 10 by 3. Three goes into 10 three times, with one (1) left over. This remainder, one, is what is returned.

Bit flag operators

The final types of mathematical operators are the bit flag operators. These operators work only with integer values and treat them as if they were a series of flags, each specifying a true or false value, instead of whole numbers. By using the bit flag operators you can find out (or change) the state of a single bit (or a set of bits) inside a value. The use of these operators is a bit complex (no pun intended) so we'll be discussing them in detail later.

Comments: The Statements That Aren't

The last type of JavaScript "statement" we need to discuss is the comment. Comments aren't really statements, they are lines or blocks of text that you put into your JavaScript code to explain what is going on. Comments can be very helpful to anyone who might have found your JavaScript code on the Internet and is trying to adapt it for their own use. Comments can also be very helpful to you. Just imagine writing a very clever piece of code and then not looking at it again for a month or longer. Without comments, there's a good chance that your own code would have you scratching your head in bewilderment.

If you want to designate a single line as a comment, you simply place two slashes (//) at the start of your comment text. For example:

```
// Now we square x
x = x * x
```

These comment markers can actually come anywhere on the line. For example:

```
x = x * x // now we square x
```

The trick is that *everything* that comes after the comment marker is treated as a comment, even JavaScript code!

```
// Both of these lines are comments and will be ignored!
// x = x * x
```

As you can see from the previous example, you can mark multiple lines as comment lines. However, if you need to mark a *lot* of lines as comment text, it can be tedious to mark each one individually. So, JavaScript allows you to mark a block of text as one big comment by enclosing it between /* and */ characters. For example:

```
/* Now we square x to achieve the desired
result */
x = x * x
```

Done!

As with single-line comments, multiple-line comments can also start anywhere on the line. Anything (even JavaScript code) between the start and ending comment markers is treated as a comment and ignored by the JavaScript interpreter.

The important thing about comments is to *use them*. Don't be afraid to sprinkle comments liberally throughout your JavaScript code. Be descriptive, be detailed, be funny if you want, just be sure to do it. The first time you have to revisit a piece of your own code, you'll be glad those comments are there.

REVIEW

In this session, you learned about simple JavaScript statements and operators. You also learned about JavaScript data types and variables. You learned how to name a variable as well as what constitutes an illegal variable name. You also found out that JavaScript variables are loosely typed. This means that they take on the type of whatever value you assign to them. It also means that any given variable can be assigned any type of data. We also went over the basic JavaScript operators and saw examples of how each one works. We'll be using these operators extensively over the next couple of days, so be sure to keep Table 2-2 and Table 2-3 earmarked for easy reference.

QUIZ YOURSELF

1. Is #_of_pies a legal JavaScript variable name? What about _numPies? Why or why not? (See "Variable names.")

2. What is wrong with the following statement? greet = "I said "Howdy!"" (See "Assignment Statements.")

3. If x is 33 and y is 67, what is the value of x after the following statement executes? x += y; (See "Other assignment operators.")

4. If x is 12, y is 4, and z is 2, what is the value of each of these variables after the following statement executes? x *= z++ * ++y; (See Table 2-2.)

5. Assuming the following is all on a single line, what is wrong with the following line of code? x = 1 y = 12 z = 100; (See "Assignment Statements.")

SESSION

3

Flow of Control Statements

Session Checklist

✔ Understanding Boolean values, expressions, and operators

✔ Understanding code blocks and flow of control statements

**30 Min.
To Go**

At this point, we've seen how JavaScript code fits into a Web page and we've seen how to create basic JavaScript statements. But, if we want to deliver truly dynamic content on our Web pages, we need to be able to make choices in our JavaScript programs.

Understanding Boolean Values and Expressions

As we saw in Session 2, JavaScript allows you to create and use variables containing *Boolean* values. "Boolean" is just a fancy word that means "true or false." So, you can create variables that look like this:

```
shoppingCartEmpty = false; readyToCheckout = true;
```

Notice that these values aren't in quotes. That's because `true` and `false` are JavaScript *keywords* that have a special meaning to the JavaScript interpreter. A *keyword* (often called a *reserved word*) is a word that is reserved for use by the

JavaScript interpreter. This means that these words can't be used for variable or function names. (We'll discuss functions in the next session.) These keywords represent Boolean or *logical* values.

If you aren't familiar with Boolean values, working with them can be a bit strange at first. Boolean values represent absolutes: A Boolean variable is either true or false — there is no middle ground. You might also want to think of Boolean values as switches representing *on* (true) or *off* (false). (You'll also find Boolean values sometimes represented by the numbers one and zero — true and false, respectively. Actually, any value other than zero can be used to represent true.)

If you compare this with a string variable (which can have an almost infinite number of values), you might think that Boolean variables are a bit useless. But, the fact that Booleans can have just two values makes them ideal for making choices in a program.

Before you can make a choice in your JavaScript program, you have to express that choice in a way that the JavaScript interpreter can understand. To do this, you have to write a Boolean (or logical) expression of some sort. Don't let this jargon scare you; a logical expression is really just a true/false question and its answer. In fact, without realizing it, you ask and answer logical questions every day of your life. Questions like, "Do I have enough money for a soda?" You answer this simply by digging the change out of your pocket, adding it up, and comparing the total to the cost of a soda. Based on the result of the comparison (true or false), you either buy the soda or you don't. Asking logical questions in a JavaScript program is just as easy. You simply compare the value of one variable (the amount of change in your pockets) to some other value (the cost of the soda) and then react based on the result (which is true or false).

Comparison operators

In the above example, the comparison we were making was to see if the amount of change we had was less than or equal to the cost of a soda. However, there are lots of other types of comparisons you can make in JavaScript. Each type of comparison has its own operator and the result of any of these comparisons will be either a true or false Boolean value. Table 3-1 shows these operators and gives an example of their use. The first four of these operators should be familiar from high school algebra class. However the last two might require a bit of explanation.

Table 3-1
Comparison Operators[1]

Operator	Operation	Sample Code	Result
<	Less than	w < z	true
>	Greater than	w > z	false
<=	Less than or equal to	w <= z	true
>=	Greater than or equal to	z >= x	true
==	Equality	x == y	true
!=	Inequality (not equal)	x != y	false

[1] *For all examples assume w is 9, x is 10, y is 10 and z is 20.*

The equality operator

In some programming languages, you can test for equality simply by using a single equal sign, like so: `areEqual = x = y;` The problem with this method is that, in this single statement, the equal sign is being used two different ways: as a test to see if x and y are equal and to assign the result of this comparison to the variable `areEqual`. This is perfectly fine for a simple statement like this one, but in more complex statements, things can become a lot more difficult to follow. JavaScript removes this problem by using distinct operators for an assignment operation (a single equal sign) and an equality comparison (two equal signs). So, in JavaScript this example statement would be rewritten as: `areEqual = x == y;` This statement says, "Compare the values of x and y. If they are equal, put a `true` into the variable `areEqual`. If they are not equal, put a `false` into `areEqual`."

In JavaScript, a single equal sign *always* represents an assignment operation, regardless of the context in which it appears. This fact is probably the largest source of errors in JavaScript programs. (We'll see an example of this later in this session.) So, if your JavaScript program is behaving strangely, the first thing to check is whether or not you have correctly used two equal signs when you are testing for equality.

The inequality operator

In other programming languages, you'll usually see a test for inequality written using a less than (<) and a greater than (>) symbol: areNotEqual = x <> y; If you read this literally, you are asking "Is x less than or greater than y?" This is, frankly, a little confusing. Fortunately, JavaScript is able to express the concept of inequality a little better. In JavaScript there is a special symbol used specifically for expressing the concept of *not*: the exclamation point (!). So, to test for inequality, you would code: areNotEqual = x != y; Which can be read literally as "Is x not equal to y?"

**20 Min.
To Go**

Logical operators

The operators you've seen so far let you compare one value to another and generate a Boolean result. But, what if you need to base your decision on two or more Boolean values? As shown in Table 3-2, JavaScript has several operators to help you do just that.

Table 3-2
Logical Operators[2]

Operator	Operation	Sample Code	Value of bool3
&&	Logical AND	bool3 = bool1 && bool2;	false
||	Logical OR	bool3 = bool1 || bool2;	true
^	Exclusive OR	bool3 = bool1 ^ bool2;	true
!	Logical negation (not)	bool3 = !bool1;	false

[2]   For all examples, assume bool1 is true and bool2 is false.

The logical AND operation

A logical AND operation returns a true if and only if all of the Boolean values you are ANDing together are true. If even one value is false, the entire expression will be false.

The logical OR and exclusive OR operations

The logical OR operation will return a true value if *any* of the values you are ORing together are true. In fact, the only way a logical OR operation will return false is if *all* of the values in the expression are false.

The exclusive OR operation is a bit trickier than a logical OR. An exclusive OR expression is `true` if (and only if) exactly one of the values in the expression is `true`. If both values are `true` (or both values are `false`), the exclusive OR expression will be `false`.

The logical negation operation

The logical negation operation is a bit different from the operations you've looked at so far. The difference is that negation simply reverses the Boolean value that it's applied to. So, if you negate a `true` value, you get `false`. Similarly, if you negate a `false` value, you get `true`. To use the variables from Table 3-2 (where `bool1` is `true` and `bool2` is `false`), here are some examples of negation (and the other operators) at work:

```
bool3 = !bool2;            // bool3 will be true
bool3 = !(bool1 && bool2);  // bool3 will be true
bool3 = !(bool1 || bool2);  // bool3 will be false
bool3 = !(bool1 ^ bool2);   // bool3 will be false
bool3 = !(bool1 && !bool2); // bool3 will be false
```

There are a couple of things to notice here:

- When you want to negate an expression or Boolean variable, you just slap an exclamation point up against its left-hand side.

- You can use parentheses to "nest" operations in the order you want them to be carried out. In the second example, the parentheses tell the JavaScript interpreter that you want the logical AND carried out first. The result of that operation (`false`) will then be negated to give the final result of `true`. Compare this with the last example, where `bool2` is negated before it is ANDed with `bool1`.

Understanding Flow of Control Statements

As I said at the beginning of this session, in order to create really interesting programs, you have to be able to make decisions. So now that you've got a basic understanding of Boolean values and how they can be tested, let's look at the JavaScript statements that use them to make decisions.

The basic idea behind flow of control statements is that they let you decide which block of code you want executed based on some condition. Of course, having said that, I now have to define what a *block of code* is.

The code block

In the simplest terms, a block of code can be one of two things:

- A single line of code.
- Zero or more lines of code that are enclosed by a set of curly braces ({}). As far as the JavaScript interpreter is concerned, all of the code between the curly braces is the same thing as a single line of code.

So, for example, this is a block of code: x = x + y; And this is a block of code too:

```
{
y = 10;
x = 20;
document.write( "Hello!");
}
```

If this is a bit confusing, don't panic! The examples to come should help clear things up.

The if and if . . . else statements

The simplest flow of control statement that JavaScript has to offer is the if statement. This statement lets you easily decide if a block of code will execute. For example:

```
strollerPrice = 199;
if (strollerPrice <= 100)
    document.write( "This stroller is cheap!");
document.write( "Thanks for shopping at Baby-Palooza.com!");
```

How does this work? Well, following the if keyword, there is a Boolean expression (also known as a *conditional expression*) contained in parentheses. (In JavaScript, conditional expressions are always in parentheses.) If this expression evaluates to a value of true, we'll execute the block of code after the condition. In this case, that's just a single statement. So, if the value of strollerPrice is less than or equal to 100, the first document.write statement will be executed. Otherwise, the first document.write statement will be skipped entirely.

It's important to note here that this if statement will only trigger the execution of one statement. The second document.write statement is *not* a part of the if statement and will be executed regardless of the outcome of our conditional expression. If you want more than one statement to be executed, you have to enclose all of those statements inside a set of curly braces, like this:

```
if (strollerPrice <= 100) {
    document.write( "This stroller is cheap! ");
    document.write( "You certainly are getting a deal . . .");
    }
document.write( "Thanks for shopping at Baby-Palooza.com!");
```

At this point, I should probably say something about coding style. You'll notice in this example that the opening curly brace is on the same line as the if state-ment and that the closing curly brace is on its own line, indented to be even with the lines above it. You'll also notice that I always put a space between an opening parenthesis and whatever comes after it. I'll be using this style throughout this book, but there isn't anything magical about it. It's purely a personal style that I've developed over the years that, for me, makes source code more readable. JavaScript ignores white space characters (spaces, tabs, and carriage returns), so you can arrange your blocks of code in the manner that's the most readable to you.

When used all by itself, the if statement is really only good for one thing: excluding a block of code from being executed. What if you need to *choose* between two blocks of code? Well, in this case, you can use the if statement along with an else statement, like this:

```
if (strollerPrice <= 100) {
    document.write( "This stroller is cheap!");
    }
else {
    document.write( "This stroller is not so cheap.");
    }
```

The concept here is very simple: if the condition in parentheses evaluates to true, then you execute the code block immediately following the condition. Otherwise, execute the block of code following the else keyword.

You might have noticed here that both blocks of code in this example are only one statement long, yet I've enclosed each in curly braces. Why do this? Well, for one thing, it's important for you to realize that you *can* do it this way. Also, it's just a good idea to enclose single-line blocks of code in curly braces. Doing so removes any ambiguity as to which statements belong to a flow of control state-ment. Plus, if you have to go back and add more statements to a block of code, you won't have to remember to add the curly braces, because they will already be there!

When you need to make a complex decision, you can nest several `if . . . else` statements For example, consider this code:

```
strollerPrice = 199;
if (strollerPrice < 100) {
    if (strollerPrice < 50) {
        document.write( "Wow! This is cheap!");
        }
    else {
        document.write( "Very affordable!");
        }
    }
else {
    if (strollerPrice > 150) {
        document.write( "This is a high-end model!");
        }
    else {
        document.write( "A bit pricey, but nice!");
        }
    }
```

In this code, we're using nested `if . . . else` statements to zero in on precisely how much a stroller costs and then print an appropriate message based on that cost.

The assignment error

Earlier in this session, when I talked about the equality operator, I noted that in JavaScript a single equal sign *always* represents an assignment operation. Why is this important to know? Consider the following code:

```
strollerPrice = 199;
if (strollerPrice = 50) {
    document.write( "This stroller is only $50!<br />");
    }
document.write( "Actually, the price is: $" + strollerPrice);
```

In this example, you'll notice that I'm using the addition symbol to "add" a number to a string. When you use the +operator like this, JavaScript will automatically convert the number to a string and concatenate it with the string! You'll also notice that I'm writing out an HTML `<br />` tag as part of our output. (Just so you know, `<br />` is the XHTML version of `<br>`. I'll be using XHTML coding conventions throughout this book.) When you run this script, you'll find that *both* document.write statements have executed. Worse still, the value of strollerPrice has been changed from 199 to 50! What happened? Well, remember, a single equal sign is an assignment statement, *regardless of context*. So, even though the single equal sign is inside the conditional expression of an if statement, the JavaScript interpreter still assigns the value of 50 to strollerPrice.

But, why does this condition evaluate to true? Remember, Boolean logic is absolute, so something is either true or false. Also remember that Boolean values are sometimes represented as numbers: 1 for true and 0 for false. Actually, *any* value (numbers or strings or whatever) other than 0 is considered to be true. Only a numerical 0 is equivalent to false. So, the result of our "conditional expression" is 50, which evaluates as true.

As I said before, this insidious problem is probably the top cause of bugs in JavaScript programs. So be sure to keep your eyes open for it in your own programs!

10 Min. To Go

The switch and break statements

A close relative of the if statement is the switch statement. This statement allows you to very quickly choose between the known values of a variable and execute a corresponding code block. It's not quite as flexible as an if statement, but it's easy to follow and fast. For example, let's rework the previous example as a switch statement.

```
strollerPrice = 199;
switch (strollerPrice) {
    case 49: {
        document.write( "Wow! This is cheap!");
        break;
        }
    case 99: {
        document.write( "Very affordable!");
        break;
        }
    case 149: {
        document.write( "A bit pricey, but nice!");
        break;
        }
    default: {
        document.write( "This is a high-end model!");
        }
    } // end of switch statement
```

First comes the `switch` keyword, followed by the variable to test in parentheses. Inside the code block that follows, there are several `case` statements. Each of these is followed by a constant value that the variable will be tested against. If the value of the variable matches any one of these constant values, the code block following that `case` statement will be executed. If the value being tested doesn't match any of the cases, the statements following the `default` keyword will be executed. (Note that if you know and list all the possible cases, you don't have to specify a `default` statement.) As shown here, `strollerPrice` doesn't match any of the specified cases, so this will jump right to the `default` statement and tell the user, "This is a high-end model!" But, if `strollerPrice` were set to 99, this same code would write out the string "Very affordable!" and then execute the `break` statement that follows.

The `break` statement will *break out of* the current flow of control statement. When the JavaScript interpreter encounters a `break` statement, it immediately halts the flow of control statement it's in and resumes execution with the next statement immediately following the flow of control statement.

The `break` statement will work with any flow of control statement, but it's especially important to know how to use it with a `switch` statement. This is because, without a `break` between `case` statements, execution will fall through to the next `case` statement and execute the code block associated with that `case`, whether or not the `case` is a match for the test variable! For example, if you were to remove all of the `break` statements from the previous example, and set `strollerPrice` to 49, *all* of the `document.write` statements in the `switch` would be executed! (Give it a try with the source code on your CD-ROM.) This behavior can be confusing, but it can also be useful in some situations where you need or want multiple cases to be selected at one time. So, always remember to put `break` statements between your cases, but keep looking for ways to use this behavior to your advantage.

The while and do . . . while statements

I've shown you how to select one block of code or another, but what if you need to perform a block of code over and over again? JavaScript has several statements that let you do just that. The first of these is the `while` statement. The `while` statement is fairly simple, it simply repeats a block of code until some conditional expression becomes `false`. For example:

```
stockPrice = 100;
while (stockPrice > 0) {
    document.write( "Our stock is currently: $" + stockPrice +
    "/share<br />");
    stockPrice -= 10;
    }
```

The key parts of this example are the conditional expression (stockPrice > 0) and the statement that lowers the stockPrice each time through the loop. The conditional expression is evaluated before the loop executes. If this expression evaluates to false, the code block after the condition is not executed. If however, the condition is true, the code block is executed. When the code block finishes, the condition is checked again, and, if it's still true, the code block executes again.

The statement that changes stockPrice is just as important. Without this statement, stockPrice would never change, our condition would never become false, and our loop would never end! This turn of events is called an *infinite loop*. If you ever accidentally introduce an infinite loop into one of your JavaScript programs, it will appear as if the browser has hung up. In most cases, the browser will, after a few minutes, tell you that the script has been running longer than expected and give you the chance to stop the script. (If not, you'll have to manually close your Web browser using whatever task management facilities are available in your operating system.)

The main problem with the while statement is that if the condition is false when you first try to execute the statement, your code block will *never* be executed. If you need to make sure that your code block is executed at least once, use a do . . . while statement instead. The following code, for example, wouldn't display anything at all if it were written as a while loop. However, in do . . . while form, it's immediately apparent that this particular stock has become worthless.

```
stockPrice = 0;
do {
    document.write( "Our stock is currently: $" + stockPrice +
    "/share<br />");
    stockPrice -= 10;
    } while (stockPrice > 0);
```

The for statement

The most powerful flow of control statement is undoubtedly the for loop. While a bit difficult to master, the for loop gives you more control over your looping operations than any of the other statements. Conceptually, the basic format of a for loop is this:

```
for (initialConditionSetup; endOfLoopTest; conditionModifier) {
    codeBlock;
    }
```

So, if I want to write a for loop to add up the value of all the strollers I have in stock, I can code something like this:

```
strollerPrice = 199; numStrollers = 15; totalValue = 0;
for (counter = 1; counter <= numStrollers; counter++) {
    totalValue += strollerPrice;
    }
document.write( "Stroller inventory is worth: $" + totalValue);
```

Notice that inside the parentheses are three JavaScript statements:

- The first statement, counter = 1;, actually creates a new variable named counter that is local to the code block used in the for loop. When the loop ends, this variable is discarded. (We'll talk about local variables in Session 4.)

- The second statement, counter <= numstrollers;, is our conditional expression that generates a Boolean result. If this result is false, then the loop ceases execution.

- The third statement, counter++, is executed once at the *end* of each trip through the loop. In this case, this statement is used to increment the counter variable by one each time through the loop.

So, when this loop executes, it will execute the statement totalValue += strollerPrice; over and over until the counter++ statement causes counter to reach a value greater than the value of numStrollers. At that point, the loop will end, the counter variable will be discarded, and totalValue will contain a value of 2985.

The continue statement

You'll often find yourself performing a series of tests in the loops you create. In many cases, a true result will mean that it's time to jump back to the top of the loop. The continue statement lets you do just that.

```
strollerPrice = 199;
while (strollerPrice > 0) {
    strollerPrice -= 50;
    if (strollerPrice > 100) {
        document.write( "More than $100" + "<br />");
        continue;
        }
    if (strollerPrice > 50) {
```

```
                    document.write( "More than $50" + "<br />");
                    continue;
                    }
            }
```

In this example, I'm using the `continue` statement to jump back to the top of my loop whenever one of my `if` statements evaluates to `true`. The `continue` statement doesn't reset any of the values in the loop, it simply skips everything up to the end of the loop.

The ?: operator

The final statement we'll look at is actually an operator. This operator, known as the conditional operator, allows you to choose between two expressions to evaluate. In abstract terms, here's how it works:

```
result = (condition) ? (evaluate if condition is true) : (evaluate
if condition is false);
```

So, before the ?, we have a condition in parentheses. If that condition evaluates to `true`, the expression between the ? and the : is evaluated. If the condition is `false` however, the expression after the : is evaluated. So, in the following example:

```
y = 10; z = 30;
x = (y < z) ? y * z : y + z;
```

Done!

The condition is `true` (10 is less than 30), so we multiply y by z and assign the result to x.

REVIEW

In this session you've looked at Boolean values, logical expressions and operators, code blocks, and JavaScript's flow of control statements. You've seen how all of these things work together to let you write JavaScript programs that can execute different blocks of code depending on the outcome of logical decisions you make in our programs. If you haven't already, take some time to play with all of the source code for this session that is on your CD-ROM. Tinker around with the values assigned to the various variables and see how your tinkering affects the outcome of the programs.

QUIZ YOURSELF

1. What is a Boolean value? (See "Understanding Boolean Values And Expressions.")

2. What is a Boolean expression? (See "Understanding Boolean Values and Expressions.")

3. What is the difference between the = and == operators? (See "The equality operator" and "The assignment error.")

4. What is a code block? (See "The code block.")

5. What is the difference between a while and a do . . . while statement? (See "The while and do . . . while statements.")

How to Write JavaScript Functions

Session Checklist

✔ Learning when to create and use a function

✔ Understanding how functions return values

✔ Understanding JavaScript variable scope

✔ Learning how to store JavaScript code in external files

**30 Min.
To Go**

When you write a program, you'll often find yourself doing the same things over and over again. For example, take a few minutes to look at the file Listing4-1.htm. (It's in the Session04 folder on your CD-ROM.) As you can see, this is a long and tedious HTML document. The thing that makes it both long *and* tedious is that the code to output our product information is repeated over and over. What's worse, all this HTML and JavaScript only produces the simple table shown in Figure 4-1.

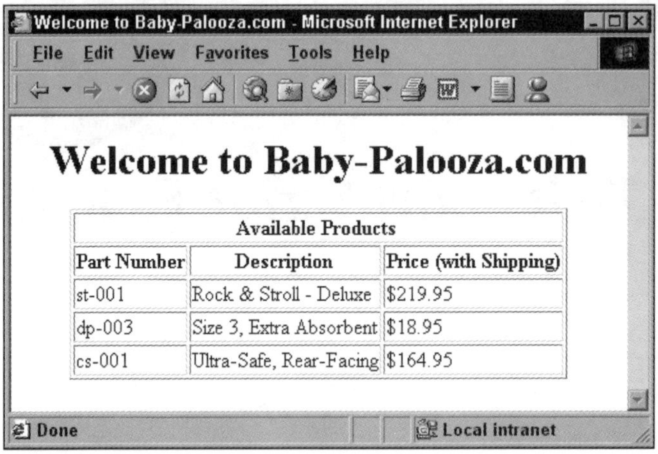

Figure 4-1
The short and sweet output of the long and tedious code

Creating a Function

So, the question is, "How can we use JavaScript to reduce the size of this code?" The answer is, "By writing a function."

In the simplest terms, a function is just a code block that you give a name to. There are a few advantages to putting your code into a function:

- You can use a function over and over again. All you have to do is call it by its name. (This is one aspect of something technical types refer to as "encapsulation.")

- Functions can perform the same operation on different sets of values. For example, if you wrote a function to square a number, you could pass it a different number to square each time you called the function. The values you pass to a function are called *parameters*.

- All of the JavaScript code we've looked at so far has been immediately executed as soon as the JavaScript interpreter gets to it. Functions, on the other hand, only execute when you call them explicitly.

In the Listing4-1.htm file, there are actually several places where functions would improve things. For instance, in each row of our table, we are adding the shipping cost to the product cost and displaying the result as a dollar amount. Here's a function that will calculate the final cost for us:

```
function calcFinalCost( baseCost, shippingCost) {
    return baseCost + shippingCost;
    }
```

This is a very simple function, but, just for fun, let's look closely at each part of it.

- First is the `function` keyword. This tells the JavaScript interpreter that the code block that follows should be treated as a function and only executed when explicitly called.

- Next is the function name, which is `calcFinalCost`. The rules for naming functions are exactly the same as the rules for naming variables that we saw in Session 2.

- In parentheses is the list of parameters that this function expects to receive. In this case the function is expecting two parameters: `baseCost` and `shippingCost`. These values are passed from the caller and are used in the body of the function to perform the function's task.

- Next, is the opening curly brace that marks the beginning of the body of the function.

- On the next line is a simple addition operation where the values of the parameters are added together.

- Also on this line is the `return` keyword. As you might guess from its name, this keyword evaluates the expression that follows it and sends the result back to whoever called the function.

- Finally, the closing curly brace marks the end of the function.

Calling a function

**20 Min.
To Go**

Now that we have this function defined, how do we actually use it? Well, the following code shows how the function would be used to help create the last row of the output shown in Figure 4-1 (You can find the complete code on your CD-ROM. Look for the file called Listing4-2.htm.):

```
<td>
<script language="javascript">
document.write( "$" + calcFinalCost(carSeatPrice, carSeatShip));
</script>
</td>
```

As you can see, we invoke our function simply by giving its name, followed (in parentheses) by the parameters we want to pass to it. These values are passed by position into the parameter variables we specified when we defined our function. (In other words, `baseCost` acquires the value in `carSeatPrice` and `shippingCost` takes on the value in `shipping`.) Those values are used to perform the calculation defined in the function. Finally, the result of the function is passed back to the point the function was called from and the result is used in our `document.write` statement.

Using a function to reduce code size

This simple function is good for discussing the concepts behind functions, but it really hasn't made our HTML file any shorter or any less tedious, has it? So, let's define another, slightly more complex function that will actually reduce our code size. The following code shows a function to display all relevant information for a product:

```
function showProductInfo( price, desc, partNo, ship) {
    document.write( "<tr>");
    document.write( "<td>" + partNo + "</td>");
    document.write( "<td>" + desc + "</td>");
    document.write( "<td>$" + calcFinalCost( price, ship) +
    "</td>");
    document.write( "</tr>");
    }
```

So, instead of defining row after row using HTML, we can simply call this function for each product and it will produce the appropriate HTML for us. To see how much this reduces the size of our code, take a look at the Listing4-3.htm file on the CD-ROM.

Understanding the finer points of functions

At this point, you've actually got all the information that you need to write functions all by yourself. However, there are a couple of additional points that I need to mention before we proceed.

In both of the examples we've seen, our functions have accepted several parameters. However, functions are not required to accept any parameters at all. But, when you define a function with no parameters, you still have to include a set of parentheses after the function name. (This is called an *empty parameter list*.) Such a function definition would look like this:

```
function noParams() {
    // function code goes here
    }
```

And you would call it like this: myResult = noParams(); (Note that, even though there are no parameters being passed, you *must* include the empty set of parentheses after the function name.)

You might have noticed that in the showProductInfo function there was no return keyword. That's because this particular function had no need to return any value. All of its work was accomplished using document.write statements, which took effect immediately. This is perfectly legal in JavaScript. In fact, you'll probably find yourself writing lots of functions that don't return any values at all!

Understanding JavaScript Scope Rules

Scope is a concept that determines if a variable or function defined in one part of your program is accessible from another part of your program. It can, for example, be very useful to be able to hide a variable created in one part of a program from a function created in another part of a program.

Most programming languages offer complex scope rules and have scope idiosyncrasies that can take months or even years to master. JavaScript, however, takes a somewhat more simplistic approach to scope. In JavaScript, there are just two types of scope:

Global Something with global scope is accessible from anywhere in your HTML file. Functions, for example, are always global. This means that any function you define can be called from any place else in the file. (As we'll see in Session 24, functions can even be accessed from different browser windows!) Variables are global if they are defined outside of a function.

Local Variables are local if they are defined inside a function. Additionally, you must use the var keyword to avoid confusing your local variable with any global variable that has the same name. Local variables are only accessible from the function in which they are defined.

Confused? The following example should help clear things up.

```
aGlobalVariable = "I'm global!<br />";
anotherGlobal = "I'm global too!<br />";
```

```
function scopeDemo() {
    var aGlobalVariable = "Actually, I'm local!<br />";
    document.write( aGlobalVariable);
    anotherGlobal = "I was changed by the function!<br />";
    }
document.write( aGlobalVariable);
document.write( anotherGlobal);
scopeDemo();
document.write( aGlobalVariable);
document.write( anotherGlobal);
```

If you run this code (it's on the CD-ROM in the Listing4-4.htm file), you'll see some output that you might not expect. First, this code sets up two global variables. (Remember, it's not their names that make them global, it's the fact that they are defined outside of any function! The names are just to help you follow what's supposed to be going on.) Then the code defines a function. After the function is defined, we output the value of aGlobalVariable and anotherGlobal. As expected, these values are unchanged. Then we call our function.

The first thing the function does is to create a new *local* variable. As you can see, this variable has exactly the same name as one of the global variables I've just created. However, since I've used the var keyword in this statement, the JavaScript interpreter knows that I'm creating a new variable that's local to this function. This means that, as long as this function is executing, any reference to aGlobalVariable is actually a reference to the local variable with that name. So, when the following statement executes, it's the value of the local variable that's output, not the value of the global variable. However, when the next statement references anotherGlobal, the JavaScript interpreter will find that there is no local variable with that name. So, as you would expect, it assigns the new value to the global variable. (Remember, global variables are available *everywhere*, even inside functions!) The moment the function finishes executing, the JavaScript interpreter throws away the local variable named aGlobalVariable. From that moment on, any further references to aGlobalVariable refer to the global variable defined in the first line of the script.

After returning from the function, the script again outputs the values in aGlobalVariable and anotherGlobal. This time however, one of them has changed; the value in anotherGlobal is now what was assigned to it inside the function. However, the value in aGlobalVariable is unchanged.

If you still find the concept of scope confusing, here are some tips to help you out:

**10 Min.
To Go**

- First of all, *never* give more than one variable the same name. Just by following this simple rule, you'll save yourself an incredible amount of heartache.

- To further avoid confusion, always use the `var` keyword when you create variables inside your functions. Of course, the `var` keyword is completely optional, so why bother? Well, some older versions of Netscape Navigator actually treat variables defined inside functions as global variables, unless you use the `var` keyword when you define the variable. By using the `var` keyword consistently, you'll never have to worry about running afoul of this strange behavior.

- You can also use the `var` keyword when defining global variables. This won't make your global variables local, but it will tell someone reading your code that you were defining a variable and not just making another assignment statement.

Using External Source Code Files

As I said at the start of this session, when you write a program, you'll find yourself doing the same things over and over again. In JavaScript programming this is true not only for a single Web page, but for entire Web sites. Therefore, it stands to reason that a function that's useful on one page might come in handy on another page as well. So, what's needed is some way to share your JavaScript functions (and other code) among all of the Web pages on your Web site. To accomplish this, the `<script>` tag supports something called the *src* attribute. This attribute (which stands for "source") allows you to specify a separate file that contains JavaScript code that you want to import into your Web page. For example, consider the `<script>` tag in the following code.

```
<html>
<head>
<title>Welcome to Baby-Palooza.com</title>
<script language="javascript" src="babyPalooza.js"></script>
</head>
<body bgcolor="white">
<!-- Remaining HTML goes here -->
</body>
</html>
```

In this example you can see that all of our JavaScript code has been removed from the first <script> block. Instead, the opening <script> tag looks like this:

```
<script language="javascript" src="babyPalooza.js"></script>
```

The src attribute tells the JavaScript interpreter that you want to include the JavaScript code that can be found in the file named "babyPalooza.js". So, the interpreter retrieves this file and parses the code it finds there just as if the code had been typed into the HTML file. (To see how all of this fits together, see the Listing4-5.htm and babyPalooza.js files on your CD-ROM.)

The .js **file extension on our external source file stands for, of course, JavaScript. It's not required that external source files use this extension, but it is a good idea to do so, simply because it will clearly identify your files as JavaScript source code.**

The babyPalooza.js file is simply all of the JavaScript variable and function definitions we have been working with throughout this session. This is what is loaded by the JavaScript interpreter in response to the src attribute in our first <script>. As you can see from looking at these last two files, using the src attribute can really help to reduce the overall size of your Web page. And, by placing your JavaScript code in a separate file, you can easily share your functions and variable definitions between files.

Done!

REVIEW

Functions and the concept of code reuse were the focus of this session. You looked at the structure of a function as well as why you would want to use functions. You learned how functions return results and discussed the fact that some functions don't need to return results at all. You saw how functions are called and how they can be used to reduce the overall size of a program by encapsulating tasks that are repeated over and over again. You learned about JavaScript's scope rules, and I pointed out ways to avoid confusion when creating local and global variables.

Finally, I told you about the src attribute of the <script> tag and showed you how it can be used to reduce the size of a Web page and to share JavaScript variables and functions among the different pages on your Web site.

Quiz Yourself

1. What are parameters? (See "Creating a Function.")

2. What does the `return` keyword do? (See "Creating a Function.")

3. How do you call a function? (See "Calling a Function.")

4. What is the difference between a local and a global variable? (See "Understanding JavaScript Scope Rules.")

5. What does the `src` attribute of the `<script>` tag do? (See "Using External Source Code Files.")

PART

I

Friday Evening

1. Where can you use the `<script></script>` tags in an HTML file?
2. What is a function?
3. What are the possible values for a variable that contains a Boolean value?
4. In your own words, describe what a code block is.
5. What rules must a JavaScript variable and function name follow?
6. What are the two ways to include comments in your JavaScript source code?
7. What file format should your JavaScript code be stored in?
8. What is the `language` attribute of the `<script>` tag used for?
9. How do you return a value from a function?
10. Write a function that takes four Boolean parameters and returns a `true` only if all four parameters are `true`.
11. Write a loop that adds the numbers from 1 to 100 and prints the result.
12. How many parameters must a function have?
13. What is the `src` attribute of the `<script>` tag used for?
14. In your own words, describe what the three expressions in the condition of a `for` loop do.
15. What is the difference between local and global variables?
16. What value will be placed in x as a result of the following statements? What will the value of y be?

    ```
    y = 75;
    x = (y = 100) ? 29 : 42;
    ```

17. What kind of data can you assign to a JavaScript variable?

18. Create a function to square a number and return the result.

19. Create a function that takes one number as a parameter. If the number is odd, the function should return `true`, otherwise, it should return `false`. (Hint: Use the modulus operator.)

20. Write a function that accepts a number as a parameter and returns the Boolean equivalent for that number.

☑ Friday

☑ **Saturday**

☐ Sunday

PART

II

Saturday Morning

Working with JavaScript Strings

Session Checklist

✔ Understanding how JavaScript implements strings

✔ Understanding how to use JavaScript string properties and methods

**30 Min.
To Go**

J avaScript supports a lot of different types of data, but the one you'll probably work with the most is the string. For that reason, I need to give you a
closer look at JavaScript strings and the different operations you can perform
on them. As you saw last evening, strings are easy to create; you simply assign
one to a variable like so:

```
var myString = "Welcome to Baby-Palooza!";
```

This simple statement creates a new variable and assigns a string value to it.
Once this is done, you can manipulate the string in this variable in just about any
way you want.

String Mechanics

Of course, at this point, I haven't told you all the different ways you can manipulate a string, have I? OK, grab your browser and let's start manipulating!

Concatenation

Perhaps the most basic string operation is *concatenation*. In the simplest terms, concatenation is an operation where you take two or more strings and jam them together to make a bigger string. Here's an example:

```
var greeting = "Welcome to Baby-Palooza!";
var beg = "Please come back soon!";
var howdy = greeting + beg;
```

As mentioned in Session 3, when used with a string, the plus sign acts as a concatenation operator. So, the last statement is saying, "Take the contents of `greeting` and tack the contents of `beg` onto the end of it. Then put the entire thing into howdy." After this code executes, what do you think the contents of `howdy` will be? If you said that `howdy` will contain "Welcome to Baby-Palooza! Please come back soon!" you were right.

No, this isn't a typo, there really shouldn't be a space between the "!" and "Please." (Remember, JavaScript is just a programming language, so it has no idea about the rules of grammar. Heck, it doesn't even know that these strings represent sentences!) In order to have a space between these strings, the last statement would have to look like this:

```
var howdy = greeting + " " + beg;
```

See what I've done here? I've explicitly placed a blank space between my two string variables. Now, the contents of `howdy` will look like this: "Welcome to Baby-Palooza! Please come back soon!" This brings up several important points:

- You can concatenate string variables with *hard-coded* strings. Hard-coded simply means something that you've typed in yourself. In this example, the blank space (" ") is the hard-coded string. (You'll find that the term *literal* is sometimes used instead of hard-coded.)

- You can concatenate as many string variables and hard-coded strings as you want into one string.

- If you build strings this way, it's entirely up to you, the programmer, to account for spaces between strings, punctuation, and so on.

Now, as you saw in Session 2, JavaScript has a lot of operators. So, you might be wondering if there is another concatenation operator. Actually, there is. Remember the += operator? When you use it with two numbers, it works like this:

```
x += y; // This is the same as . . .
x = x + y;
```

So, assuming that greeting and beg are still defined as you saw earlier, what do you think the following statement will do? greeting += " " + beg;

That's right, it will take the value of greeting and concatenate it with a blank space followed by the value in beg. Then the whole thing will be put back into the greeting variable. The end result is that greeting will contain "Welcome to Baby-Palooza! Please come back soon!"

Simple numeric conversion

Strings can also be used to do simple conversions of numbers into strings. For example:

```
var descAndPrice = "Stroller: $" + 199;
```

As I've said before, in a case like this the JavaScript interpreter will take the number, convert it into a string and concatenate that with the string "Stroller: $". The result of all this will be that the descAndPrice variable will contain the string "Stroller: $199". As you might expect, this also works for numbers with decimal places in them:

```
var descAndPrice = "Stroller: $" + 199.95;
```

If you have a number that you need to quickly convert into a string, you can do this by concatenating it with the *empty string*. The empty string is a string that contains, well, nothing. (I suppose that's why it's called the empty string.) At any rate, the empty string is represented by an empty set of either double "" or single '' quotes. (Notice that there is no space between either set of quotes.) Since the empty string is still a string, the simple act of concatenating it with the number changes the number into a string. For example:

```
var cost = 199;
cost += "";
```

20 Min. To Go

String Methods and Properties

In JavaScript, strings are implemented as *objects*. So, when you create a string, you are actually creating a JavaScript object, a *String object*. (Note the capital S here. A String object is different from the string data that you find inside it.) I'll be discussing objects in much greater detail in Session 17, so I'm not going to delve too deeply into this aspect of strings right now. But, if I want to tell you about String object methods and properties, you've got to know a little about methods and properties and how they relate to objects.

In the simplest terms, an object is a chunk of data that has some sort of functionality attached to it. That functionality is implemented as one or more *properties* and *methods*. Properties are straightforward; they are just variables that hold information about the data in the object. Strings, for example, have only one property, the length property. As the name implies, this property simply tells you how many characters are in the string data.

Methods are a bit trickier. At this point, the best way to think of methods is as if they are functions that belong to an object.

So, when you create a String object, you are creating a chunk of data (the characters of the string) that has a bunch of properties and methods predefined for you to use with it. The properties give you details about the data in the object and the methods allow you to perform tasks using the data in the object. For Strings, those tasks include things like searching for a character in the string data, extracting a portion of the string data, or converting the string data to upper or lower case.

Using String methods and properties

How do you actually call one of these methods? Let's look at an example:

```
var prez = "Thomas Jefferson";
var upperPrez = prez.toUpperCase();
```

Here I've created a String object named prez. On the next line, I've invoked the String method that will convert the contents of prez to upper case. As you might guess, the result of this second statement is that the variable upperPrez will contain "THOMAS JEFFERSON." However, let's look at how to invoke the method that makes this happen.

First, there's the name of my String object, prez, followed by a period. The period tells the JavaScript interpreter that I want to access a property or method inside the String object that I have named. So, after the period, I name what it is that I want to access, in this case, that's the toUpperCase method.

Earlier I said that methods are like functions that belong to objects. As you can see in this example, as with a function, the method name is followed by a set of parentheses. Some methods take parameters, just like functions do. So, just like a function, you would pass those inside the parentheses. It's important to realize that *every* string you create gets access to every method that is defined for the String object. But, when you invoke a String method, it only does its work on the data in the String object that you've named. For example, consider this code:

```
var prez1 = "George Washington";
var upperPrez1 = prez1.toUpperCase();
var prez2 = "Thomas Jefferson";
var upperPrez2 = prez2.toUpperCase();
```

After this executes, upperPrez1 will be "GEORGE WASHINGTON" and
upperPrez2 will contain "THOMAS JEFFERSON." This is just as simple as it looks
and works exactly the way you think it should. The prez1.toUpperCase() statement tells JavaScript that you want an upper case copy of the data in prez1.
Similarly, prez2.toUpperCase() tells JavaScript that you want an upper case
copy of the data in prez2.

With that under your belt, getting at the length property should seem pretty
simple:

```
document.write( prez1.length); // writes out the value 17
document.write( prez2.length); // writes out the value 16
```

Again, it's just a simple matter of specifying which String object you want to
work with and then following that with a period and the name of the property you
want to extract.

> **Many programming languages number the characters in a string
> starting with the number 1. JavaScript, however, begins number-
> ing characters with the number 0. So, for example, the string
> "Baby" has a length of 4 characters, but those characters are
> numbered from 0 (the *B*) to 3 (the *y*).**

String methods you can use

**10 Min.
To Go**

Now that I've shown you how to call a String method, what methods are there to
call? (Note that, because you've only got a weekend to learn about JavaScript, this
book is only going to cover the most useful aspects of the language. If you want to
dig deeply into every nook and cranny of JavaScript (including the string methods
that you won't find in this book), check out the official language specification for
JavaScript that is on your CD-ROM. It's in the file ECMA-262.pdf.)

The charAt() method

This method allows you to extract a single character from a specified position in a
String object. For example, give this code a try (it's on your CD-ROM if you don't
feel like typing it in):

```
var greeting = "!azoolaP-ybaB ot emocleW";
for (x=greeting.length - 1; x >=0 ; x--) {
    document.write( greeting.charAt( x));
    }
```

When you run this code, you'll see it prints out "Welcome to Baby-Palooza!" If you take a close look at the for loop, you'll see why: I've begun the loop at the *end* of the greeting string by setting x equal to the length of greeting minus one. (Remember, JavaScript character string positions are numbered starting with 0. So, the position of the final character is the length minus one.) The loop then progresses downward (note the x-- statement in the loop condition) until it goes below 0. (Again, remember that the position of the first character in a string is 0.)

Each time through the loop the charAt method extracts the character found at position x in greeting. The end result is that the string data is printed out backwards, giving us a now familiar salutation.

The indexOf() method

This method searches a String for a substring. If the substring is found, the position at which it was found is returned. If the substring isn't found, the method will return a value of negative one (-1). There are actually two different forms for calling this method. Here's an example of the first one:

```
var itemDesc = "Stroller and SunShade";
var sunPos = itemDesc.indexOf( "Sun");
if (sunPos != -1) {
    document.write("Found 'Sun' at position: " + sunPos);
    }
else {
    document.write( "Could not find 'Sun'!");
    }
```

Here I'm checking to see if the characters "Sun" exist in the itemDesc string variable. They do, so I output a short message telling me the position (13) where "Sun" was found in the string data. (As with every other part of JavaScript, each of the String methods you are seeing here is case-sensitive. So, if I had searched for "sun" instead of "Sun," the indexOf method would not have found a match and would have returned a -1 result.)

As you might imagine, the indexOf method begins looking for your substring at the start of the string data. This is usually fine, but there might be a time when you want to exclude a portion of the string from your search. The second form of the indexOf method is intended for just such a situation:

```
var custEmail = "somebody@aol.com";
var atPos = custEmail.indexOf( "@");
var aolPos = custEmail.indexOf( "aol", atPos);
if (aolPos != -1) {
    document.write( "Welcome AOL User!");
    }
else {
    document.write( "Welcome non-AOL User!");
    }
```

In this example, I'm testing an e-mail address to see if it belongs to a specific domain. So, since I only need to test what's after the @ symbol, I use the first form of indexOf to find the @. I then use that position information in the second form of indexOf. In this second form, I pass a start position after the substring you are looking for. This start position tells the method where in the string data to begin looking for the substring.

The lastIndexOf() method

This method does the exact same thing as the indexOf method, except it starts searching from the end of the string data, not the beginning. As with indexOf, there are two forms of the lastIndexOf() method. In the first form, you simply specify the substring you are searching for. In the second form, you specify the substring along with a starting position. If you specify a starting position, the search will progress from that point backwards toward the beginning of the string data. Here's an example:

```
var itemDesc = "Stroller and Stroller Carseat Adapter";
var strollPos = itemDesc.lastIndexOf( "Stroller");
if (strollPos != -1) {
    document.write("Found 'Stroller' at position: " + strollPos);
    }
else {
    document.write( "Could not find 'Stroller'!");
    }
```

If you run this code, you'll find that "Stroller" is reported as found at position 13 and not at position 0. (Regardless of which end the search begins from, the position returned is always counted from the start of the string data.)

The split() method

The `split` method takes a string and splits it into an array. I haven't told you about arrays yet, but we'll get to them soon, in Session 6.

The substring() method

The `substring` method extracts a new String from the interior of an existing String.

```
var greeting = "Welcome to Baby-Palooza";
document.write( greeting.substring( 11, 15) + "<br />"); // "Baby"
document.write( greeting.substring( 8, 10) + "<br />"); // "to"
document.write( greeting.substring( 16)); // "Palooza"
```

The first parameter of the `substring` method is the starting position of the String that you want to extract. The second parameter is the position that's *one greater than* the last character you want to extract. This is an important point: The character specified in the first parameter *will* be a part of the extracted String, but the character specified in the second parameter will *not*.

Another thing to notice is that the second parameter is entirely optional. If you omit it (as I've done in the last line of this example) the remainder of the source String will be extracted.

The toLowerCase() and toUpperCase() methods

Done!

As you've already seen, the **toUpperCase** method returns an all UPPER CASE version of the data in a String object. As you can probably guess, the **toLowerCase** method returns an all lower case version of the data in a String object.

REVIEW

You've just taken a long look at JavaScript Strings. You learned that JavaScript Strings are actually objects that have a `length` property and many different methods. You also learned how to access the `length` property and how to call the different String methods.

Quiz Yourself

1. How do you concatenate two strings together? (See "Concatenation.")

2. What happens when you concatenate a number with a string? (See "Simple numeric conversion.")

3. How do you call a String method? (See "Using String methods and properties.")

4. What does the `length` property tell you about a String? (See "String methods and properties.")

5. How are the character positions in a JavaScript String object numbered? (See "String methods and properties.")

Working with JavaScript Arrays

Session Checklist

✔ Understanding what arrays are and how to process their contents

✔ Understanding the kinds of data you can store in an array

✔ Understanding multidimensional arrays

✔ Learning about array methods

**30 Min.
To Go**

U p to this point, I've been creating a new variable every time I needed to store a new value. For example, in Session 4, I used the following code to hold product information:

```
strollerPrice = 199.95;
strollerDesc = "Rock & Stroll - Deluxe";
strollerPartNo = "st-001";
strollerShip = 20;
diaperPrice = 13.95;
diaperDesc = "Size 3, Extra Absorbent";
diaperPartNo = "dp-003";
diaperShip = 5;
carSeatPrice = 149.95;
carSeatDesc = "Ultra-Safe, Rear-Facing";
carSeatPartNo = "cs-001";
carSeatShip = 15;
```

While this is very descriptive, it's also a very cumbersome way to do things. Worst of all, if my inventory should ever change, I would have to create a new set of variables (each with an appropriate name) for each product. Wouldn't it be nice if there were a type of variable that could hold a bunch of related, but different, data all at once? Well, there is, and it's called an *array*.

What Is an Array?

An array is a variable that has numbered or named *slots* that you can put data in. You can think of these slots as a set of individual variables inside the array. For example, the following code shows how one of the above products looks when it's placed in an array:

```
var strollerInfo = new Array();
strollerInfo[0] =  199.95;
strollerInfo[1] = "Rock & Stroll - Deluxe";
strollerInfo[2] = "st-001";
strollerInfo[3] = 20;
```

As with strings, JavaScript arrays are implemented as objects. Unlike strings, however, you can't just create an array by assigning a value to a variable. Instead, you have to actually create an Array object. So, how do you create an Array object? The answer is in the first line of our example: var strollerInfo = new Array();

As usual, I use the var keyword to signify that I am creating a new variable, and then I give that new variable a name (strollerInfo). This is followed by the new keyword. This keyword tells the JavaScript interpreter that I want to create a new object of some type. In this case, I want to create a new Array object. So, I follow the new keyword with a call to the Array() constructor method.

A *constructor method* is a special method that every type of object has. The first thing that makes it special is that it has the same name as the type of object to which it belongs. (Yes, String objects have a constructor method named String().) Basically, a constructor method tells JavaScript what steps to take to build a specified type of object. That's why it's called a constructor method; it's actually building the object you've requested. So, after this line is finished, I've got a new Array object stored in the strollerInfo variable.

How to use an array

As I said earlier, an array can be thought of as a variable with a bunch of named or numbered slots in it. Each of these slots can hold its own chunk of data, just as if it were itself a variable. (Actually, the slots and the data in them are most often referred to as *elements* of the array.) To access these slots you simply give the name of the array variable, followed in square brackets by the number or name of the slot you want to access. (The number or name you assign to a slot in an array is called the *index* of that slot.)

Using numbered array elements

In the previous example, I'm using numbered slots to hold my product data. Notice that I've started numbering my slots with zero. (You can actually begin numbering your slots with any number you like, but beginning with zero is standard practice.)

You've seen how to get data into an array, but how do you get data out of an array? Well, there are lots of ways to do this, but the most common way is to process each slot in the array from inside a loop of some sort. Of course, to do that, you have to know how long the array is. That's why, as with String objects, every Array object has a `length` property that tells you how many slots exist in the array. (The JavaScript interpreter automatically updates the value in this property as you add slots to the Array object.) So, with the previous example in mind, take a look at this:

```
for (x=0; x<strollerInfo.length; x++) {
    document.write( strollerInfo[x] + "<br />");
    }
```

When you run this code (it's in the Listing6-2.htm file on the CD-ROM if you don't want to type it in), you'll get a list of the contents of the array. The `for` loop simply steps through each of the slots in the array and, using the number stored in x, extracts and displays the data in each slot of the array.

Using named array elements

In my first example, I used numbered slots to hold my product data rather than named slots. However, I could have just as easily have used named slots, as seen here:

```
var strollerInfo = new Array();
strollerInfo["price"] =  199.95;
strollerInfo["desc"] = "Rock & Stroll - Deluxe";
strollerInfo["partNo"] = "st-001";
strollerInfo["shipCost"] = 20;
```

One advantage of this approach is that, instead of a meaningless number, each slot's name tells the programmer exactly what the slot holds. The downside, however, is that you can no longer use a numeric counter to retrieve the contents of the array. To solve this problem, JavaScript provides a special variant of the `for` loop designed specifically for this sort of task. An example of this is shown below.

```
for (x in strollerInfo) {
    document.write( strollerInfo[x] + "<br />");
    }
```

In this version of the `for` loop, the three expressions that would normally control the loop are replaced by the expression (x in strollerInfo). This expression tells the JavaScript interpreter that each time through the loop, the value of x should become the name of the next slot in the strollerInfo array. So, the first time through the loop, x contains "price." The second time through it contains "desc," and so on. An added benefit of this approach is that, since x will take on the name of each slot, you can inspect x and use its contents to display the name of each slot. Like this:

```
for (x in strollerInfo) {
    document.write( x + " is " + strollerInfo[x] + "<br />");
    }
```

It's important to note that if you are going to use named slots you can give your slots any name that will fit between a set of quotes. Even if that name isn't a valid JavaScript variable name! So, for example, the code shown here would be perfectly legal:

```
var strollerInfo = new Array();
strollerInfo["Price"] = 199.95;
strollerInfo["Product Description"] = "Rock & Stroll - Deluxe";
strollerInfo["Baby-Palooza Part Number"] = "st-001";
strollerInfo["Shipping Cost, Ground"] = 20;
for (x in strollerInfo) {
    document.write( x + " is " + strollerInfo[x] + "<br />");
    }
```

This would yield the much nicer output shown in Figure 6-1.

Unfortunately, there are a couple of drawbacks to using named slots:

- With named slots, you can only step through your array in one direction, from top to bottom. With numbered slots, you can step through from the bottom (length - 1) to the top (0).

- Directly accessing an array element with a named slot requires that you know the name of the slot. If you are using verbose slot names, this can make for some very difficult programming. A better solution is to use numbered slots and set aside one slot for a detailed description of the array's contents.

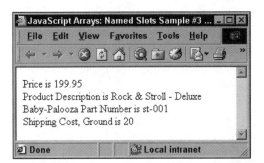

Figure 6-1
The output of the code using verbose slot names

**20 Min.
To Go**

What kind of data can you put into an array?

Actually, since JavaScript variables are loosely typed (as mentioned in Session 2), you can actually put any kind of data into any slot of a JavaScript Array object. As you've already seen, you can even assign a different type of data to each slot in an array. This makes JavaScript arrays very powerful. It also lets you create a *multidimensional array*.

What's a Multidimensional Array?

Think of a multidimensional array as an array of arrays. Why would you ever need something like this? Well, consider our product data: In the examples I've shown you so far, I've actually only been assigning the data for *one* product into my array. Given what you've seen thus far, the information for each of the other products would also have to be placed into its own Array object and you would then have to manipulate each of these individually. Here again, it would be very nice if there were a way to wrap all of the data into a single variable that could be easily manipulated. With that in mind, take a look this:

```
var strollerInfo = new Array();
strollerInfo[0] =  199.95;
strollerInfo[1] = "Rock & Stroll - Deluxe";
strollerInfo[2] = "st-001";
strollerInfo[3] = 20;
var diaperInfo = new Array();
diaperInfo[0] = 13.95;
diaperInfo[1] = "Size 3, Extra Absorbent";
diaperInfo[2] = "dp-003";
diaperInfo[3] = 5;
var carSeatInfo = new Array();
carSeatInfo[0] = 149.95;
carSeatInfo[1] = "Ultra-Safe, Rear-Facing";
carSeatInfo[2] = "cs-001";
carSeatInfo[3] = 15;
var productInfo = new Array();
productInfo[0] = strollerInfo;
productInfo[1] = diaperInfo;
productInfo[2] = carSeatInfo;
```

As expected, I've created separate Array objects to hold the information for each product. However after that's done, I've also created a fourth array called productInfo. I then take this array and fill its slots with the three product information arrays I've already created. After doing this, I end up with an array of arrays. I can then access all of the information about all of my products through the productInfo variable.

How to access data in a multidimensional array

Accessing the data in a multidimensional array is a simple matter of specifying each index needed to drill down to the slot you want in the appropriate array. For example, the price for the car seat is kept in slot one of the third array in productInfo. So if we wanted to print this out, we would code:

```
document.write( "Car seat price: " + productInfo[2][0]);
```

See how this works? After the name of the multidimensional array (productInfo), I've specified the index ([2]) of the subarray I want to access. If you look back at the code that created this array, you'll see that this is the slot containing my car seat information. Once I've zeroed in on the correct array, I simply specify the index of the slot I want to extract data from ([1]). For another example, if I wanted to change the price of the diapers to $15.95, I would code:

```
productInfo[1][0] = 15.95;
```

As our final example, the following code will take the arrays I just created and display the contents of each slot.

```
for (x=0; x<productInfo.length; x++) {
    for (y=0; y<productInfo[x].length; y++) {
        document.write( productInfo[x][y] + "<br />");
        }
    }
```

Here I'm using a couple of nested `for` loops to display all of the data in my multidimensional array. The outer loop moves through the main array (`productInfo`), while the inner loop displays the contents of each subarray.

Array Methods

As we've seen, JavaScript arrays are actually pretty easy to work with. However, since they are objects, JavaScript arrays also come with a variety of methods that make them even more useful and powerful. In this section, we'll look at these methods as well as the `split()` method that belongs to the String object. (Note that examples of each of these methods can be found on your CD-ROM in the Session06 folder.)

The Array() constructor method

There are actually a couple of different ways to use the `Array()` constructor method.

`new Array()`	With no parameters. As you've already seen, this simply creates an empty Array object.
`new Array( length)`	With a `length` parameter. This creates a new Array object with `length` empty slots.
`new Array( item1, item2, etc.)`	With multiple parameters. This creates an Array object whose slots are filled with the items you pass as parameters.

The concat() method

This `concat()` method will join multiple arrays together into a single new Array object.

The join() method

This method will combine the individual elements of an array into a single string. This string will be delimited by a character that you specify when you call the join() method.

```
var bpArray = new Array( "Diapers", "Baby Wipes", "Rattle");
var prodList = bpArray.join( "-");
```

After this code executes, prodList will contain the string "Diapers-Baby Wipes-Rattle." If you don't specify a delimiter, the join() method will use a comma by default. (Compare this with the String.split() method discussed at the end of this section.)

The pop() method

This method removes and returns the last element in an Array object. After this method executes, the Array's length property will be one less than before. For example, the following code will result in lastProduct containing the string "Rattle."

```
var bpArray = new Array( "Diapers", "Baby Wipes", "Rattle");
var lastProduct = bpArray.pop();
```

Internet Explorer 5 on the Macintosh does not support this method or these (described later): push(), shift(), splice(), and unShift().

The push() method

This method puts a new item at the end of an Array. Afterwards, the Array's length property will be one greater than before. After the following code executes, the bpArray variable will have a new element at its end containing the string "Diaper Cream."

```
var bpArray = new Array( "Diapers", "Baby Wipes", "Rattle");
bpArray.push( "Diaper Cream");
```

The reverse() method

This method will reverse the order of the elements of an Array object.

The shift() method

This method will remove the first element of an array (element 0) and move the other elements up one. Afterwards, the Array's length property will be one less than before.

10 Min. To Go

The slice() method

The slice() method will return a new Array object containing a subset of the elements in your original array. You simply specify a starting and ending element and this method will return a new Array object containing each element from the starting position to the end position minus one. In the following example the cleanUp variable will be an Array object with two elements: "Diapers" and "Baby Wipes." Again, note that the specified ending element (element 2, "Rattle") is *not* included in the new Array object.

```
var bpArray = new Array( "Diapers", "Baby Wipes", "Rattle",
"Stroller", "Booties");
var cleanUp = bpArray.slice( 0, 2)
```

The sort() method

The sort() method will let you sort the contents of an Array object using whatever sorting process you want. You simply have to specify an appropriate sorting function when you call the sort() method.

```
function simpleSort( item1, item2) {
    var result = 0;
    if (item1 > item2)
        result = 1;
    if (item1 < item2)
        result = -1;
    if (item1 == item2)
        result = 0;
    return result;
```

```
    }
var bpArray = new Array( "Diapers", "Baby Wipes", "Rattle", "Car
Seat", "Stroller");
bpArray.sort( simpleSort);
```

The sorting function (which you must write) will be called again and again by the sort() method until all elements are sorted. Each time it's called, it will receive two parameters (here called item1 and item2). The sorting function must compare these items and return a result based on that comparison. Note that the comparison logic you use is totally up to you, but it should make sense for the type of data you are sorting. In the above example, I'm just sorting strings, so a simple string comparison is all that's required. (JavaScript uses an alphabetical order rule to compare strings. So, "ape" is less than "zebra.")

- If item1 is *greater than* item2, the function should return a positive number.
- If item1 is *less than* item2, the function should return a negative number.
- If item1 is found to be *equal to* item2, the sorting function should return a zero.

The sort() method uses these results to rearrange the contents of the Array in sorted order. (It's important to note that you can write as many sorting functions as you want and use them with whichever Array objects you want. For example, you can write one function to sort items in ascending order while another sorts them in descending order.)

The splice() method

The splice() method is the most complex of the Array object methods. It allows you to delete items from an Array and, optionally, insert new items in place of the old ones. In its simplest form, the splice() method can delete one or more array elements, like this:

```
var bpArray = new Array( "Diapers", "Baby Wipes", "Rattle",
"Car Seat", "Stroller");
bpArray.splice( 2, 1);
```

The first parameter tells the method which element to start the delete operation with. (In this case, it's element 2, "Rattle".) The second parameter tells splice() how many elements to delete. In this case, I've specified a value of 1, so only the "Rattle" element will be deleted. This effectively removes the element from the middle of the array.

The second form of the `splice()` method doesn't actually remove any elements, it merely replaces their contents. For example:

```
var bpArray = new Array( "Diapers", "Baby Wipes", "Car Seat",
"Stroller");
bpArray.splice( 1, 3, "Booties", "Sun Shield", "Baby Sling");
```

Here again, the first parameter tells `splice()` where to start the operation. The second parameter tells it how many elements, including the specified starting element, need to be replaced. The remaining parameters are the new values that should be assigned to the specified elements. So, after this code runs, bpArray[0] will contain "Diapers", bpArray[1] will contain "Booties", bpArray[2] will contain "Sun Shield", and bpArray[3] will contain "Baby Sling".

The toString() method

This method will combine all of the elements in an Array object into a single string. Each element will be separated by a single comma. This is exactly the same as calling the `join()` method without specifying a delimiter character.

The unShift() method

This method will add a new element to the beginning of the array and move all the old elements up one. Afterwards, the Array's `length` property will be one more than before. So, after the following code executes, bpArray[0] will contain the string "Stroller."

```
var bpArray = new Array( "Diapers", "Baby Wipes", "Rattle");

bpArray.unshift( "Stroller");
```

The String.split() method

The final method you need to know about isn't an Array object method at all, it's the `split()` method of the String object. As you might have guessed by now, this method takes a string and breaks it into an Array object. The trick is: How does it know where to break the string up? Well, when you call the `split()` method, you specify a delimiter that the method will use to determine the start of each new element. For example, the following code will create an Array with "Diapers", "Baby Wipes," and "Rattle" as the elements.

```
var productList = "Diapers-Baby Wipes-Rattle";
var bpArray = productList.split( "-");
```

Putting It All Together

At this point, you've got all the pieces you need to really start making things happen. Two files in the Session06 folder of your CD-ROM (the babyPalooza.js and index.htm files) take everything you've seen so far and combine it all to lay the foundation of the Baby-Palooza.com storefront. Due to the length of these files I won't be showing them here, so load them into your editor (and your web browser) so that you can follow along.

Looking first at the babyPalooza.js file, you'll see that I've reorganized all of the store data in terms of Array objects. This will allow me to manipulate all of my product information through a single variable: productInfo.

I've also updated the showProductInfo function to take advantage of the fact that it is now being passed an Array. As a result, it now pulls the product data that it displays directly out of the Array object it receives, rather than processing a bunch of parameters. As part of that process, I've also used a call to the split() method along with a switch statement to determine the product's category ("Stroller," "Rattle," etc.) Displaying this information will give my customers a slightly better idea of what they are buying.

Tying all of this together is the index.htm file. The main difference between the current version of this file and what you saw in Session 4 is that I no longer explicitly call showProductInfo for each product. Instead I simply loop through my productInfo array and pass each product's information Array object to the function. (Remember, productInfo[x] actually refers to an entire subarray in my multidimensional array.)

Done!

REVIEW

In this session you've learned about arrays, the JavaScript Array object, and all of the different operations and methods they can use. You saw how arrays can be used to hold a lot of data in a single variable while still allowing easy access to that data. You also learned how to create and use an array whose slots are named instead of numbered. You even saw a variant of the for loop that will let you work with arrays that have named slots. Finally, we looked at an example of how everything you've seen so far can be used together to lay the groundwork for a flexible Web storefront.

Quiz Yourself

1. What exactly is an array? (See "What is an Array?")

2. How do you access the contents of an array? (See "How to use an array.")

3. Why might you want to use named slots? (See "Using named array elements.")

4. What is a multidimensional array? (See "What's a Multidimensional Array?")

5. What does the `join()` method do? How does it relate to the `split()` method of the String object? (See "Array Methods.")

Understanding the Browser Object Model

Session Checklist

✔ Understanding what the Browser Object Model is

✔ Understanding the structure of the Browser Object Model

✔ Understanding how JavaScript works with the Browser Object Model

**30 Min.
To Go**

Up to now, I've been telling you about JavaScript the programming language. Now it's time to talk about the environment that JavaScript actually lives in. If you are thinking that means the Web browser, you are only partially correct. While it's true that the Web browser is the host for your JavaScript programs, your programs will never interact directly with the Web browser. Instead, you'll be working with a collection of JavaScript objects that act as an intermediary between your JavaScript programs and the Web browser. This collection of objects is sometimes called the *Browser Object Model*. The purpose of the Browser Object Model is to provide a simple, consistent interface between your JavaScript programs and the Web browser.

Why do things this way? Well, consider the personal computer industry. Programs written for one platform (like the Macintosh) won't run on another platform (like Windows) without a lot of conversion work. This is because they use very different programming interfaces to accomplish the same tasks.

Now consider the Web browser industry. The JavaScript code you create for Internet Explorer should be able to work perfectly well on Netscape's Navigator. (There are of course, some differences, but they are minor compared to moving software between the Mac and Windows!) You can even use the code you wrote for Navigator on Linux with Internet Explorer on the Macintosh. This is because both browsers support the same programming interface, namely, the Browser Object Model.

What's in the Browser Object Model?

You've already been exposed to one part of the Browser Object Model: the document object. As you'll remember from Session 1, the document object represents the actual HTML document that's loaded into the Web browser. Just like the other objects you've looked at (the String object in Session 5 and the Array object in Session 6), the document object has a whole host of properties and methods all its own. (In fact, the document object is so important, we're going to discuss it in detail in Session 9 a bit later this morning.)

There's more to the Browser Object Model than just the document object. The Browser Object Model is made up of a whole slew of objects that allow your JavaScript programs to peek and poke into just about every nook and cranny of the Web browser. All of these objects are arranged in what looks like an upside-down tree structure. The window object sits at the top of this tree and all of the other objects in the Browser Object Model can be found inside it. Figure 7-1 illustrates the main objects found in the Browser Object Model for Netscape Navigator 6 and Internet Explorer 5 (other browsers will be a bit different).

As you can see from Figure 7-1, the Browser Object Model is very big and rather complex. So, the purpose of this session is to simply get familiar with the Browser Object Model and the capabilities it offers. You'll be learning about the individual parts of the Browser Object Model over the remainder of the weekend. In the discussion that follows, I'll give the names of the major objects in the Browser Object Model along with a brief description of each. I'll also tell you in which session number that object is discussed.

The window object

The window object represents the Web browser window. It also encapsulates all of the other objects we'll be talking about in the remainder of this session. (Remember the "array of arrays" from the end of Session 6? The concept behind the window object is very similar to that. Think of it as an object that contains a bunch of other objects.) Most of the objects inside the window object represent the various controls that you see in your browser window. For example, the history object (discussed in Session 27) holds the addresses of the Web pages you've visited. Other objects and properties inside the window object include the following.

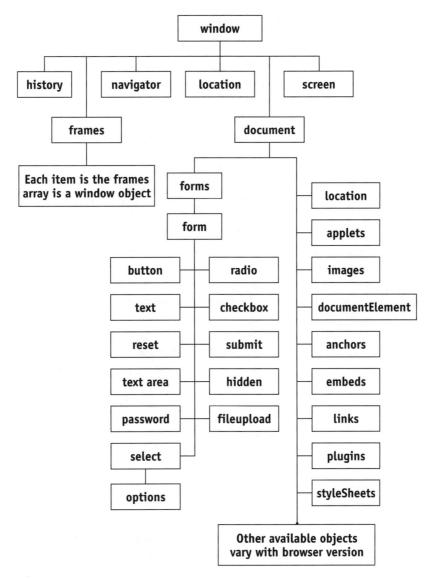

Figure 7-1
The Browser Object Model

The document **object:** As mentioned in Session 1, the document object represents the currently loaded HTML page. There's more information on the document object to come later in this session, and we'll be discussing it in detail in Session 9.

The frames **array:** JavaScript treats each frame that appears in the browser window as a window object all to itself. So, if your Web site uses frames, the JavaScript window object that represents the actual browser window (that is, not one of the frames) is known as the parent window. This parent will contain an Array object called the frames array. Each slot in the frames array will contain a window object corresponding to one of the frames in the Web browser. While it might sound confusing to have window objects inside window objects, it's quite easy to work with, as you'll see in Session 23.

The location **property:** This is a String object that contains the address of the Web page currently loaded into the Web browser. (The location object is discussed in Session 27.)

The navigator **object:** This object holds details about the brand, version, and capabilities of your Web browser. In addition to this basic information, it also contains detailed lists of the plug-ins that are installed and the MIME types that the browser knows about. Your JavaScript program can use this information to determine if a particular type of multimedia file will work in the browser. (The navigator object is discussed in Session 26. Support for plug-ins and MIME types is discussed in Session 29.)

At this point, an illustration might help. Figure 7-2 shows a typical browser window, frames and all, and how the parts of the window correspond to the objects you've just been introduced to.

Another important aspect of the window object is the fact that it goes by several different names. Usually if you want to refer to the window object, you just use the name *window*. However, you don't *have* to name the window object at all. If JavaScript doesn't know which object you are talking about, it will assume that you are talking about the window object and use it by default. For example, the following two statements are equivalent:

```
document.write( "Howdy!"); window.document.write( "Howdy!");
```

As mentioned earlier, when you are working with frames, the window object representing the actual browser window can be referred to as "parent." You can use this name even if you aren't using frames.

Finally, you can also refer to the window object as "self" or "top." (The name "top" is also useful in the context of frames. We'll talk more about that in Session 23 as well.) So, all of the following statements are equivalent.

```
document.write( "Howdy!"); parent.document.write( "Howdy!");
self.document.write( "Howdy!"); top.document.write( "Howdy!");
```

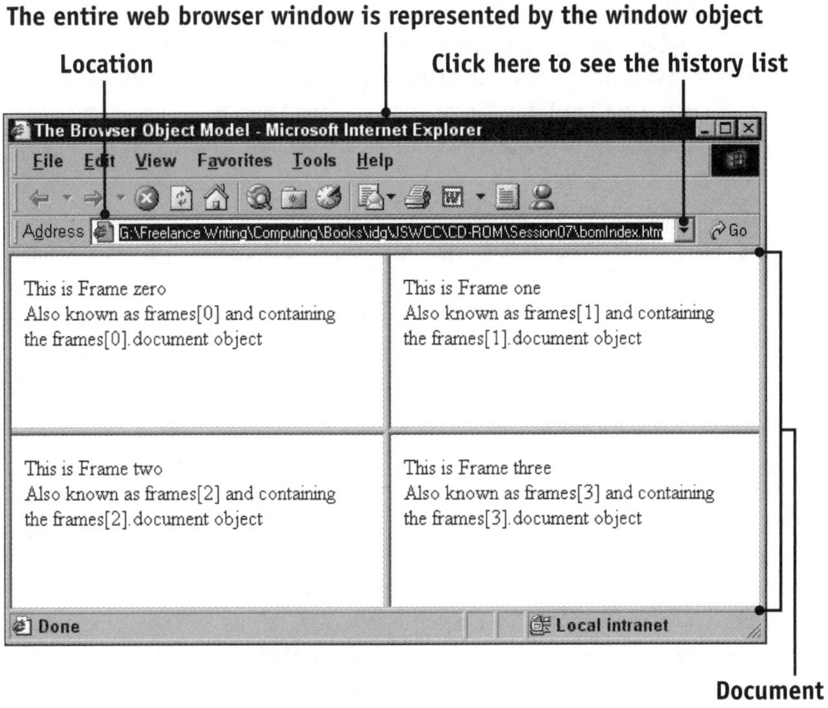
The entire web browser window is represented by the window object
Location
Click here to see the history list
The Browser Object Model - Microsoft Internet Explorer
File Edit View Favorites Tools Help
Address G:\Freelance Writing\Computing\Books\idg\JSWCC\CD-ROM\Session07\bomIndex.htm
Go
This is Frame zero
Also known as frames[0] and containing the frames[0].document object
This is Frame one
Also known as frames[1] and containing the frames[1].document object
This is Frame two
Also known as frames[2] and containing the frames[2].document object
This is Frame three
Also known as frames[3] and containing the frames[3].document object
Done
Local intranet
Document

Figure 7-2
Parts of a browser window and corresponding JavaScript objects

20 Min. To Go

The document object

You've already seen how the `document` object can be used to write a string out to the browser window. However, the `document` object can do much more than just this. The `document` object allows your JavaScript program to do the following.

Interact with HTML forms: This includes manipulating all of the various controls available to HTML forms (text boxes, buttons, and so forth). You can even validate the data in a form (Session 15) and change the location that a form is submitted to. This is probably the single most useful aspect of JavaScript on the Web page, so we're going to be looking at this in extremely fine detail in Sessions 12, 13, and 15.

Manipulate cookies: The `document` object gives you direct control over the cookies that are saved on the Web browser client's machine. We'll be looking at this in Session 16.

Interact with images: The document object allows you to directly access and manipulate the images that are loaded into your Web documents. In Session 14, we'll see how JavaScript will let us load images and even create simple animations.

Interact with Java applets: The document object also gives you access to any Java applets that might be loaded by your Web page. We'll look at this in Session 30.

JavaScript and the Browser Object Model

Now that you've got an idea of what's in the Browser Object Model, you might be wondering how you actually use it. I've already shown you a small sample of this, in the discussion of the window object. Consider again, this line of code:

```
window.document.write( "Howdy!");
```

What exactly is this code telling JavaScript to do? Well, remember from our discussion of String object methods that the period is an operator that tells JavaScript to *look inside* an object so that you can access something contained in it. So, this code says, "Look inside the window object and get me the document object. Then, look inside the document object and call its write() method." This is how you access the parts of the Browser Object Model with JavaScript: Starting with the window object, you list the names of the objects that will lead to the object you want to access. All you have to remember is to separate the object names with periods. This list of object names will tell JavaScript the path to follow to access the Browser Object Model object you want.

A simple example

How does an HTML file map to the Browser Object Model? Here's an example.

```
<html>
<head><title>Browser Object Model</title></head>
<body bgcolor="white">
Welcome to Baby-Palooza!
<form name="order">
Number of Strollers:
<input type="text" name="strollCount" value="0" /><br />
```

```
Number of Diapers:
<input type="text" name="diaperCount" value="0" /><br />
Number of Rattles:
<input type="text" name="rattleCount" value="0" />
</form>
</body>
</html>
```

When the Web browser loads this file, it actually creates a complete set of Browser Object Model objects to represent it. For this file, the following objects are created:

Object	Meaning
The window object	This represents the Web browser itself.
The document object	This represents the HTML file.
A form object named "order"	This represents the <form> tag defined in our HTML file. Note that the name of this object is the same as the name you specify in the name attribute of the <form> tag. (If you have more than one <form> in your HTML file, you need only give them each a unique name attribute to access them through JavaScript.)
Three input objects named "strollCount," "diaperCount," and "rattleCount"	These objects represent the text boxes defined inside the order form. Each of these objects has a value property that holds the number that's currently typed into the text box. Again, the name for each of these JavaScript objects is taken directly from the name attribute used in its corresponding HTML <input> tag.

Of course, there are other objects created. For example, a forms array is created as well. But, since there are no corresponding definitions in the HTML file, those objects will be empty. (In this case, the forms array will have a length of zero.) In Figure 7-3, you can see how these objects are nested one inside the other.

10 Min. To Go

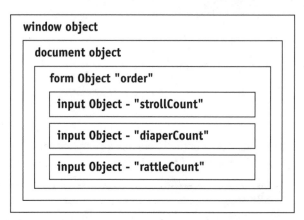

Figure 7-3
Objects created by our simple HTML file

Knowing all of this, you can then write code that will access these objects. For example:

```
var numStrollers = document.order.strollCount.value;
var numDiapers = document.order.diaperCount.value;
```

In each line of code, I'm "drilling down" from the outermost object (in this case, the document object, remember that the window object is implied) to the property I want to access (the value property of the individual text box objects). The first line, for example, says, "Look in the document object and you'll find an object named order. Look inside the order object and you'll find another object named strollCount. Look inside this object and get the contents of its value property. Finally, place that result into the numStrollers variable." Of course, you can also assign values to these properties as well:

```
document.order.strollCount.value = 10;
document.order.diaperCount.value = 95;
```

However, these are more than just simple assignment statements. Remember, these objects correspond to HTML elements that are actually on the screen while your JavaScript program is executing. So, if you assign a new value to the value property of the rattleCount text box, that number will immediately appear on screen in the text box! This is what makes the combination of JavaScript and the Browser Object Model so very powerful. By using them together, your JavaScript program can easily interact with the elements of the HTML page and dynamically change the information that the user sees.

Done!

REVIEW

In this session, you learned about the Browser Object Model. You learned that, as far as JavaScript is concerned, the Web browser and everything in it is just a collection of JavaScript objects. You also learned how to create statements to access the various parts of the Browser Object Model. Finally, you saw how interaction between your JavaScript code and the Browser Object Model can change what the user sees in the Web browser.

QUIZ YOURSELF

1. What does the `window` object represent? (See "The window object.")
2. What is kept in the `frames` array? (See "The window object.")
3. What does the `self` object refer to? (See "The window object.")
4. How is the name attribute of an HTML tag used by the Browser Object Model? (See "A simple example.")
5. What happens when you assign a value to the value property of a text box object? (See "A simple example.")

Working with the window Object

Session Checklist

✔ Understanding what the window object is
✔ Learning about window object properties and methods

**30 Min.
To Go**

As you've seen in the previous session, the window object is a JavaScript object that represents the entire Web browser window. By working through the window object, your JavaScript code can effectively control just about every aspect of the browser. As you might imagine, Session 7 only scratched the surface of what's in the window object. In this session, we're going to dig quite a bit deeper into the window object so you can see how to use its properties and methods in your JavaScript programs. (Examples of these properties and methods can be found on your CD-ROM in the Session08 folder.)

Both Netscape and Internet Explorer have added proprietary properties and methods to the window object. So I'll restrict myself to only those properties and methods that work in both browsers. If you need to write JavaScript that's specific to a browser, refer to Session 26.

Properties of the window Object

As you read the following descriptions, keep in mind that a window object and its properties can be assigned to a JavaScript variable just like any other object. Many of the examples in this session make use of this fact to open and track multiple windows.

The closed property

This tells you if a particular window object represents an open browser window. If the window is open, the closed property will be false. If the window is closed, it will be true.

The defaultStatus property

This property specifies a string that will be displayed in the browser's status bar. (The status bar is typically found in the lower left-hand corner of the browser window.)

The document property

This is the document object. It represents the HTML document that is currently loaded into the browser window or the HTML document that is loaded into a particular frame. The document object is discussed in detail in the next session.

The frames array

This array holds one window object for each frame in a multiframe Web site. (The frames array is discussed in detail in Session 23.)

The history property

The history property is an object that contains the history list — that is, a list of Web sites visited by that window object. Each window object (including those in the frames array) has its own history property. (The history object is discussed in Session 27.)

The location property

The location property holds the Web address of the page you are currently viewing. If you assign this property a new Web address, the Web browser will load that Web page. (The location object is discussed in detail in Session 27.)

The name property

This property contains the name of the window object. Note that this is not the same as the name of the JavaScript variable that actually holds the window object. For example:

```
var catalogWindow = window.open();
catalogWindow.name = "catalog";
```

Once you assign a name to a window object, you can use that name in the target attribute of an anchor tag. So, in the following example, clicking on the "See the Catalog" link will load the catalog.htm file into the window that was opened by your JavaScript code.

```
<a href="catalog.htm" target="catalog">See the Catalog</a>
```

The navigator property

The navigator object contains information about the Web browser including its version, brand information and platform information. The following simple script will reveal everything contained in the navigator object. (We'll discuss how to use this information to write browser-specific scripts in Session 26.)

```
for (x in navigator)
    document.write( x + " = " + navigator[x] + "<br />");
```

The opener property

When one window creates another (using the window.open() method, discussed later in this session) the first window becomes the *opener* of the new window. This allows you to actually communicate between windows. (We'll look at this process in Session 24.)

```
self.name = "original";
var newWindow = window.open();
document.write( newWindow.opener.name);
```

The parent property

If your site is arranged in frames, each frame is considered to be its own window. So, each frame has its own window object. These window objects are all "children" of the frameset document that loaded those frames into the Web browser. The window object representing the frameset document is therefore said to be the *parent* of each frame. The parent property holds the window object representing the frameset document. This is shown in Figure 8-1. (The source code for Figure 8-1 is in the file framesNparent.htm.)

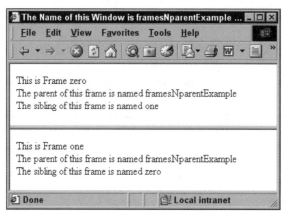

Figure 8-1
Frames and the parent property

The screen property

The screen property contains information about the screen settings on the client monitor. You can use this information to determine the resolution of the client monitor and load the appropriately sized graphics. (We'll discuss the screen property in Session 14.)

The status property

This property holds a string that will be temporarily displayed in the browser's status bar. After a brief period, the string in the defaultStatus property will replace this message.

The top property

The top property refers to the top-most window in a set of frames-based windows. This is essentially the window object that represents the actual Web browser window. How is this different from the parent property? Consider Figure 8-2.

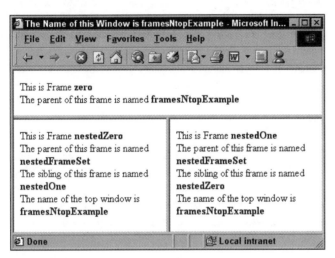

Figure 8-2
Frames within frames and the top property

This window shows a frameset within a frameset. As you can see, the innermost set of frames (the bottom row) have a parent that is itself a frame in the browser window. In this case, the parent for these frames is not the same thing as the actual browser window. The top property, on the other hand, always represents the actual browser window.

20 Min. To Go

Methods of the window Object

The window object provides several methods. In this section, we'll look at these methods and see how they can be used to interact with the user and the web browser itself.

The alert() method

This method displays a dialog containing a message that you specify along with a single OK button. Calling this method will halt execution of your JavaScript program until the user clicks the OK button to proceed. (Note that in the Linux version of Netscape Navigator, the alert() method does *not* halt execution of your program!) The alert() method is extremely useful as a debugging tool. If you need to know the value of a variable, simply slap it into an alert() call and you'll see the value pop up on the screen in front of you. For example, if you wanted to know the value of a variable named price, you could simply code alert(price).

The blur() method

The blur() method will remove the focus from the associated window object. This means that the window object will no longer receive any keystrokes that the user types. If you call blur() for a window in a frame, the focus will go to the top object in its browser window. If you call blur() for a top level window (that is, the window that represents the browser) that window will usually be sent to the back of all other open browser windows.

The clearInterval() and clearTimeout() methods

See the discussions for the setInterval() and setTimeout() methods later in this Session.

The close() method

Calling the close() method will close the associated browser window. As a security measure, most Web browsers will only let you close the windows you create yourself. If you try to close a browser window created by the system, you'll usually get a confirmation dialog telling you that the Web page you are viewing is trying to close the window. For example, assuming that you start Internet Explorer (for Windows) and immediately load in a file containing the following code:

```
var newWindow = window.open();
newWindow.close();
self.close();
```

The first close() call will proceed as expected. However, the second close() call will bring up a dialog asking you to confirm that you want the window to close.

The confirm() method

The confirm() method lets you ask the user a simple "OK" or "Cancel" question. You pass the confirm() method a string containing your question and it presents that question to the user along with a set of OK and Cancel buttons. If the user clicks the OK button, a true is returned. If the user clicks the Cancel button, a false is returned.

```
if (confirm("Would you like to proceed?")) {
    alert("Here we go...");
    }
else {
    alert("I understand. These things can be scary!");
    }
```

The focus() method

The focus() method will tell the Web browser to direct keystrokes to the specified window object. If the window object specified isn't the front-most window, the focus() method will bring that window to the front.

The moveBy() method

Calling this method will move the specified window by a specified number of pixels.

```
self.moveBy(10, 30); self.moveBy(-10,-30);
```

The first statement will move the window 10 pixels to the right and 30 pixels down from its current position. The second statement will move the window 10 pixels up and 30 pixels to the left of its current position. Note that most browsers will not let you move the window off of the screen.

The moveTo() method

This method moves a window to an absolute position on the screen. For example:

```
self.moveTo(0, 0); self.moveTo(100,300);
```

The first statement will move the window to the upper left corner of the screen. The second statement will move the window to a position 100 pixels from the top of the screen and 300 pixels from the left-hand side of the screen. Here again, most browsers will not let you move the window off of the screen.

The open() method

As you've seen in several of the other examples in this Session, the open()
method opens a new browser window and returns a window object to represent it.
If you call the open() method with no parameters, you will get an empty browser
window. If you want something more interesting, you can pass up to four parameters in the following order:

url   This is the Web address of a Web page that you want to
               automatically load into the new window.

name   This is a string that will be placed into the window.name
               property of the new window.

featuresList   This is a string specifying the features the new window
               should have. This parameter lets you specify how big the
               window should be, if it should have toolbars, scroll bars,
               and so on. (We'll discuss these features in Session 24.)

replace   This is a Boolean value that specifies if the Web address
               specified in the first parameter should replace the current
               entry in the history list.

As an example, the following code would create a new window object named
"hungryMinds" which would display the Hungry Minds Web site.

```
var bookSite = window.open( "http://www.hungryminds.com",
"hungryMinds");
```

The prompt() method

The prompt() method allows you to ask the user a question, and get back an
answer. You pass two parameters to the prompt() method: a message string and a
default response value. The following statement will present the user with the dialog shown in Figure 8-3.

```
var response = prompt( "What is your favorite color?", "black");
```

Note the default response specified in the call to prompt() is shown in the text
box. The user can type over this value, or click OK to accept it as their reply. If
they click OK, the value typed into the text box will be returned to your script. If
the user clicks Cancel, a special value called *null* is returned to your script. A null
tells your program that nothing was returned by prompt(). (The null value is
used in JavaScript to represent "nothing" or an empty object.) Since null is a
JavaScript keyword, you can check for it like this:

```
var response = prompt( "What is your favorite color?", "black");
if (response == null) {
    alert( "You clicked the Cancel button");
    }
else {
    alert( "Your response was " + response);
    }
```

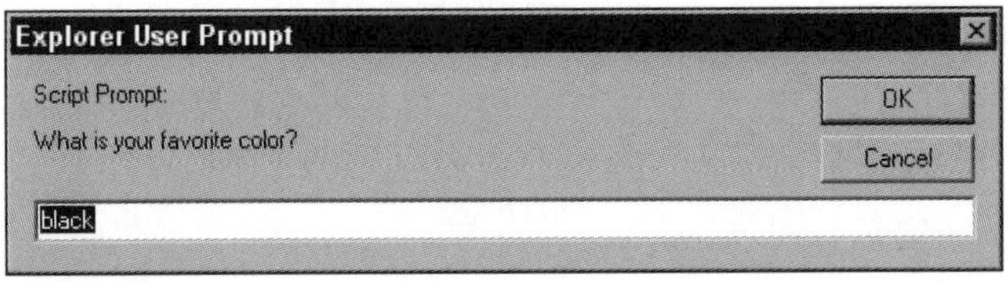

Figure 8-3
A dialog created by the prompt() method

The resizeTo() method

This method will resize a browser window to the width and height specified.

```
self.resizeTo(50, 325); // Set width to 50 and height to 325
```

Note that the size you specify represents the *entire* browser window (including toolbars, buttons, and so forth) not just the document portion of the window!

The scroll() and scrollTo() methods

Each of these methods will let you scroll the content of a window to a specified point. The point specified will appear in the upper left-hand corner of the window.

```
scroll( 0, 0); scrollTo( 0, 30);
```

The first statement will scroll to the top of a document while the second statement will scroll 30 pixels down the document.

The scrollBy() method

The scrollBy() method will scroll a document a specified number of pixels from its current position. The following statement will scroll a document up 25 pixels.

```
scrollBy( 0, -25);
```

**10 Min.
To Go**

The setInterval() and clearInterval() methods

The `setInterval()` method is almost exactly like the `setTimeout()` method. (In fact, you should read the description of the `setTimeout()` method before continuing here.) The main difference is that the JavaScript statement you pass to `setInterval()` is executed over and over again. After each execution, the timer resets and the countdown begins again. So, this statement will scroll down a document, 100 pixels at a time, every two seconds.

```
var intervalID = setInterval( 'scrollBy( 0, 100);', 2000);
```

The only ways to stop this process is to either close the browser window or to use the `clearInterval()` method to stop the timer from counting down.

```
clearInterval( intervalID);
```

The setTimeout() and clearTimeout() methods

This method is one of the most useful, and confusing, methods in the `window` object. The `setTimeout()` method takes two parameters: The first is a string that represents a valid JavaScript statement. The second is a number representing a time period expressed in milliseconds. (A millisecond is 1/1000th of a second. So, 1000 milliseconds is 1 second.)

The `setTimeout()` method takes the first parameter and sets it aside in a special queue. It then takes the second parameter and uses it to start a countdown. For example, if you pass 2000 milliseconds for the second parameter, you'll get a two-second countdown.

Once the countdown is finished, the first parameter is retrieved and passed to the JavaScript interpreter. The JavaScript interpreter then executes the statement in the string just as if you had typed it directly into your source code.

In this example, the `setTimeout()` method will set up a five-second counter. When this expires (that is, when it *times out*) the statement `alert('Hello World!')` will be executed.

```
setTimeout( "alert('Hello World!')", 5000);
```

Notice that the string we are passing is a valid JavaScript statement. Also note how I've nested my quotes in this example. If I had written the statement this way:

```
setTimeout( "alert("Hello World!")", 5000);
```

The statement would have failed because you can't have two sets of the same type of quotes in a single string.

Another thing to note is that the setTimeout() method does *not* set up a recursive call to the statement you specify in the first parameter. The JavaScript statement in the first parameter is only executed once, and only after the specified number of milliseconds has passed. To execute a statement over and over again, use the setInterval() method instead.

It's not shown in any of these examples, but the setTimeout() method also returns a result. This result is a timer ID that you can either hold onto or ignore completely. If you decide to hold onto it, you can pass this timer ID to the clearTimeout() method and the timer will be stopped and the associated JavaScript statement will not be executed.

The setTimeout() method is an extremely powerful and important part of the window object. In fact, it's so useful, you'll find it used in a large number of the sample files for this session. (We'll be talking more about the setTimeout() method and its close cousin, the eval() function, in Session 20.)

You should *never* write a recursive function in JavaScript! If you do, you'll quickly generate an error message to the effect that the JavaScript interpreter has run out of memory. In a worst-case scenario, you can even crash the browser! Instead, always use the setInterval() or setTimeout() methods to set up a repeating function or code block. (For an example of a recursive function, see the recurseBad.htm file in the Session08 folder. Just be sure to save all of your work before you load this file!)

Done!

REVIEW

It's been another information-packed session, but the result is that you now know just about everything there is to know about the window object. You've learned about the properties and methods that make up the window object, and, if you've loaded any of the source files on the CD-ROM, you've seen how to use them.

QUIZ YOURSELF

1. What is the difference between the parent and top properties? (See "Properties of the window Object.")

2. What is in the `navigator` object? (See "Properties of the window Object.")

3. What does the `opener` property contain? (See "Properties of the window Object.")

4. What does the `alert()` method do? (See "Methods of the window Object.")

5. What do the `setTimeout()` and `setInterval()` methods do? (See "Methods of the window Object.")

Working with the document Object

Session Checklist

✔ Understanding what the document object is

✔ Learning about document object properties and methods

**30 Min.
To Go**

The document object is a JavaScript object that represents the HTML page that's currently loaded into the Web browser. As with the other objects you've seen, the document object contains a whole host of properties and methods that let you investigate and manipulate the HTML page. In this session, we'll look at these properties and methods to see how you can use them from JavaScript. (Examples showing the use of each property and method can be found on your CD-ROM in the Session09 folder.)

As with the window object, each of the major Web browsers defines several proprietary properties and methods for the document object. Again, I'll be restricting my discussion to those items that should work in the latest versions of Internet Explorer and Netscape Navigator.

Properties of the document Object

In the sections that follow, you'll see how the properties of the document object can be used to affect the way your HTML documents are seen by your users.

The alinkColor property

The alinkColor property specifies the color that should be used to display the currently active link. The currently active link is the link that will be followed if you press the return key or click the mouse on it. To change this, just assign it a new color value:

```
document.alinkColor = "gray";
```

If you need a bit more control over the color you want to use, you can also assign a hexadecimal color value. Note however that these hex values need to be preceded with a pound sign and not the 0x that you would use when assigning a hexadecimal value to a JavaScript variable. So, an equivalent statement using a hex value would look like this:

```
document.alinkColor = "#808080";
```

When you assign a color this way, you are specifying the red, green, and blue (RGB) color values that will be mixed to create the final color. In the above example, all three colors are being assigned a value of 0x80 (128 decimal). In the following example:

```
document.alinkColor = "#00FF77";
```

The value for red is 0x00 (zero, the lowest possible value), the value for green is 0xFF (which is 255 decimal and is the highest possible value) and the value for blue is 0x77 (which is 119 decimal). These values will be mixed to arrive at the final display color.

However, if you don't want to muck about with numbers, there are several standardized color values that have been assigned names that you can use for your colors. Table 9-1 shows the standard color names (and their equivalent hexadecimal values) that you can use for this and the other color-related properties of the document object.

Table 9-1
Standard Color Names and Numbers

Color Name	Hexadecimal Color Number (#RRGGBB)	Color Name	Hexadecimal Color Number (#RRGGBB)
aqua	#00FFFF	navy	#000080
black	#000000	olive	#808000
blue	#0000FF	purple	#800080
fuchsia	#FF00FF	red	#FF0000
gray	#808080	silver	#C0C0C0
green	#008000	teal	#008080
lime	#00FF00	white	#FFFFFF
maroon	#800000	yellow	#FFFF00

The anchors array

The anchors array holds one Anchor object for each set of `<a name="someName"></a>` tags that are in the document. Each Anchor object has a name property that contains the name specified in the name attribute of the HTML anchor tag. So, the following HTML

```
<a name="top">This is the top</a>
<!-- Lots of content would go here -->
<a name="bottom">This is the bottom</a>
```

would create an anchors array with two Anchor objects in it. The first anchor object would have a name property of "top" and the second would have a name of "bottom."

The applets array

The applets array holds all of the Java applets that are embedded in the HTML document. (Each item in this array corresponds to an `<applet>` tag in the HTML document.) The properties and methods that you can access for these Java applets will be the same as the properties and methods that each applet makes available to the outside world. We'll be discussing the relationship between Java and JavaScript in more detail in Session 30.

The bgColor property

This property lets you set the background color of the HTML document.

```
document.bgColor = "red";
```

Note that in Netscape Navigator, you can only assign a value to bgColor at the start of your HTML document (that is, in a script block located between the <head></head> tags.) In Internet Explorer however, you can assign a value to this property at any time. This will result in an immediate change of the background color in your document.

The cookie property

The cookie property lets you read and set the client's cookie value for an HTML document. Reading and writing a cookie is very simple:

```
var theCookie = document.cookie; // read the cookie
document.cookie = theCookie; // write the cookie
```

However, as you'll see in Session 16, actually using a cookie is a bit more complex.

The domain property

This property contains the host name of the Web server that the HTML document was loaded from. (If the document was loaded from a local file, this property will contain the empty string.) As I've hinted at previously, JavaScript code in one browser window can communicate with JavaScript in another window. However, this is allowed only if the document.domain property is the same for each window that wants to communicate. So, if the two HTML files you want to communicate come from two different servers on your site (that is, two different domains), this can present a problem. In Session 24, I'll show you how to use the document.domain property to work around this restriction.

The embeds array

The embeds array contains one entry for each of the <embed> tags in the HTML document. If an individual embedded item has a Java-style interface, you can interact with it in the same way that you would a Java applet in the applets array. However, this is entirely dependent on the embedded item.

The fgColor property

This property lets you change the foreground color of the HTML document.

```
document.fgColor = "blue";
```

**20 Min.
To Go**

(Unlike the bgColor property, only older versions of Netscape Navigator restrict the use of this property to the start of an HTML document. In Navigator v6 and later, you can assign a value to fgColor whenever you like.)

The forms array

The forms array contains one form object for each set of <form></form> tags in the HTML document. These form objects themselves contain objects representing the various controls (text boxes, select menus, etc.) that the user interacts with in the form. The form object and its contents are one of the most important and useful parts of the document object, so I'll be going over them in great detail in Sessions 12, 13, and 15.

The images array

The images array contains one entry for each <img> tag in the HTML document. Each entry is a JavaScript Image object that you can use to load new images or create simple animations. You'll find information on the images array and how to use it in Session 14.

The lastModified property

This is a String object containing the date that the HTML file was last changed on disk.

The linkColor property

This property holds the color that will be used to display links (`<a href="somedestination"></a>` tags) in the document. As with the `fgColor` property, older versions of Netscape Navigator restrict the use of this property to the start of an HTML document. In the latest browsers, you can assign a value to `linkColor` whenever you like.

The links array

This holds a `Link` object for each `<a href="somedestination"></a>` tag in the HTML file.

The Link object

A JavaScript `Link` object contains lots of different properties that can provide you with a ton of information about the HTML link it represents. This information can be used to write all sorts of interesting scripts. (The linksArray.htm file on your CD-ROM shows one use for this information.) The properties of the Link object vary from browser to browser, but the most common (and useful) are described in the following sections.

The Link.hash property This contains a String object containing the *hash* part of the Web address specified in the link. For example, in this link, the hash portion is #top.

```
<a href="http://www.baby-palooza.com/index.htm#top">Baby-
Palooza</a>
```

The Link.host property This contains a String object containing the host information from the link's Web address. For example, in this link, the host portion is www.baby-palooza.com:80.

```
<a href="http://www.baby-palooza.com">Baby-Palooza</a>
```

The Link.hostname property This contains a String object containing just the host name information from the link's Web address. For example, in this link, the hostname portion is www.baby-palooza.com.

```
<a href="http://www.baby-palooza.com">Baby-Palooza</a>
```

The Link.href property This String object contains the entire Web address specified in the link. For example, in this link, the href portion is `http://www.baby-palooza.com/`.

```
<a href="http://www.baby-palooza.com">Baby-Palooza</a>
```

The Link.pathname property If the Web address points to a file that's buried in a folder somewhere on the server, this property will contain the path to that file. In this link, the `pathname` property would contain the string `strollers/index.htm`.

```
<a href="http://www.baby-
palooza.com/strollers/index.htm">Strollers</a>
```

The Link.port property This is a String object containing the port specified in the link's Web address.

```
<a href="http://www.baby-palooza.com:80">Baby-Palooza!</a>
```

Here, the port property would contain the value 80.

The Link.protocol property The protocol (http, ftp, etc.) specified in the link's Web address.

The Link.search property This is the query string specified in the Web address.

```
<a href="http://www.baby-
palooza.com/search.htm?type=stroller">Show Strollers</a>
```

In this example, the search property would contain the string `?type=stroller`. Note that the question mark *is* included at the start of the string.

The Link.target property This is a String object containing the name of the target window that is specified in the link. In the following link, the `target` property will contain the string `goodBooks`.

```
<a href="http://www.hungryminds.com" target="goodBooks">Hungry
Minds</a>
```

The Link.innerHTML Property This property is available in Netscape Navigator v6 and Internet Explorer v5 and later. Basically, it's the text that shows up in the Web browser for a particular link. For example, in this link, the string "Hungry Minds" will be in the `innerHTML` property.

```
<a href="http://www.hungryminds.com">Hungry Minds</a>
```

The really neat thing about this property is that you can actually assign a new string to it, and change the link's text on the screen!

The location property

This holds the Web address the HTML document was loaded from. Assigning a new Web address to `location` will force the browser to load the page stored at that address.

```
document.location = "http://www.hungryminds.com";
```

**10 Min.
To Go**

The plugins array

This is another name for the `embeds` array. Netscape Navigator 6 doesn't support this property, probably to avoid confusion with the `navigator.plugins` array (which you'll be learning about in Session 29). The `navigator.plugins` array holds information about extensions installed in the browser itself, while the `plugins` array (and the `embeds` array) holds information about the items embedded in an individual HTML document. (Even though only Internet Explorer supports this property, I mention it here to draw the distinction between the `plugins` array and the `navigator.plugins` array.)

The referrer property

The `referrer` property is a String object that holds the Web address of the document from which the current HTML document was reached. (Note that this property is in the latest versions of Internet Explorer and Netscape Navigator, but does not seem to work .)

The title property

This property holds a String containing the title of the HTML document. This is the title that is specified between the `<title></title>` tags. (In Internet Explorer v5+ and Netscape Navigator v6, you can assign this a new string and the title of the window will change.)

The URL property

This property contains the same information as the location property. The main difference is that, in Netscape Navigator, assigning a new Web address to the URL property has no effect. (In Internet Explorer, assigning a new address to the URL property will force the browser to load that page.)

The vlinkColor property

This property specifies the color to be used to display the links that have been visited.

Methods of the document Object

In addition to the properties discussed in the previous sections, the document object also contains several methods that allow you to manipulate the actual body of the document.

The clear() method

In the past, the clear() method was used to clear the contents of a browser window. Now however, the clear() method doesn't really do much of anything. In fact, the clear() method will be removed from JavaScript in the near future. So, why mention it? Well, there's a lot of JavaScript out there that uses the clear() method, so I thought you should know about it. However, don't use the clear() method in your own JavaScript code!

The open() and close() methods

When you use the write() or writeln() method to write a string to the document object, you are actually sending data to something called a *stream*. A stream is really just a holding place for data. The data sits in the stream until the browser is ready for it. In this case, your string data sits in the stream until the browser can write it out to the browser window. The act of preparing a stream for use is called *opening* the stream. Conversely, when you finish using a stream, you should *close* it. That's what these methods do.

The open() method tells the browser that you want to write some new string data to the current document object. The close() method tells the browser that you have finished writing your data. It also forces the browser to output any data that's left in the stream.

Normally, you don't have to bother with either method. When the browser loads an HTML file, it automatically opens an output stream and begins filling it with the contents of the HTML file along with the output of any document.write() or document.writeln() calls you make in your JavaScript code. Then, when the HTML file is completely loaded (and your JavaScript code has finished creating its output), the browser will close the stream and display the page. However, if you want to send any text to the browser window, *after* the HTML page is loaded, you need to proceed in the following manner:

1. Call document.open(). This will open the document object for writing once again.

2. Make your document.write() or document.writeln() calls. This will let you write out whatever HTML or plain text you wish.

3. Call document.close(). This tells the browser that you are finished writing your output to the browser window. In response, it will close the output stream and write any characters left in the stream to the browser window.

As you might guess, this combination of calls will actually let you create your own HTML pages on the fly. While this is a very powerful feature of JavaScript, there is one side effect of the open() method that you need to be aware of: When you call the open() method, the contents of the document are cleared from the browser window. (This is why the clear() method is no longer used. The open() method does exactly the same thing.) Then whatever you write to the browser window will actually *replace* the old contents of the browser window as soon as the close() method is called! Consider the following:

```
<html>
<head>
<title>The document Object: the open() and close() Methods</title>
<script language="javascript">
function writeNewStuff() {
    document.open();
    for (x=0; x<5; x++) {
        document.write( "Oh dear! I seem to have overwritten
        everything!<br />");
        }
    document.close();
    }
```

```
</script>
</head>
<body bgcolor="white">
<script language="javascript">
for (x=0; x<5; x++) {
    document.write( "Shop at Baby-Palooza!<br />");
    }
setTimeout( 'writeNewStuff()', 5000);
</script>
</body>
</html>
```

Here, the code at the bottom of the file writes out five lines of propaganda and then sets up a timer that will call the writeNewStuff() function five seconds later. When this function executes, it calls the open() method and then writes out five more lines of text. Finally, it calls close() to send that text to the browser window. If you load this file into a browser, you'll see the initial text on screen for a few seconds and then it will suddenly be replaced by the output of the writeNewStuff() function. If you then view the source of the browser window, you'll find the original contents of the HTML document are gone, including your JavaScript code!

The moral of this story is that it's a *very* bad idea to call the open() and close() methods for the document that your code resides in. As we'll see in Session 23, a better approach is to have your JavaScript code in a *control frame* and your content in another *display frame*. This way, your JavaScript code can use the open(), write() and close() methods to change the contents in your display frame while your JavaScript code remains untouched.

The write() method

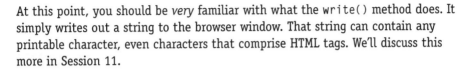

Done!

At this point, you should be *very* familiar with what the write() method does. It simply writes out a string to the browser window. That string can contain any printable character, even characters that comprise HTML tags. We'll discuss this more in Session 11.

The writeln() method

The writeln() method is just like the write() method, with one addition. At the end of the string you specify, it adds a new line character. While this doesn't appear in your final HTML output, it will help format the underlying HTML code by placing a new line at the end of each line of output (this causes subsequent lines of output to start on the next line).

REVIEW

In this session, you learned about the properties and methods of the `document` object. First, you saw how to use the properties to examine and change characteristics of the currently loaded HTML document. Then, you saw how to use the `document.open()`, `document.write()`, and `document.close()` methods to create new contents for the browser window.

QUIZ YOURSELF

1. What is the `document` object? (See "Working with the document object.")
2. What is kept in the `forms` array? (See "The forms array.")
3. What does the `links` array represent? (See "The links array.")
4. What happens when you assign a new Web address to the `document.location` property? (See "The location property.")
5. What is the major side effect of the `document.open()` method? (See "The open() and close() methods.")

SESSION

10

Reacting to Events

Session Checklist

✔ Understanding what events are and how JavaScript can handle them

✔ Learning which events you can handle with JavaScript

✔ Learning how to use events to respond to user actions

**30 Min.
To Go**

You've seen how the JavaScript language works, and you've also learned a lot about how the Browser Object Model allows JavaScript to interact with the browser. However, almost everything I've shown you thus far has required you, the programmer, to take the initiative in making things happen. In this session, you're going to learn how to write JavaScript code that actually waits for things to happen and then reacts accordingly.

What Are "Events?"

To paraphrase a popular colloquialism, "stuff happens." This is true not only in life, but in the Web browser as well. When something interesting happens in the Web browser, it's called an *event*. For example, when the user clicks the mouse on a button in a form, that's an event. However, events aren't just created by the user.

When the browser finishes loading a Web page, that's an event too. In fact, in the Web browser environment, there are over a dozen different types of events that can occur. There are events that tell you when keys have been pressed, when a form has been submitted and even when the contents of a text box have changed! The point of this is that an event exists to represent just about everything that can occur in the Web browser. For example, each and every HTML control you create will generate its own set of events. Because of this, you can write JavaScript code to respond to each control's events individually. This gives you an incredible amount of control over the behavior of your Web pages.

Responding to an event is called *handling* the event, and the JavaScript code you write to handle an event is called an *event handler*. So, for example, you can write one event handler that's called when your HTML document finishes loading, and another that's called when a new item is chosen from a select menu in one of your forms. Of course, you don't have to create event handlers for *every* event, but if you really need to, you can.

Creating Event Handlers

An event handler usually takes the form of a JavaScript function that you create specifically to handle a certain type of event. An event handler can also be one or more JavaScript statements that are embedded in the HTML that defines the event.

The first step in creating an event handler is to actually define the event you want to handle. Event definitions always begin with the letters on and are usually defined as part of an HTML tag. For example, a *load* event occurs when the Web browser finishes loading an HTML document. So, this event will be defined as an *onload* event for the body of the document. So, the onload event is defined as part of the <body> tag, like so:

```
<body onload="alert('Welcome to Baby-Palooza.com!')">
```

Here I have the name of my event (onload) followed by an equal sign. After that, in quotes, I have the JavaScript statement I want to execute in response to the event. Almost all event definitions follow this same basic format.

The question now is, "What exactly does this do?" Well, the onload event for an HTML document occurs after the last character of that document is loaded into the Web browser. So, as soon as the Web browser has loaded the last character of the HTML file, it looks to see if I have defined an onload event handler in the <body> tag. I have, so at that point it actually executes the JavaScript statement that is in quotes after the equal sign. The end result is that after the page loads, an alert window will appear to welcome the user to the Baby-Palooza.com site.

The act of triggering an event is sometimes referred to as *firing*
the event. So, you might hear someone say something like,
"When the `onload` **handler fires, you'll be directed to a new Web**
site."

Event handlers can be more that just one JavaScript statement. So, this is perfectly legal:

```
<script language="javascript">
var pageLoaded = false;
</script>
<body onload="alert('Welcome!'); pageLoaded = true;">
```

This event handler consists of a call to the `alert()` method, followed by an assignment statement. (Remember, as shown in Session 2, you can have multiple JavaScript statements on a single line, just separate them with a semicolon.) There are just two statements in this handler, but it could just as easily contain three statements or a dozen.

Another important point to notice in this example is that the code in my event handler has full access to my global variables (in this case, the `pageLoaded` variable). Remember, JavaScript global variables are accessible *everywhere*, including inside event handlers.

Of course, if your event handler needs to do something complex, you'll probably want to place it in a function. As you might expect, that would look something like this:

```
<script language="javascript">
var pageLoaded = false;
function doLoad( isLoaded) {
    pageLoaded = isLoaded;
    alert( 'Welcome!');
    }
</script>
<body onload="doLoad( true);">
```

In this case, I've simply defined a function (`doLoad()`) to handle the event. So, my event handler simply calls the function. To prove that this is the same as any other function call, I've even passed it a parameter (`true`). (You don't have to pass a parameter if your function doesn't require one.) It should be noted that there's no magic in the name I've given this function. You can give your event handling functions whatever names you wish (as long as those names are valid JavaScript function names). I've simply gotten into the habit of naming all of my event handling functions "do*EventName*()". This really helps me identify my event handling functions when I'm looking through my code.

**20 Min.
To Go**

Events You Can Handle

Now that you know how events work in general, it's time to learn about the different events there are and how you can actually handle them with JavaScript. As with the `window` and `document` objects, each of the major browsers defines several proprietary events that the other browser simply doesn't support. So, here again, I'll restrict the discussion to those events supported in the latest versions of the major browsers.

Another important point is that most events can be fired by lots of different objects in the Browser Object Model. For example, not only can you define an `onload` event for the `<body>` tag, you can also define one for every `<img>` tag in your HTML document (as you'll see in Session 14). So, as you look over the following descriptions, remember that, unless explicitly stated otherwise, any given event will probably work for most HTML tags. (The trick is to experiment and see which events a given tag will support.)

Finally, in the list of events that follows, I'm going to refer to each event as you'd actually see it in a JavaScript program. For example, instead of talking about the "load" event, I'll simply refer to it as the "onload" event. (Note that the following discussion covers the available events in a fairly generic fashion. While there are examples of how to use each event on your CD-ROM in the Session10 folder, more detailed examples of how to use each event can be found in later sessions.)

The onabort event

This event is unique to the JavaScript Image object. It fires when the user aborts the loading of an image. In other words, if an image has not finished loading and the user clicks the browser's Stop button, each unloaded image will fire off an `onabort` event.

```
<img src="bigImage.jpg" onabort="alert('Why did you do that?')" />
<img src="bigImg2.jpg" onabort="alert('You stopped them all!')" />
```

Assuming these images are in the same document, clicking the Stop button before either has loaded will cause both alert windows to display. (However, if one image has finished loading before the Stop button is clicked, only the unfinished image's `onabort` handler will fire off.) We'll be discussing the Image object and its related events in Session 14.

The onblur event

In the world of programming, the term *blur* is used to indicate that an object on the screen has had the user's attention shifted away from it. When a window gets *blurred,* that usually means that the window has been sent behind all of the other windows that are on the screen. Coding an `onblur` handler for a window is actually fairly simple. You simply define your handler in either the `<body>` or `<frameset>` tag that is loaded into the window. For example:

```
<body bgcolor="white" onblur="doBlur()">
```

For the controls in a form, *getting blurred* means that the user's keystrokes no longer go into a particular control. For example, consider the following form:

```
<form>
    <input type="text" name="fname"
    onblur="alert('Enter your last name')" />
    <input type="text" name="lname"
    onblur="alert('Thanks!')" />
</form>
```

Here I have two text fields. When I'm typing in the first field, it's said to have the *focus.* (See the discussion of the `onfocus` event later in this session.) This simply means that any keys I press will be sent to this control. If I press the tab key to move to the next field (or if I click the mouse in the second field to select it), the focus will shift to the second field and first field will fire an `onblur` event. It's important to note here that the `onblur` event can be fired for just about any control that you can put into a form, not just for text boxes.

The onchange event

The `onchange` event can be fired by any control in a form. However, it will only fire when the contents or selected value of the control actually changes *and* the control becomes blurred. If the contents don't change or the control doesn't become blurred, the `onchange` event will not fire. See the onchangeEvent.htm file for a detailed example.

The onclick and ondblclick events

These events will fire in response to a click or double-click on the HTML element in which the event is defined. This is normally used to assign some sort of action to a button in a form, like so:

```
<input type="button" value="Click Me!" onclick="doClickMe()" />
```

However, this can also be used with just about *any* nonempty tag (that is, any tag that has an opening and closing tag) to make a block of text clickable. For example:

```
<b ondblclick="alert('take things too far!')">You can...</b>
```

For other bizarre permutations of this concept, see the anyTagCanHaveEvents.htm file on your CD-ROM. Also, see "The Anchor Tag's Nonevent" at the end of this session for information on how to use the onclick event with your <a></a> tags.

The onerror event

There are two uses for the onerror event: telling when an image has not been loaded properly and handling JavaScript errors in a particular window.

Trapping image errors

For images, the onerror event fires if an image fails to load due to an error. For example, if an image doesn't exist, an onerror event will fire for that <img> tag.

```
<img src="dontExist.jpg" onerror="alert('Could not load')" />
```

Trapping JavaScript errors

As you've probably noticed by now, when an error occurs in your JavaScript program (for example, if you try to execute a document.writ() call), the type of error report you get depends on which browser you are using. In Internet Explorer, you'll get a dialog telling you what the error was, while Netscape Navigator will simply halt the execution of your script and won't do much beyond that. (To get actual JavaScript error information from the most current versions of Netscape, you have to type **javascript:** into the address box and press the return key.) If you would like your error reporting to be a bit more consistent, you can define your own JavaScript interpreter error handling function. Then, when an error occurs in your program, your function will be called to handle the error.

Unfortunately, defining such an error handler is a bit different than what we've seen so far, but it's still pretty simple to do. You simply assign the name of your error handling function to the onerror property of the window object, like so:

```
window.onerror = doWindowError;
```

Then, you simply define your error handling function as you would any other function. The only difference is that this function must accept three parameters: a message string that details what the error was, the Web address of the file that caused the error, and the line number where the error occurred. A simple example might look like this:

```
function doWindowError( msg, url, line) {
    // Handle the error any way you want here
    return true;
    }
window.onerror = doWindowError;
```

Note that, at the end of my error handling function, I return a `true` to the JavaScript interpreter. This tells the interpreter that I handled the error myself and that it shouldn't process it any further. Of course, if you return a `false`, the JavaScript interpreter will go ahead and do whatever else it thinks is necessary to handle the error.

The onfocus event

This is the counterpart to the `onblur` event. When a window comes to the front, or a control becomes the target of a user's keystrokes, it is said to have gained the focus. The `onfocus` event allows you to respond to this occurrence.

The onkeydown, onkeypress, and onkeyup events

These events allow you to detect when a key has been pressed inside a control. We'll discuss these events in more detail in Session 25.

The onload event

This event fires in two different instances: when an HTML document finishes loading and when an image finishes loading.

Trapping HTML document loads

To define an `onload` handler for an HTML document, just define it in the `<body>` tag.

```
<body onload="doLoad()">
```

Then, when the last character of the HTML document has been loaded by the browser, the `onload` event handler will execute.

It's important to realize that, for a complex HTML document, one with lots of forms and other elements, having a document's last character loaded by the browser may not be the same as having the document ready to use. Before a document is ready to use, its contents must be parsed by the JavaScript interpreter to create all of the Browser Object Model objects needed to properly represent the contents of the document. For example, if there are five forms in a document, all five corresponding `form` objects might not exist when the `onload` handler fires. This can cause big trouble if you try to use a not-yet-existent element from your `onload` handler. We'll see how to solve this problem in Session 24.

Trapping image loads

When used with `<img>` tags, this event can tell your JavaScript program when an image has finished loading. (In Session 14, you'll see how this is used to create animations.)

```
<img src="../images/happyBaby.jpg" onload="alert('Happy Baby')" />
```

The onmousedown event

This is similar to the `onclick` event. It fires when the mouse is clicked inside an element.

The onmousemove event

This event tells you when the mouse has been moved inside an element.

The onmouseout event

This event is triggered when the mouse leaves an element. Typically, you use this event to undo whatever you might have done in response to an `onmouseover` event.

The onmouseover event

This event fires when the mouse moves over an element. You can define this event for almost any nonempty HTML tag. Typically, it's used to change the window's status line when the mouse passes over a link. Like so:

```
<a href= "http://www.baby-palooza.com"
onmouseover="window.status='Visit baby-palooza.com!'; return
true">Baby-Palooza.com</a>
```

When the mouse passes over this link, the status bar at the bottom of the window will change to contain the message "Visit baby-palooza.com!" (Note that after changing the `window.status` property, my event handler returns a `true` value. This is required when changing the `window.status` property from inside an event handler.)

The onmouseup event

In contrast to the `onclick` and `onmousedown` events that tell you when an element has been clicked, this event tells you when the mouse button has been released in an element.

The onreset event

This event only fires in response to a click on a form's Reset button. For example:

```
<form onreset="return doReset()">
<input type="reset" value="Reset Form" />
</form>
```

**10 Min.
To Go**

Notice that I'm defining the `onreset` event in the `<form>` tag and that I'm using a `return` keyword as part of the event handler. The `return` keyword actually returns the Boolean result of the event handler to the JavaScript interpreter. If that value is `true`, the JavaScript interpreter will pass the reset event on to the browser, which will then reset the form to its original state. However, if that returned value is `false`, the JavaScript interpreter will tell the browser not to bother with resetting the form. This means that your `onreset` handler can set the form to whatever state it wishes, regardless of the original state of the form.

The onresize event

This event fires when the user resizes the browser or frame that the HTML document is in. You define it as part of the `<body>` tag, like so:

```
<body onresize="alert('You resized the window!')">
```

The onsubmit event

This is another event that belongs to forms. It fires when the user clicks a form's Submit button. It's defined similarly to the onreset event.

```
<form onsubmit="return doSubmit()">
<input type="submit" value="Submit Form" />
</form>
```

Like the onreset event, this event handler returns its result to the JavaScript interpreter. If that value is true, it tells JavaScript to go ahead and let the browser submit the form and its data. If the value returned is false, the JavaScript interpreter will *not* allow the browser to submit the form. This allows your onsubmit handler to actually validate the data in the form before the browser submits it. If the data is good, you return a true and the form goes on its merry way. If the data is bad, you return a false, and you can then force the user to correct the data and try again. Of course, what constitutes good and bad data is totally up to you. (In Session 15, we'll take a look at different data validation techniques.)

The onunload event

This event fires when an HTML document is being removed from the browser window. This can happen when the user clicks a link to go to another HTML document or when the browser window is being closed. You specify an onunload handler in the <body> tag.

```
<body bgcolor="white" onunload="alert('Bye-Bye...')">
```

Receiving this event is a good indication that it's time for your JavaScript program to do any cleaning up that might be necessary. As you'll see in Session 16, it's a great time to save out the information I need to preserve the contents of my shopping cart.

The Anchor Tag's Nonevent

While all of the above events can make your Web site more interactive, what about intercepting a simple click on a regular link? Actually, there are a couple of very interesting ways that you can use JavaScript to enhance the behavior of links.

First, you can execute one or more JavaScript statements instead of jumping to another HTML page. Consider the following example:

```
<a href="javascript:doSomething()">Click here to do something</a>
```

In this example, I've replaced the normal Web address in the `href` attribute with a JavaScript statement. Notice however that, unlike a standard event handler, I've started my statement with `javascript:`. This tells the HTML interpreter that what follows is a JavaScript statement, and not a standard Web address.

Another thing you can do is to combine a Web address with an `onclick` event handler.

```
<a href="http://www.hungryminds.com" onclick="alert('This handler
will return false'); return false">This link goes nowhere. . .</a>
```

Here I've added an `onclick` handler that first displays an alert window and then returns a `false`. Because this `onclick` handler returns `false`, the link specified in the `href` attribute will *not* be followed when the user clicks on this link. On the other hand, this link

```
<a href="http://www.hungryminds.com" onclick="alert('This handler
will return true'); return true">This link works as expected</a>
```

Done!

will display the alert window and then the link specified in the `href` attribute will be followed, just as you would expect it to. So, by combining an anchor tag with an `onclick` handler you can create links that only work when a specific condition has been met.

REVIEW

In this session, you learned how to write JavaScript that responds to events. You learned what events are available in the Web browser environment and what each signifies. You also saw how to create individual event handlers for each and every event that you want to react to. Finally, you learned how to use an `onclick` event handler to create hyperlinks that are followed conditionally, based on the Boolean result of the `onclick` handler.

QUIZ YOURSELF

1. What is an event? (See "What are "Events?")

2. What is an event handler? (See "Creating Event Handlers.")

3. How does the onblur event differ for the browser window and a control in a form? (See "The onblur event.")

4. How can you use the onerror event to create your own error handling routine? (See "The onerror event.")

5. How can you use an onclick event handler to create a hyperlink that is followed only if some JavaScript function returns true? (See "The Anchor Tag's Nonevent.")

PART

II

Saturday Morning

1. What is the empty string?

2. After the following statement executes, what will be stored in myVar?

   ```
   var myVar = 9 + "";
   ```

3. Write a statement that will extract the letters "Script" from the following sentence, "I think JavaScript is neat!"

4. Write a function that accepts a string and returns true if the word "JavaScript" is in the string. If the word "JavaScript" is not found, return a false. Note that you should check for any variation of "JavaScript" including "JAVASCRIPT," "javascript," or any other combination of upper- and lower-case letters.

5. In your own words, describe the Browser Object Model.

6. Write a statement (or statements) that will create an array from the following string, "Strollers:Diapers:Rattles:Bottles."

7. How do you create a multidimensional array with JavaScript?

8. Write and test a function that will sort an array of strings in reverse order (that is, from "Zebra" to "Apple").

9. How do you move through the items of an array that uses named slots?

10. How does the document object relate to the window object?

11. What is the alert() method used for?

12. What does a Link object represent?

13. What are the document.open() and document.close() methods used for?

14. Write a function that prompts the user to type in her name.

15. What is the difference between the `document.write()` and `document.writeln()` methods?

16. Write a function that uses the `confirm()` method to decide if an alert window should be displayed. (The contents of the alert window don't matter.)

17. What does the `onclick` event represent?

18. What is the difference between the `onblur` and `onfocus` events?

19. Create a link that sends the user to `http://www.hungryminds.com`. Include an `onclick` handler that asks the user if they really want to visit the Hungry Minds home page. If the handler returns `true`, jump to the page. If the handler returns `false`, do not jump to the page.

20. What does the `onload` event signify when used with an `<img>` tag?

PART

III

Saturday Afternoon

Dynamically Creating an HTML Page

Session Checklist

✔ Understanding how JavaScript can dynamically create an HTML document

✔ Understanding how JavaScript can dynamically create JavaScript

✔ Learning tips for debugging dynamically created HTML and JavaScript

**30 Min.
To Go**

The initial idea behind JavaScript was that it would be used to enhance the functionality of Web pages. In fact, JavaScript can do much more than just enhance a Web page; it can actually be used to create a Web page from scratch. For example, you've already seen (in Sessions 4 and 6), how the docu- ment.write() method could be used to write out the HTML tags needed to create a table. However, you aren't restricted to just creating tables. You can use JavaScript to dynamically build and output just about *any* HTML tag that you want. For example, you can create forms, image tags, headings, and even blocks of additional JavaScript code — all from within your JavaScript program.

Not Dynamic HTML

It's extremely important to note that what I'm talking about here is "dynamically created HTML," *not* Dynamic HTML (also known as "DHTML"). What's the difference?

Dynamically created HTML is HTML that is created and output by your JavaScript code as your HTML document is loading. In other words, you are using JavaScript to actually create the HTML that defines what the Web page initially looks like.

Dynamic HTML is a combination of JavaScript and the Browser Object Model that allows your JavaScript program to manipulate the appearance and properties of the HTML that is already loaded into the browser. You'll be learning about Dynamic HTML in Session 22.

Dynamically Creating HTML

As you saw in Session 9, when the browser begins to load an HTML document, it essentially makes a call to the document.open() method and then begins to parse the HTML code in the document. As it parses the HTML, it sends any output that's generated to the browser window for the user to see. During this process, if any document.write() calls are made, the output of those calls is sent to the HTML parser and processed accordingly. The key phrase here is "processed accordingly." If the output of a document.write() call contains one or more HTML tags, those tags will be rendered by the HTML parser and the result sent to the browser window, just as if the tags had been hard-coded in the original HTML file. So, the following JavaScript statement:

```
document.write("<b>This is bold text!</b>");
```

has the same overall effect as the following line of HTML:

```
<b>This is bold text!</b>
```

The important thing to realize here is that, as far as the HTML parser is concerned, these are both just streams of characters to be parsed. Consider the following combination of JavaScript and HTML.

```
<script language="javascript">
document.write("<b>This is bold text!");
</script>
</b>
```

Here, my opening boldface tag is generated by the call to `document.write()` and my closing boldface tag is a part of the enclosing HTML document. However, all the HTML parser sees is a stream of characters to process. This continues until every bit of HTML in the document (including any JavaScript-generated HTML) has been processed. At this point, the browser closes the document and the page is displayed in the browser. After the document is closed, there are only two ways to change the contents of the window:

- Use `document.open()` to reopen the document. This would be followed by the `document.write()` calls needed to output the desired HTML. After everything was output, you would then call `document.close()` to tell the browser to display the new contents. As we saw in Session 9, the drawback to this approach is that this combination of calls will actually erase the current contents of the window.

- The only other option is to use Dynamic HTML (DHTML) to modify the structure of the HTML document. We'll discuss this in detail in Session 22.

The point here is that if you want to dynamically generate the contents of your HTML page, the best time to do so is while the page is being loaded.

HTML == JavaScript string

The key to dynamically creating HTML is to realize that, as far as the browser is concerned, an HTML document is just a stream of characters. In terms of JavaScript, this means that the HTML you'll be creating can be thought of as one or more strings. This means that you can manipulate the HTML you want to output just as easily as you can manipulate any other JavaScript variable.

Storing HTML tags in string variables

The simplest, yet most powerful, trick to creating HTML with JavaScript is placing HTML tags in string variables. For example, in Session 6, I showed you a function, `showProductInfo()`, that created a table row by using a series of `document.write()` calls. That section of the function looked like this:

```
document.write( "<tr>");
document.write( "<td>" + category + "</td>");
```

```
document.write( "<td>" + pInfo[2] + "</td>");
document.write( "<td>" + pInfo[1] + "</td>");
document.write( "<td>$" + calcFinalCost( pInfo[0], pInfo[3]) +
"</td>");
document.write( "</tr>");
```

Here I have the strings "<td>", "</td>", "<tr>", and "</tr>" repeated over and over again. However, if I use a few variables to hold these strings, my code might look like this:

```
var tag_tr = "<tr>";
var tag_tr_end = "</tr>";
var tag_td = "<td>";
var tag_td_end = "</td>";
document.write( tag_tr);
document.write( tag_td + category + tag_td_end);
document.write( tag_td + pInfo[2] + tag_td_end);
document.write( tag_td + pInfo[1] + tag_td_end);
document.write( tag_td + "$" + calcFinalCost( pInfo[0], pInfo[3])
+ tag_td_end);
document.write( tag_tr_end);
```

Of course, this change hasn't really saved any keystrokes. In fact, my code has actually gotten larger. However, this isn't about saving space: it's about flexibility. Assuming that the variables I've just defined are still hanging around, consider the following code:

```
var tableRow = tag_tr;
tableRow += tag_td + category + tag_td_end;
tableRow += tag_td + pInfo[2] + tag_td_end;
tableRow += tag_td + pInfo[1] + tag_td_end;
tableRow += tag_td + "$" + calcFinalCost( pInfo[0], pInfo[3]) +
tag_td_end;
tableRow += tag_tr_end;
document.write( tableRow);
```

As you can see, in this example I've placed the entire string representing my table row into a single variable. Then, after I've built the string, I simply make one call to document.write() to send the string to the HTML parser. This is nice, but again, the fact that I've dropped to a single document.write() call isn't the point.

The point is that I now have the definition for a fairly complex HTML structure (an entire table row) inside a single JavaScript variable! This means that I can reuse this HTML structure over and over again as I build my HTML page.

Creating customized controls

While it's nice to be able to reuse HTML structures at will, the real power of dynamically created HTML comes from creating customized controls for your Web page. For example, it would be nice if the baby-palooza.com product listing contained links that the user could click to obtain more information on a given product. Assuming that the part number for a product is the basis for the name of its information page, this becomes a simple thing to do, as shown below:

```
var tag_tr = "<tr>";
var tag_tr_end = "</tr>";
var tag_td = "<td>";
var tag_td_end = "</td>";
var tableRow = tag_tr;
tableRow += tag_td + category + tag_td_end;
tableRow += tag_td + pInfo[2] + tag_td_end;
tableRow += tag_td;
tableRow += "<a href='" + pInfo[2] + ".htm'>" + pInfo[1] + "</a>";
tableRow += tag_td_end;
tableRow += tag_td + "$" + calcFinalCost( pInfo[0], pInfo[3]) +
tag_td_end;
tableRow += tag_tr_end;
document.write( tableRow);
```

With this code in place, each table row that's written to the browser will contain a link to a page containing more information about the product listed in that row of the table. And you don't have to stop at simple links. You can also create a more user-friendly link:

```
tableRow += "<a href='" + pInfo[2] + ".htm'";
tableRow += " onmouseover='window.status=";
tableRow += '"View more information about ' + pInfo[1] + '";return
true' + "'";
tableRow += ">" + pInfo[1] + "</a>";
```

With this additional code, in addition to giving users a link to more information, when they move the mouse over that link, they get a user-friendly description (in the status bar of the browser) of where the link will be taking them.

In these examples, I've only been showing you how to build custom links. If you wanted to, you could just as easily build some other type of custom control. For example, assume that instead of creating a table row, you wanted your function to create a menu item for use in a select list in a form. The JavaScript to do that might be as simple as this:

```
var optionItem = "<option value='" + pInfo[2] + "'>";
optionItem += pInfo[1] + "</option>";
```

The point is that you can create *any* type of HTML element you want and it can be as customized as you want.

Debugging your dynamically created HTML

One problem you might have noticed in the above examples is that the JavaScript code required for creating really useful HTML can quickly become very confusing. This can make it difficult to find the cause of any problems that might come up when you are testing your JavaScript code.

For example, the code required to create a link with an onmouseover event handler is almost unreadable due to all of the nested quotes that you have to work around. One way to make this type of quote nesting easier is to use *escaped* quotes inside the string you want to build. An escaped quote is one that is preceded by a backslash character (\). When the JavaScript interpreter sees an escaped quote, it knows that that quote should not be considered as the end of the string. For example, this is an illegal JavaScript string:

```
var msg = 'That's already in your shopping cart.';
```

While this version, with an escaped single quote, is perfectly legal:

```
var msg = 'That\'s already in your shopping cart.';
```

The backslash tells the JavaScript interpreter that it shouldn't consider this quote to be the end of the string. Instead, it should be treated just like another character in the string. You can also escape double quotes:

```
var quote = "Maia says, \"I love shopping at baby-palooza.com!\"";
```

So, the earlier example of a complex link could be rewritten like this:

```
tableRow += " onmouseover='window.status=\"View more information
about " + pInfo[1] + "\";return true'>" + pInfo[1] + "</a>";
```

While making your code more readable isn't exactly a debugging tip, it can certainly help prevent bugs from occurring in the first place.

This technique can place any character into a string. For example, \n is a new line character and \t is a tab. You can also include a character by its hexadecimal character code. Simply code *\xHH* **(where** *HH* **is the hexadecimal character code) and the character will be inserted into your string. For example, \x20 will put a blank space into your final string. (To see the values for all characters, see the charCodes.htm file.)**

Another problem with dynamically generated HTML is that, in some browsers, the HTML that's generated never actually shows up when you view the source for the page in the Web browser. This can lead to all sorts of problems, because it's very difficult to debug source code that you can't actually see! The solution here is to create a dummy text box control and, after you have built the HTML you are going to output, shove that HTML into the text box so that you can examine it. You'll also need to put a line feed (\n) at the end of each line of HTML you are placing in the text box, so that it won't all be strung together.

A complete example

In the Session11 folder on your CD-ROM, you'll find updated versions of the babyPalooza.js and index.htm files. These files bring all of these concepts together in an updated version of the baby-palooza.com product listing. (Due to the length of these files, I can't present them here, so be sure to open them in your HTML editor so you can follow along with the discussion.) While these files are basically the same as the ones you saw at the end of Session 6, there are a few new things going on here. If you look in the babyPalooza.js file, you'll notice that the showProductInfo() function has been changed to build a single output string instead of using multiple document.write() calls. Beyond that, two new global variables have been added: debugFlag and debugInfo. If the debugFlag variable is set to true, the showProductInfo() function will place the string it builds into the debugInfo variable, followed by two carriage returns. The new index.htm file also checks to see if the debugFlag variable is true. If it is, a completely new HTML form is output to the browser. Inside this form is a <textarea> control that contains all of the information in the debugInfo variable. This allows me to see exactly what the HTML I've built looks like. If you load the index.htm file into your browser you'll see something like Figure 11-1.

Figure 11-1
The shopping cart with dynamically generated HTML displayed

Dynamically Creating JavaScript

**10 Min.
To Go**

Now, if you can dynamically create HTML, you should be able to dynamically create JavaScript, right? Well, yes, you can. However there is one major "gotcha" to watch out for when dynamically creating a block of JavaScript.

When you output your `<script>` and `</script>` tags, you should *never* output these tags as complete strings. That is to say, you should never ever code something like this:

```
document.write( "<script>");
document.write( "</script>");
```

If you do, the HTML and JavaScript interpreters will get hopelessly confused. They'll actually think that you are starting a new script block inside your current script block. Since this is a big no-no, you'll either be presented with an error dialog or your code will simply stop executing for no apparent reason.

The solution to this problem is actually very simple, just break the "tags" up in your `document.write()` calls, like this:

```
document.write( "<scrip" + "t>");
document.write( "<" + "/script>");
```

Done!

By breaking these strings up like this, you prevent the HTML and JavaScript interpreters from mistaking them as HTML tags. This ability to dynamically generate JavaScript code is a very powerful feature, so I'll be discussing it in much more detail in Sessions 20 and 23.

REVIEW

In this session, you learned how to use JavaScript to dynamically create HTML code. You saw how to generate links and other HTML controls that have been customized to reflect the information that you are presenting to your users. You also learned how to use a text area control to display the HTML that your JavaScript has dynamically created. Finally, you learned that JavaScript can also dynamically generate more JavaScript code, but that there are potential problems that come with generating a new set of `<script></script>` tags.

QUIZ YOURSELF

1. What is the difference between dynamically created HTML and DHTML? (See the opening paragraphs of this session.)
2. How does the HTML parser see the output of a `document.write()` call? (See "Dynamically Creating HTML.")
3. Why would you want to store an HTML tag in a JavaScript variable? (See "Storing HTML tags in string variables.")
4. What kinds of HTML elements can you dynamically create with JavaScript? (See "Creating customized controls.")
5. Why should you not code a statement like `document.write( "<script>")`? (See "Dynamically Creating JavaScript.")

Working with HTML Forms

Session Checklist

✔ Learning about the JavaScript form object

✔ Understanding how JavaScript interacts with HTML forms and input controls

**30 Min.
To Go**

F orms are the basis for just about every sort of activity on the Web. For example, when your users subscribe to an e-mail newsletter or purchase a new computer, you'll have to present them with a form in order to get the job done. So, to build a truly effective Web site, you have to understand how to use HTML forms and the JavaScript form object.

How the form Object Relates to the <form> Tag

By now, you should have a pretty good idea of what the form object is. It's simply a JavaScript object that represents a set of HTML <form></form> tags. As you saw in Session 9, the document object actually contains an array of form objects, which goes by the clever name of forms. After an HTML document is loaded and parsed, this array will contain one form object for each set of <form></form> tags in the HTML document. The following code shows a simple HTML document with three form objects:

```
<html>
<body>
<form></form>
<form></form>
<form></form>
</body>
</html>
```

This will create a `forms` array with three entries. Since the `forms` array is a property of the `document` object, you can reference these `form` objects like this:

```
var firstForm = document.forms[0];
var secondForm = document.forms[1];
var thirdForm = document.forms[2];
```

Give it a name

If you would rather not refer to your forms by number, you can also give each form object a name. For example, given the simple HTML document I just defined, I could code something like this:

```
document.forms[0].name = "formZero";
```

Here, I've simply assigned a string to the `name` property of the first entry in my `forms` array. I could then access this `form` object like so:

```
var firstForm = document.formZero;
```

Being able to assign a name is nice, but you can also specify a name for your form objects inside your HTML document, as shown here:

```
<html>
<body>
<form name="formZero"></form>
<form name="formOne"></form>
<form name="formTwo"></form>
</body>
</html>
```

When this HTML document is parsed, the resulting JavaScript `form` objects will have their `name` properties automatically set to the names specified in the `name=` attributes of each `<form>` tag. You can then access these form objects like so:

```
var firstForm = document.formZero; // Same as document.forms[0]
var secondForm = document.formOne; // Same as document.forms[1]
var thirdForm = document.formTwo; // Same as document.forms[2]
```

What's in a name?

One thing that's important to note here is that the names I've given my form objects are all valid JavaScript variable names. While this isn't absolutely necessary, it's a very good idea to make sure you only use valid JavaScript variable names for your form objects, as well as the other HTML-based objects you work with. Why? Consider this:

```
<html>
<body>
<form name="form Zero"></form>
<form name="form One"></form>
<form name="form Two"></form>
</body>
</html>
```

Since HTML doesn't place any restrictions on the values that can be used for an attribute, these three name attributes are perfectly valid HTML. However, if I were to try to use these names from JavaScript, I would have to code something like this:

```
var firstForm = document.form Zero;
var secondForm = document.form One;
var thirdForm = document.form Two;
```

Unfortunately, none of these statements will work, because the JavaScript interpreter will have a very hard time with the blank space in the middle of each name. So, the only way to access these form objects will be through the forms array. The moral of the story is, if you are going to give names to the elements in your HTML documents try to use names that are also valid JavaScript variable names!

How Controls Relate to the form Object

When you build a set of `<form></form>` tags on your HTML page, you rarely leave it empty. In most cases, you'll fill a form with text boxes, check boxes, pop-up menus and other controls that the user can interact with directly. Each of these has a corresponding HTML tag (or tags) that defines the control. When the HTML document is loaded and parsed by the browser, these tags lead to the creation of corresponding JavaScript objects. As you might expect by now, these control objects can be found inside the `form` object that they are associated with. For example, take a look at the following HTML document.

```
<html>
<body>
<form name="formZero">
    <input type="text" name="userName">
</form>
<form name="formOne">
    <textarea name="address"></address>
</form>
<form name="formTwo">
    <input type="checkbox" name="spamMe">Add me to your mail list
</form>
</body>
</html>
```

Here again, I've defined three `form` objects. However, each of these `form` objects now contains an object that represents the control inside the form. As with my forms, I've specified a name attribute for each control. So, if I want to access these objects I can simply code something like this:

```
var uNameObject = document.formZero.userName;
var addressObject = document.formOne.address;
var spamMeObject = document.formTwo.spamMe;
```

After these statements execute, the new variables I've created will hold the objects representing the controls in my three forms.

Suppose that you load that last HTML document into a Web browser and type your name into the `userName` text box. How would you actually retrieve that value? Actually, it's pretty simple to do.

**20 Min.
To Go**

Every type of control that you can create in a form has a corresponding type of JavaScript object. While these objects do differ somewhat, they all follow the same basic format. In particular, they all have a property named `value`. This property contains the current value that the control is set to. The concept of a control's *value* differs from one type of control to the next, but, in the case of a text box or text area, the `value` property will hold the string that's currently typed into the control in the browser window. So, if I wanted to extract the user's name, I could code:

```
var uNameString = document.formZero.userName.value;
```

Similarly, if I wanted to set the user's name, I could code:

```
document.formZero.userName.value = "John Doe";
```

For the most part, this is the way you use JavaScript to get and set the value of any HTML control. However, as I said before, each type of control object has a slightly different set of properties and methods that allow you do much more than just get or set their value. So I'm going to go over each type of control in detail in the next session.

Inside the form Object

There's a lot more to the form object than just the name property. Here's a detailed look at the properties and methods that will give you total control over the forms on your HTML pages. (As always, you'll find example programs for each of these properties and methods in the Session12 folder on your CD-ROM.)

Properties of the form object

A <form> tag has a lot of different attributes that you can set to control its behavior. The form object has properties that correspond to each of these attributes so that you can work with them from JavaScript.

The action property

This property holds a Web address that tells the browser where to send the form when the user clicks the Submit button. The initial value for this property is taken from the action= attribute of the <form> tag. For example, given the following HTML definition

```
<form name="orderForm" action="processOrder.cgi"></form>
```

the value of document.orderForm.action will be "processOrder.cgi." If you assign a new Web address to this property, the form will be sent to that new address when the form's Submit button is clicked.

The elements array

While it's nice to be able to access a control directly using a name, there might come a time when you want to process your controls in a more automatic fashion.

It's also possible that your controls might not have names, or they might have names that aren't valid JavaScript variable names. For those situations, the `form` object provides the `elements` array.

The `elements` array is an array that contains all of the control objects defined in the form. You can access the items in this array two ways: by index number or by name. For example, take a look at the following form definition.

```
<form name="myForm">
    First Name:<input type="text" name="fname"
    value="Maia" /><br />
    Last Name:<input type="text" name="last name"
    value="Disbrow" /><br />
    Favorite Food:<input type="text" name="favorite food"
    value="Bananas" />
</form>
```

In this form I've defined three controls. Two of these controls have names that simply aren't valid JavaScript variable names. However, I can easily access these controls by using the `elements` array. Accessing a control by its index in the elements array works just like any other array access:

```
for (x=0; x<document.myForm.elements.length; x++) {
    document.write( document.myForm.elements[ x].name);
    document.write( " contains ");
    document.write( document.myForm.elements[ x].value);
    document.write( "<br />");
    }
```

However, if I wanted to use the name of a control, I can do that as well:

```
document.write( document.myForm.elements[ "fname"].name);
document.write( " contains ");
document.write( document.myForm.elements[ "fname"].value);
document.write( "<br />");
document.write( document.myForm.elements[ "last name"].name);
document.write( " contains ");
document.write( document.myForm.elements[ "last name"].value);
document.write( "<br />");
document.write( document.myForm.elements[ "favorite food"].name);
document.write( " contains ");
document.write( document.myForm.elements[ "favorite food"].value);
```

In this case, the `elements` array is acting like an array with named slots... because it is!

**10 Min.
To Go**

The encoding property

This property is equivalent to the enctype= attribute in a <form> tag. This attribute tells the Web browser what encoding scheme should be used to transmit the forms data when the Submit button is pressed.

A discussion of encoding types is beyond the scope of this book, but you can find a complete discussion of them at the World Wide Web Consortium's Web site. Start your investigation at the following link:

www.w3.org/TR/html4/interact/forms.html#form-content-type

The length property

This property tells you how many controls are in a form object. This is essentially the same as the length property of the form's elements array.

The method property

This property is the same as the method= attribute in a <form> tag. This property tells the browser which method (post or get) to use when sending the form's data after the Submit button is clicked.

The name property

As you've seen already in this session, the name property is the same as the name= attribute of a <form> tag.

The target property

This property corresponds to the target= property in the <form> tag. This property lets you specify the name of a browser window or frame that should be used to present the results of the form submission. For example, if your <form> tag looks like

```
<form target="resultWindow">
```

when the user submits the form, a new browser window with the internal name "resultWindow" will open up and the results of the form submission will be seen in that window. (If a browser window named "resultWindow" already exists, it will come to the front and the results of the submission will be displayed there.)

Methods of the form object

The form object also has several methods that allow you to trigger the various actions that a form can perform. These methods make it easy to automate most form actions.

The reset() method

When a user clicks on a form's Reset button, the Web browser fires an onreset event (as shown in Session 10) and resets the controls in the form to their default values. If you would like to reset a form from your JavaScript program, calling the reset() method for that form is exactly the same thing as clicking on the form's Reset button. In fact, the following control definitions have the same effect:

```
<input type="reset" value="Reset" />
<input type="button" value="Reset"
onclick="document.formName.reset()" />
```

Of course, it's easier to simply define an actual Reset button, but using the reset() method gives you a lot more control over the process of resetting the form. By using the reset() method, you the programmer get to decide when your form should be reset.

The submit() method

Whereas the reset() method simulates clicking the Reset button, the submit() method simulates clicking a form's Submit button. Calling the submit() method is almost exactly the same as waiting around for your user to click the Submit button, but there is one difference. When the user clicks the Submit button, an onsubmit event is fired. However, when your JavaScript program calls the submit() method, there is no onsubmit event generated.

This actually makes quite a bit of sense. The onsubmit event is intended to give your program a chance to validate the data in a form before it's submitted. However, if you are calling the submit() method explicitly, you will already be in the middle of your JavaScript program. So, you should have already validated the form's data before attempting to call the submit() method.

Done!

REVIEW

In this session, you looked at the JavaScript `form` object and how it relates to the HTML `<form>` tag. You learned about the properties and methods of the `form` object and how they can be used to control the behavior of a form. You also saw how the controls defined in a form relate to the `form` object and how you can access those controls either by using the name of the control or the `elements` array.

QUIZ YOURSELF

1. Where are `form` objects kept in the `document` object? (See "How the form Object Relates to the <form> Tag.")

2. Why should you always give your forms and controls names? (See "Give it a name.")

3. What property holds the current value of an on-screen control? (See "Inside the form Object.")

4. How can you use the `elements` array to get at a control with a name that isn't a valid JavaScript variable name? (See "The elements array.")

5. What happens when you call the `submit()` method for a form? What, if anything, does *not* happen? (See "The submit() method.")

Working with HTML Controls

Session Checklist

✔ Learning how to use HTML controls with JavaScript

**30 Min.
To Go**

N ow that you've seen how to use your forms from JavaScript, it's time to learn the details of how each HTML control can be used from JavaScript. As you'll see, most controls are very easy to work with. You simply respond to one or two events or you just get or set the control's value property to determine its current state. However, some controls, like a select list, require a bit more work to use effectively.

Working with Buttons

Buttons are probably the simplest HTML controls that you can define. However, buttons can be very useful to your JavaScript program. By defining an onclick handler for a button, you can have that button trigger any number of actions by your JavaScript code. As you saw in Session 10, you can define an onclick handler for a button like this:

```
<input type="button" value="On Screen Button Name"
onclick="handler()" />
```

So, when the user clicks the button, the handler function will be executed. (Remember, an event handler doesn't have to be a function call, it can simply be one or more JavaScript statements that are coded right into the HTML definition for your control. Refer back to Session 10 for the details on how to create an event handler.)

You'll notice here that, contrary to the advice I've given in Session 12, I haven't given this example button a name= attribute. You *can* give a button a name if you want, but there usually isn't any need to. The main reason you would want to give a control a name is if you want to store data in it. The name will simply make retrieval of that data easier. In a button, the value property of the button actually shows up on screen as the text the user sees in the button. So, it's really not a good idea to go changing the value of a button. However, you can give each of your buttons names if you need to differentiate between them easily. (For example, a function that could be called by several buttons might need to know exactly which button called it.)

In addition to simple buttons like the one shown above, there are two specialized buttons: the Submit button and the Reset button. These buttons have a pre-defined role in your HTML forms, so they don't actually support onclick handlers (or any other type of event handler).

While you can't code an event handler directly into the definitions for these buttons, they still generate events that your JavaScript code can latch on to. When the user clicks the Submit button for a form, an onsubmit event is generated. Similarly, when the user clicks the Reset button for a form, an onreset event is generated. As you saw in Session 10, instead of specifying the handlers for these events in the buttons themselves, you specify them in the <form> tag.

```
<form onsubmit="return doSubmit()" onreset="return doReset()">
<!-- other controls go here -->
<input type= "submit" value= "Submit This Form" />
<input type="reset" value="Reset This Form" />
</form>
```

When the onsubmit handler is called, your program has a perfect opportunity to check the data in the form to see if it's valid or invalid. Data validation is an important topic in its own right, so I'll be discussing it in detail in Session 15.

Working with Check Boxes

Working with check boxes is almost as simple as working with buttons. There are a few important differences though. For example, consider this HTML definition of a simple check box:

```
<input type="checkbox" name="overnight" value="Y" checked />
Overnight shipping?<br />
```

The first thing to notice is that the text label ("Overnight shipping") that will appear next to this check box is not defined in the tag itself. Instead, it's simply a string of characters that appears after the tag. (The label could also come before the tag; it simply depends on how you want your form to be laid out.) This means that our `value` property can hold actual data. In this, case that data is a single character, "Y".

While I've given my check box a value, that `value` is only valid if the check box is actually checked. Now, when I say "valid," I'm speaking of being "logically" valid. That is to say, the `value` property of this check box will always be "Y", but, if the check box isn't checked, the user obviously doesn't want anything to do with this option I've given them. So, I'll just ignore whatever `value` is held in the check box.

The question then becomes, "How do you know if a check box is checked?" This is where the `checked` property comes in. This is a Boolean property that simply tells you if a check box is checked or not. If `checked` is `true`, the check box is checked. If it is `false`, the check box isn't checked. You can even assign a value to this property and the on-screen appearance of the check box will change accordingly.

If a check box is not checked and you submit the form that it is in, no information about that check box will be sent to the server. That is to say, neither the name of the check box nor its value will be transmitted to the server-side process that's invoked when the form is submitted. Check box information is transmitted only if the check box is actually checked.

Like buttons, check boxes also generate an `onclick` event when they are clicked. This gives your program a chance to instantly reset other parts of your form whenever the user selects or deselects a check box. The trick to using an `onclick` handler with a check box is to remember that the code for your `onclick` handler is called *after* the check box has been checked or unchecked on the screen. The following code shows all of these aspects of check boxes working together.

```
<script language="javascript">
function doStandard() {
    if (document.delivery.standard.checked) {
        // turn off overnight check box
        document.delivery.overnight.checked = false;
        }
    }
```

```
function doOvernight() {
    if (document.delivery.overnight.checked) {
        // turn off standard check box
        document.delivery.standard.checked = false;
        }
    }
</script>
<form name="delivery">
    Select a Delivery Method<br />
    <input type="checkbox" name="standard" value="Y"
    onclick="doStandard()" /> Standard Shipping<br />
    <input type="checkbox" name="overnight" value="Y"
    onclick="doOvernight()" /> Overnight shipping?<br />
</form>
```

In this example, I've defined two check boxes. One representing standard delivery and the other representing overnight delivery. Each check box has an onclick handler that fires when that check box is clicked. The structure of each handler is similar, so I'll just go over the handler for the standard delivery check box.

When the standard check box is clicked, the doStandard() function executes. The first thing it does is inspect the checked property of the standard check box. If checked is true, it then assigns a false to the checked property of the overnight check box. When this happens, the overnight check box immediately becomes unchecked on screen.

Another way to set a check box is to call its click() method. This will toggle the state of the check box, just as if it had been clicked. The advantage of using the click() method (as opposed to simply assigning a true to the checked property) is that this method will also fire an onclick event for the check box.

Check boxes also support the onblur, and onfocus events (with corresponding blur() and focus() methods to simulate these events). For more on these events, be sure to refer to Session 10.

Finally, if you need to know whether or not a check box was initially checked, you can inspect its defaultChecked property. If this property is true, the check box was checked when the HTML file was first loaded. If the property is false, the check box was not checked.

Working with the File Upload Control

If you aren't familiar with the HTML file upload control, don't worry. Very few people even know that it exists, let alone how to use it. Basically, the file upload control presents the user with a text box and a Browse... button. If users know the path to the file they want to upload, they can type it directly into the text box. However, it's more likely that users will not know the path to the file, so they will probably just click the Browse... button. When this button is clicked, the browser will present a standard file open dialog. Users can then use this dialog to select a file from their local file system. As soon as a user has selected a file, the path to that file will appear in the text box. Then, when the user submits the form, the file itself will actually be sent to the server.

It's beyond the scope of this book to investigate what happens once the file gets to the server. The main reason for this is that beyond that point, the process is dependent on the Web server software that is being run. Since I can't know what kind of Web server software you'll be running, I'll just have to tell you to refer to the documentation for your Web server.

If you aren't familiar with the file upload control, your first question might be, "What does the HTML for one look like?" Well, it looks like this:

```
<input type="file" name="fileUploadField" />
```

Like most of the other controls you'll see in this session, a file upload control supports various events like `onclick`, `onblur`, and `onfocus`. However, the most interesting event that this control supports is the `onchange` event. This event fires after the user selects a different file to upload. If you need to restrict the type of files that can be uploaded, this gives you a great opportunity to check the file to see if it is one of the types you want to allow. The path name of the selected file can be found in the `value` property of the file upload control. All you have to do is extract this information and use some combination of JavaScript's string methods to determine if the file's name fits your criteria. (For an example of using a file upload control, see the fileUpload.htm file on your CD-ROM.)

Working with Radio Buttons

The check box example that you saw earlier ensured that only one check box was checked at a time. This behavior is similar to that exhibited by another type of HTML control, the radio button. Radio buttons are actually very similar to check boxes. In fact, you can think of radio buttons as sets of related check boxes. The difference is that only one of these check boxes can be checked at any given time. The simple act of turning one radio button on turns off all the others that are related to it.

Groups of related radio buttons are called *families*. You create a family of radio buttons by giving all of the radio buttons in the family exactly the same name. For example, the check boxes I defined earlier could be redefined as a family of radio buttons like so:

```
<input type="radio" name="dMethod" value="standard" checked />
Standard Shipping<br />
<input type="radio" name="dMethod" value="overnight" /> Overnight
Shipping<br />
```

Here, I've created two radio buttons and placed them both into the family named "dMethod" (short for "delivery method"). Now, when one radio button is checked, the other will be unchecked automatically. (The Web browser handles all of this checking and unchecking. Your JavaScript program doesn't have to do anything.)

Another thing to notice is that the value of each radio button holds information that directly reflects the meaning behind the check box. So, if the "Standard Shipping" check box is checked, the entire family of radio buttons has a "logical" value of "standard."

Unfortunately, while a family of radio buttons can be thought to have a logical value that's equal to the value of the selected radio button, there isn't a radio button method that will tell you which radio button in a family is selected. To determine which radio button is selected, you have to examine the checked property of each radio button in a family until you find the one where checked is true.

How can you do this? After all, every radio button in a family has exactly the same name, so how do you tell them apart? Actually, it's fairly easy to do, because when you create a radio button family, the JavaScript interpreter creates an array to hold information about each radio button in the family. So, in the above example, dMethod[0] is the "Standard Shipping" button and dMethod[1] is the "Overnight Shipping" button.

 When you submit a form containing a family of radio buttons, the value that's transmitted for that family is the value associated with the selected radio button (that is, the values of the other radio buttons in the family are not sent to the server).

And, as with check boxes, radio buttons can have an onclick handler. So, knowing all of this, it's actually a fairly simple matter to process a family of radio buttons:

```
function doDelivery() {
    var dLen = document.delivery.dMethod.length;
    for (x=0; x < dLen; x++) {
        if (document.delivery.dMethod[ x].checked) {
            methodValue = document.delivery.dMethod[ x].value;
            alert( "You have selected " + methodValue +
```

```
              " shipping");
              break;
              }
          }
      }
</script>
<form name="delivery">
    Select a Delivery Method<br />
    <input type="radio" name="dMethod" value="standard"
    onclick="doDelivery()" checked /> Standard Shipping<br />
    <input type="radio" name="dMethod" value="overnight"
    onclick="doDelivery()" /> Overnight Shipping<br />
</form>
```

Here, I've added an `onclick` handler to my radio button definitions. Since these radio buttons each belong to the same family, they each call the same event handler. (Note that they don't have to call the same `onclick` handler, but it's rare to have different `onclick` handlers for radio buttons in the same family.)

When the handler begins to execute, the first thing it does is determine the `length` of the array that holds the radio button family. (This tells it how many radio buttons are in the family.) At that point, it's simply a matter of using a `for` loop to inspect the `checked` property of each radio button in the array until it finds one that is `true`. At that point, it can extract the `value` from that radio button and present it in an alert window. The `break` statement terminates the loop so that it doesn't spend time looking at any remaining radio buttons. (Remember, only one radio button in a family can be checked.)

**20 Min.
To Go**

Other Radio Button Tips

As I mentioned before, radio buttons and check boxes have a lot in common. As with check boxes, you can assign a `true` to the `checked` property of a radio button and that radio button will become checked. (And all of the other radio buttons in the family will turn themselves off.)

You can also use the `click()` method to simulate a mouse click on a radio button and you can use the `defaultChecked` property to tell if the radio button was selected when the HTML document was loaded.

And, just like check boxes, radio buttons also receive `onblur` and `onfocus` events (and have the corresponding `blur()` and `focus()` methods).

Working with Select Lists

One of the most useful HTML controls available is the select list. A select list lets you present your users with a menu of items that they can pick from. Before going further with this discussion, take a look at this HTML definition for a simple select list.

```
Select a Product<br />
<select name="products" size="1">
    <option value="st-001">Rock & Stroll - Deluxe</option>
    <option value="dp-003">Size 3, Extra Absorbent</option>
    <option value="cs-001">Ultra-Safe, Rear-Facing</option>
    <option value="rt-001">UberNoise 5000</option>
    <option value="bw-001">Clean and Fragrant</option>
</select>
```

In this example, I've defined a simple select list with five items in it. (Each set of <option></option> tags defines an individual menu item.) Each of these items corresponds to one of the products in the Baby-Palooza.com inventory. As you can see, I've placed the part number of each product into the value= attribute of each option and I've used the description for the product to specify the text that will show up in the select list when this is loaded into the Web browser. While this is a fairly simple select list, it's a very complicated control in and of itself. So, the question becomes, "How does JavaScript interact with this control?"

The select object

As you might expect, the Browser Object Model defines a JavaScript object called the Select object. This object has several properties and methods that allow you to interact directly with the select lists you define in your HTML forms.

The length property

This tells you how many sets of <option></option> tags are defined for the select list.

The name property

This is the name that is specified in the name= attribute of the <select> tag.

The options array

This is an array of Option objects. Each item in the array corresponds directly to one set of <option></option> tags in the select list. Understanding the options array is the key to working with select lists, so I'll be discussing it in more detail in just a moment.

The selectedIndex property

This property holds the numeric index of the selected item in the options array. So, if the user has selected the first item in the list, the selectedIndex property will have a value of zero. (Remember, JavaScript array index numbers begin with zero.) If no item in the list is selected, this property will contain a negative one (-1).

The blur() and focus() methods

These remove the focus from a select list and give the focus to a select list, respectively. They also generate the corresponding onblur and onfocus events for the select list.

The click() method

As with the other controls you've seen, this simulates a mouse click on the select list.

The onchange event

There is one additional event defined for a select list: the onchange event. This event fires when the user actually changes her selection in the list. If the user clicks on the list, but doesn't change her selection, the event never fires. Compare this to an onclick event, which will fire regardless of whether or not the selection in the list is changed. (Note also that older versions of Netscape Navigator simply don't support the onclick event for use with select lists, all they support is the onchange event.)

Understanding the Options array

As I said, the options array is the key to working with select lists. Because it's an array, the options array has a length property (which tells you the same thing as the length property of the Select object). Each item in the options array is a JavaScript Option object, each of which represents a single set of <option> </option> tags. Each individual Option object has the following properties:

The defaultSelected property

This property holds a Boolean value that tells you if the corresponding menu item was selected by default — that is, when the HTML file was first loaded by the Web browser.

The selected property

This is a Boolean value that tells you if the corresponding menu item is currently selected or not. If this is `true`, the menu item is selected, if it's `false`, the menu item is not selected.

The text property

This is a String object that holds the text that you defined between the `<option>` `</option>` tags. For example, in the definition `<option value="rt-001">` `UberNoise 5000</option>` the `text` property of this Option object will be the string "UberNoise 5000". It's important to note that you can assign a new value to this property, effectively changing the text that is displayed for that menu item.

The value property

As with the other tags you've seen, this property holds the contents of the `value=` attribute in the original tag. The main difference is that, since each Option object has its own value attribute, a select list can hold a lot of different possible values.

 When you submit a form containing a select list, only the value associated with the selected menu item is transmitted to the server. If the select list allows multiple selections, the values of all selected items are transmitted.

A simple select list example

Since the `options` array is just that, an array, you might be thinking that the simplest way to interact with a select list is to simply loop through all of the items in the `options` array until you find the item where `selected` is `true`. You can do this, but don't forget about the `selectedIndex` property. Since this property already contains the index number of the selected menu item, you can use it to jump directly to the menu item you are interested in. (This code comes from the selectList.htm file on your CD-ROM.)

```
<script language="javascript">
function doProductPick() {
    var si = document.order.products.selectedIndex;
    var partNo = document.order.products.options[ si].value;
    var desc = document.order.products.options[ si].text;
    alert("You selected part number "+ partNo +", '"+ desc + "'");
    }
</script>
<form name="order">
    Select a Product<br />
    <select name="products" size="1" onchange="doProductPick()">
        <option value="st-001">Rock & Stroll - Deluxe</option>
        <option value="dp-003">Size 3, Extra Absorbent</option>
        <option value="cs-001">Ultra-Safe, Rear-Facing</option>
        <option value="rt-001">UberNoise 5000</option>
        <option value="bw-001">Clean and Fragrant</option>
    </select>
</form>
```

In this code, I've added an `onchange` handler to my select list definition. So when the user changes the selected item in the list, an `onchange` event will fire and my handler function will be called. When the handler function executes, the first thing it does is to retrieve the value kept in the select list's `selectedIndex` property. I can then use this information to directly access the `value` and `text` properties of the item that is selected in my select list and report that information back to the user.

Selecting an item in the list

As you've just seen, it's actually pretty simple to read information from a select list. But, what if you want to actually cause an item in the list to become selected? Your first impulse might be to assign a new value to the `selectedIndex` property of the list. However, that won't actually make anything happen. Instead, you need to assign a `true` value to the `selected` property of the Option object you want to become selected. The following bit of code from the selectAnOption.htm file shows one way you might do this.

```
function pickNext() {
    var si = document.order.products.selectedIndex;
    if (si == (document.order.products.length - 1)) {
        next = 0;
```

```
        }
    else {
        next = ++si;
        }
    document.order.products.options[ next].selected = true;
    }
function pickPrev() {
    var si = document.order.products.selectedIndex;
    if (si == -1) {
        si = 0;
        }
    if (si == 0) {
        next = (document.order.products.length - 1);
        }
    else {
        next = --si;
        }
    document.order.products.options[ next].selected = true;
    }
</script>
<form name="order">
    Select a Product<br />
    <select name="products" size="5">
        <option value="st-001">Rock & Stroll - Deluxe</option>
        <option value="dp-003">Size 3, Extra Absorbent</option>
        <option value="cs-001">Ultra-Safe, Rear-Facing</option>
        <option value="rt-001">UberNoise 5000</option>
        <option value="bw-001">Clean and Fragrant</option>
    </select><br />
    <input type="button" value="Next" onclick="pickNext()" />
    <input type="button" value="Previous" onclick="pickPrev()" />
</form>
```

If you load this example file into your Web browser and then click on the "Next" and "Previous" buttons, you'll see that the selected item changes as you click the buttons. One additional thing to note is that, when this select list is first loaded into the Web browser, no item will be selected by default. This means that the selectedIndex property of the Select object will be a negative one. So, I have to check for that occurrence explicitly in the code for the pickPrev() function.

While this example doesn't include an `onchange` handler, it's important to note that when you select a menu item in this fashion, an `onchange` event is *not* generated! (So, if you need to completely duplicate an `onchange` event, you'll have to call your `onchange` event handler after you select your new menu item.)

Multiple-select lists

Thus far, all the examples you've seen have involved single-select lists. That is to say, lists that can only have one item selected at a time. HTML however, provides for another type of selection list, the multiple-selection list. As the name implies, in a multiple-selection list, the user can select as many items from the list as they want. In HTML, the only difference between the two is the addition of a "multiple" attribute to the select list definition. In JavaScript however, the differences are a bit more substantial.

The selectedIndex property and multiple-select lists

First and foremost, in a multiple-select list, the role of the `selectedIndex` property becomes even more important. In a single-select list, the odds of running into a list with nothing selected are a fairly low. If the HTML definition of the list specifies an initially selected item or if the user selects an item, then the list will always have an item selected from there on out. In a multiple-select list however, the user can select or deselect as many items as she wants. So, it's entirely possible to have a list with no items selected. Because of this, you should always check the `selectedIndex` property before performing any operation on a multiple-select list. If the value is negative one (-1), you'll know that there is nothing selected in the list and can act accordingly.

If the value of `selectedIndex` is not negative one, then you know that at least one item in the list is selected. In this case however, the `selectedIndex` property is only telling you the index of the *first* selected item in the list. It's up to you to determine what the other selected items are. The following code is from the multipleSelectList.htm file on your CD-ROM. It shows a typical multiple-select list and how you might use it.

```
function showSelected() {
    var si = document.order.products.selectedIndex;
    if (si == -1) {
        alert( "No items are selected!");
        }
    else {
```

```
        var report = "You have selected: \n";
        var partNo = "";
        var desc = "";
        for (x=si; x < document.order.products.length; x++) {
            if (document.order.products.options[ x].selected) {
                partNo = document.order.products.options[x].value;
                desc = document.order.products.options[x].text;
                report += partNo + " - " + desc + "\n";
                }
            }
        alert( report);
        }
    }
</script>
<form name="order">
    Select a Product<br />
    <select name="products" size="5" multiple>
        <option value="st-001">Rock & Stroll - Deluxe</option>
        <option value="dp-003">Size 3, Extra Absorbent</option>
        <option value="cs-001">Ultra-Safe, Rear-Facing</option>
        <option value="rt-001">UberNoise 5000</option>
        <option value="bw-001">Clean and Fragrant</option>
    </select><br />
    <input type="button" value="Show All Selected"
    onclick="showSelected()" />
</form>
```

As you can see from this example, working with a multiple-select list isn't really too difficult. The main thing is to check the selectedIndex property immediately before attempting to work with the list. If it turns out that there is at least one item selected, I then enter a simple for loop to check each item in the list. (Note however that the for loop starts its work at the index number reported in the selectedIndex property. This lets me skip over the unselected items at the top of the list.)

**10 Min.
To Go**

Adding or removing options in a select list

The last bit of select list information that I want to give to you in this session is how to add and remove items in a select list. That's right; JavaScript will allow you to add new items to a select list or to remove old items from the list.

To remove an item from a select list, all you have to do is assign a null value to the options array element that holds the item you want to remove. This will remove that item from the list and move all the items below it up to fill the newly emptied space.

Adding an item is a bit more complex. It requires two steps:

1. Create a new Option object using the Option object's constructor method. (Remember, we discussed constructor methods in Session 6.)

2. Assign this new Option object to the end of the options array of the select list you want the new item to appear in.

The constructor method for the Option object is actually pretty simple. You pass it up to four parameters, and it will return a new Option object that you can add to the end of a select list. Those parameters, in the order that they must appear, are:

1. text: This is the text you want to appear in the menu when the new item is added.

2. value: This will be placed into the new item's value property.

3. defaultSelected: This is used to set the defaultSelected property of the new item.

4. selected: This tells the JavaScript interpreter if the new item should be selected or not when it is placed into the select list.

All of these parameters are optional, but you should usually provide at least the first two. (If you don't provide any parameters, you can set the appropriate properties after the new Option object is created.)

The addRemoveOptionsSelectList.htm file shows you how all of this can be used to create dynamic select lists. (Be sure to open this file in your HTML editor so that you can follow along with the next paragraph.) Looking at the HTML portion of this file, you'll see that I have two select lists, one containing my product information and the other an empty list that will hold the items in the user's shopping cart. When the user selects an item in the product list and then clicks the "Add to Cart" button, the addToCart() function is called. First, this function checks to see if an item in the product list is selected. If there isn't a selected item, an alert window is displayed to tell the user to select an item first. If there is an item selected however, the function retrieves the value and text properties of that item and passes them to the Option constructor method to create a new Option item. This new Option item is then assigned to the end of the select list representing our shopping cart. This causes the new item to appear immediately in the shopping cart. Finally, I assign a null to the appropriate element of the products select list, which removes the originally selected item from that list. (removeFromCart() works much the same way. The names of the select lists are reversed to move the selected item from the shopping cart back to the products list.)

Working with Text-Based Controls

Well, after that, you're probably in the mood to tackle something a bit more simplistic. You're in luck, because it's time to talk about how JavaScript interacts with the various text-based HTML controls. When I say "text-based," I'm talking about the controls whose job it is to handle lines or blocks of text. These include text boxes, text areas, password fields, and hidden fields. Here's an example of each one:

```
<!-- Text box -->
<input type="text" name="aTextBox" value="Hello World!" />
<!-- Text Area -->
<textarea name="aTextArea" rows="5" cols="60">Howdy
Terra!</textarea>
<!-- Password field -->
<input type="password" name="aPassword" />
<!-- Hidden Field -->
<input type="hidden" name="hiddenField" value="I'm Hidden!" />
```

While these are all different types of controls, JavaScript sees them all as controls that handle text. Because of this, you use each of these controls in a very similar fashion.

The most useful thing you can do with a text-based control is simply get or set the text string that's in it. Because the user can type directly into all of these controls (except for hidden field controls) this ability gives you the opportunity to interact directly with the user. As you've no doubt guessed by now, to get or set the information in one of these controls, you simply access the value property of the control. When you read the value property, you'll get back the text as it appears at that moment in the control. When you assign a string to the value property, you'll change the contents of that control on the screen. (For examples of how to use these controls, see the textBasedControls.htm file.)

Text-based control tips

When you work with a password field, remember that what appears on screen will be shown as all asterisks (*) or some other character. This is to prevent someone from stealing a password by looking over someone's shoulder. However, when you access the value property of a password field, you'll get the actual text of the password. So, if you display that information on the screen, you'll be revealing the user's password! Most users won't like that, so be careful when you work with password fields.

Hidden fields have slowly become the workhorse of HTML controls. They can contain just about any type of string or numeric data and the length of the data they hold depends only on how much memory the Web browser is willing to let them have. As you cruise the Internet looking at JavaScript code, you'll see lots of programmers hiding lots of crucial information in hidden fields. So, be on the lookout for it.

Text-based control events

Done!

Like most of the other controls you've seen, the text-based controls (with the exception of hidden fields) support the `onblur` and `onfocus` events. Another interesting event supported by text-based controls is the `onchange` event. This event fires when the contents of a text-based control are changed and then the control loses the focus. As we'll see in Session 15, these events give your program the perfect opportunity to react to user input and validate the values that they type into your forms.

REVIEW

In this session, you've gotten a detailed look at how JavaScript interacts with each type of HTML control. Although all of the controls work in much the same way (by keeping the really good stuff in the `value` property), you saw how each different control requires a slightly different approach from your JavaScript code. You learned the differences between check boxes and radio buttons as well as how to use a select list. You also learned how to use each of the different text-based controls. In Session 15, you'll build on this knowledge and learn how to ensure that the data a user enters into your form controls is valid for your application.

QUIZ YOURSELF

---

1. What property do you examine to see if a particular check box or radio button is selected? (See "Working with Check Boxes" and "Working with Radio Buttons.")

2. What is held in the value property of a file upload control? (See "Working with the File Upload Control.")

3. What exactly is a family of radio buttons? (See "Working with Radio Buttons.")

4. What does the `selectedIndex` property tell you about a select list? (See "Working with Select Lists.")

5. How can you dynamically add a new item to a select list? (See "Adding or removing Options in a select list.")

Working with Images

Session Checklist

✔ Learning how to use JavaScript to control images on the HTML page

✔ Understanding the JavaScript Image object

✔ Understanding how to create JavaScript-based rollover buttons and animations

***30 Min.
To Go***

The ability to transmit images is one of the most popular aspects of the World Wide Web. Because of their popularity, pictures have infiltrated almost every part of the Web browsing experience. For example, instead of HTML buttons, most Web sites feature clickable images that change when you move the mouse over them. While you might know and love all of these neat little graphic tricks, you might not know that JavaScript is the power behind almost each and every one of them. In this session, you'll learn how to use JavaScript to interact with the images in an HTML document and how you can create these simple animations to enhance users' experiences on your site.

Understanding the Image Object

The key to manipulating the images in your HTML documents is the JavaScript Image object. When your HTML document loads into the Web browser, the JavaScript interpreter creates an Image object for each `<img>` tag that it finds in the document. It places all of these Image objects in an `images` array (which you'll find in the `document` object). If you don't want to use the `images` array, you can specify a `name=` attribute for each `<img>` tag and access your Image objects directly. For example, assuming that the following tag is the first image in a document:

```
<img src="happyBaby.jpg" name="happyBaby" />
```

You can access the associated Image object by using either `document.images[0]` or `document.happyBaby`. If, for some reason, you can't give your images names that are also valid JavaScript variable names, you can still access them by name by using the `images` array just like you would use the `elements` array in a `form` object. For example, if you have an image defined like this:

```
<img name= "poorly named" src= "somePic.jpg" />
```

You can access it by using the images array, like so:

```
var poorlyNamedImage = document.images[ 'poorly named'];
```

Properties of the Image object

Now that you know how to get to an Image object, you'll want to know exactly what it is that you'll find there. (You'll find sample source code that exercises all of these properties in the Session14 folder on your CD-ROM.)

The border property

This property contains the border value that was set for the image in the `<img>` tag. For example, given this tag, the `border` property for `document.happyBaby` will be 10:

```
<img src="happyBaby.jpg" name="happyBaby" border="10" />
```

The complete property

This is a Boolean property that tells you if an image has completed loading.

The height and width properties

These properties tell you the current height and width (in pixels) of the picture. If you specify height and width attributes in your <img> tag, these properties will reflect those values. If you do not specify these attributes, these properties will be the actual height and width of the image. Note that after an image loads, you can assign a new value to either property and the image will be resized accordingly. (For an example of both properties, see the heightNwidthProperties.htm file on your CD-ROM.)

The hspace and vspace properties

These represent the the amount of horizontal and vertical padding used to offset the image from the content around it. Note that these properties can be changed after the image finishes loading and the image will be repositioned accordingly. (See also the discussion of the vspace property, below.)

The name property

This is the name of the image. If name is a valid JavaScript variable name, you can use it to access the image directly rather than having to go through the images array.

The src and lowsrc properties

This is the Web address of the picture that should be loaded for this image. If you assign a new value to this property, the Web browser will actually load the picture stored at that address. This is the basis for all JavaScript-based animations. For more information, see the sections "Creating Rollovers with JavaScript" and "Creating an Animation with JavaScript" later in this session.

The lowsrc property is the Web address of a low-resolution version of the image. If the browser is running on a device with a low resolution, this image will be used instead of the one specified by the src property.

Image object events

As you saw in Session 10, <img> tags support several events that allow you to detect if and when an image actually loads successfully. I'm listing them again here to be complete, but you should refer back to the sample source code for Session 10 to see a simple example of each of these event handlers in action.

The onabort event

This event fires if the user stops the loading of an image — that is, if the user clicks the browser's Stop button before the image is fully loaded.

The onerror event

This event fires if there is an error during the loading of an image.

The onload event

This event fires after an image has been successfully loaded into the browser.

Images without the <img> tag

As I said at the start of this session, the JavaScript interpreter creates an Image object for each `<img>` tag that it finds in your HTML document. However, if you want, you can create Image objects that don't have an associated `<img>` tag. You do this by using the Image object constructor, like so: `var myImage = new Image();` This statement will create a new Image object without an associated `<img>` tag. At this point, you can load an actual image file into this Image object simply by assigning a Web address to its `src` property, like this: `myImage.src = "happyBaby.jpg";`

When this picture finishes loading, you'll have an Image object with a picture loaded into it. However, that picture will *not* show up in the Web browser! In order for an image to show up in the Web browser, it *must* be associated with an `<img>` tag somewhere in the HTML document. Without this association, the Web browser simply doesn't know where to draw the image. Assume that the code you've just looked at has executed and that in your HTML file, you have the following `<img>` tag:

```
<img src="indifferentBaby.jpg" name="babyFace" />
```

If you execute the following JavaScript statement

```
document.babyFace.src = myImage.src;
```

the graphic that was contained in `document.babyFace` will be replaced by the graphic in `myImage`. Furthermore, because `document.babyFace` is associated with an `<img>` tag in the HTML document, the new graphic will replace the old graphic in the Web browser!

Creating Rollovers with JavaScript

Now that you've seen how one graphic can replace another, you'll probably want to see how to use that fact to do something useful. The simplest thing you can do with this technique is to create what's called a *rollover button*. These are called *rollovers* because when you roll the mouse over them, they change somehow. The effect can be as simple as a change in highlighting or you can actually switch to a completely different graphic.

The first step in creating a rollover button is to create a link that just happens to be an image. This is as simple as surrounding an <img> tag with a set of <a href=""></a> tags. For example, suppose I wanted to create a "More Info" image that would let my users jump to a page with further information on a product. Such a link might look like this:

```
<a href='st-001.htm'><img src='moreInfo.jpg' border='0' /></a>
```

This will place an image on an HTML page that is surrounded by a standard link. When the user clicks this image, the link will activate and she will jump to the specified page.

In order to create a rollover, you have to tell the browser to swap this image with another one when the mouse moves on top of the image. Then, to complete the rollover effect, you need to restore the original image when the mouse moves away. If you remember what you learned in Session 10, you've probably realized that the key to creating this effect is to use the onmouseover and onmouseout events to detect when the mouse has moved over and off of the image.

Now, both the <a> and <img> tags support the onmouseover and onmouseout events, so its really a matter of personal preference as to which tag you associate these events with. When creating a rollover, I personally prefer to hook the events to the <img> tag. By doing so, I've created a complete little animation all in one tag. For example:

```
<a href='st-001.htm'>
<img name='stMore' src='moreInfo.jpg' border='0'
onmouseover="document.stMore.src='moreInfoOn.jpg'"
onmouseout="document.stMore.src='moreInfo.jpg'" /></a>
```

While this might look like a very complex bit of code, it's actually fairly simple. As before, the <a></a> tags create a link that surrounds our <img> tag. So, when the image is clicked, the user will jump to the specified page.

The <img> tag is given the name "stMore" and told (by the "src=" attribute) to initially load the graphic file moreInfo.jpg. The border property is set to zero so that no border will appear around the image.

The event handlers are where all the action is. The onmouseover handler says, "When the mouse comes over this tag, change the src property of the document.stMore Image object to be moreInfoOn.jpg." As you learned earlier, when you change the src property of an Image object, the browser will actually load the specified image. If the Image object is associated with an <img> tag (like this one is), the new image will then replace the old one in the Web browser.

When the mouse moves over this image, the new image will be loaded and replace the old image. All that's left to complete the effect is to restore the old image.

When the mouse moves off of the image, the onmouseout event handler will execute. As you can see, this handler is almost the same as the onmouseover handler. The only difference is that this handler assigns the original graphic back to the src property of the Image object. This forces the browser to redraw the original graphic, and completes the rollover effect. (Note that you'll find the source code for this example in the simpleRollover.htm file on your CD-ROM.)

Creating an Animation with JavaScript

By now, you've probably already figured out how to do animations all by yourself. It's just a rollover with a lot more images, right? Well, sort of. When you are performing an animation, there are a couple of other things to consider besides just switching images. First, you have to decide how you will keep track of all the images in your animation. Second, you have to somehow preload the images in your animation, so that the first time it runs, there won't be a noticeable lag between frames. Finally, you have to decide how fast your animation is going to be.

Store your animation frames in an array

The answer to the first problem is actually pretty simple: Just store each frame of your animation in an array. Remember, JavaScript arrays can hold any type of data, so it's a simple matter to build one that holds a series of Image objects. Of course, storing your images in an array implies that you'll be stepping from frame to frame using a numeric index into the array. This in turn means that you'll have to load the images into the array in some sort of order. The upshot of all this is that the frames of your animation need to be stored in a series of files that are numbered in the order in which the frames should be played. For example, if you have a three-frame animation, you might number the individual graphic files like this:

```
myAnim0.jpg, myAnim1.jpg, myAnim3.jpg
```

(Of course, you can start your numbering with "1," but, since JavaScript starts numbering arrays with zero, I always find it easier to start my numbering with zero as well.)

Preloading images

The second problem is that of preloading the images that make up your animation. Solving this problem is as simple as creating the Image objects that will hold the frames and then setting each one's src attribute to the appropriate file name. This will begin the process of loading each frame while your HTML page is still being loaded into the browser. You can then delay the start of the animation until the complete property of the last frame becomes true.

An example of creating and loading animation frames

At this point, it's probably a good idea to go ahead and show you how what I've discussed so far fits together. The following code shows you how to create an array of images and begin loading all of your animation frames into it.

```
var titleFrames = new Array();
var titleNumFrames = 16;
for (x=0; x < titleNumFrames; x++) {
    titleFrames[ x] = new Image();
    titleFrames[ x].src = "titleAnim" + x + ".jpg";
    }
```

The first thing to notice is that none of this code is part of a function. In fact, when you look at the actual source file that this code comes from (the simpleAnimation.htm file), you'll see that these lines of code are in a <script> block that's at the top of my HTML document. So, these lines execute immediately as the document is being loaded. The first line creates a new Array object called titleFrames. (The purpose of this example is to create a title animation for the baby-palooza.com site, so all of the associated variable names begin with the string "title.") Next, I set up a global variable that tells the program how many frames there are in my animation. In this example there are 16 frames, named titleAnim0.jpg through titleAnim15.jpg.

After I've set up my variables, I enter a for loop. Each time through this loop, I create a new Image object and assign it to the next slot in my array. After creating the Image object, I immediately set its src property to the name of the next image file in my animation. Notice how I'm using JavaScript's ability to concatenate strings with numbers to generate the correct file name each time through the loop. Each time I assign a value to one of these `src` properties, the Web browser begins loading the specified image file.

Timing your animation

Now it's time to actually start and run the animation. To properly discuss how this is done, I need to show you *all* of the source code involved. So, here it is:

```
<script language="javascript">
var titleFrames = new Array();
var titleNumFrames = 16;
var titleAnimSpeed = 200;
var titleCurrentFrame = 1;
for (x=0; x < titleNumFrames; x++) {
    titleFrames[ x] = new Image();
    titleFrames[ x].src = "titleAnim" + x + ".jpg";
    }
function titleAnimate() {
    if (titleFrames[ titleNumFrames - 1].complete) {
        document.titleAnim.src = titleFrames[
titleCurrentFrame++].src;
        if (titleCurrentFrame == titleNumFrames) {
            titleCurrentFrame = 0;
            }
        }
    else {
        setTimeout('titleAnimate()', titleAnimSpeed);
        }
    }
</script>
<img name='titleAnim' src='titleAnim0.jpg' border='0'
onload="setTimeout('titleAnimate()', titleAnimSpeed)" />
```

At the top of this code, you can see that I've specified two other global variables. The first, `titleAnimSpeed`, holds the number of milliseconds delay that should come between frames. The second, `titleCurrentFrame`, tells the program which frame of the animation to display next. After the set up of the global variables, you'll find the `for` loop that loads the animation frames into my array of Image objects.

After this is the `titleAnimate()` function. This function actually performs the image swapping in my animation. I'll come back to this in a few moments.

Finally, you see the `<img>` tag that actually drives the animation. I've given this `<img>` the name `titleAnim` and the picture that's initially loaded into it is titleAnim0.jpg (which is the first frame of my animation).

Now, how can an `<img>` tag drive my animation? Well, look at the `onload` handler that's defined for this tag and remember that the `onload` event for an `<img>` tag only fires when the image has actually finished loading. When the image finishes loading, the `onload` handler will call the `setTimeout()` method and pass it the name of my animation function and tell it to wait 200 milliseconds before calling it. (Remember the value in `titleAnimSpeed` is 200.)

So, 200 milliseconds after the first frame of my animation loads, the `titleAnimate()` function is called. The first thing this function does is check and see if the last frame of my animation has finished loading. If it has *not,* the function makes another call to the `setTimeout()` method, which delays the start of the animation another 200 milliseconds. This continues until the final frame of the animation has finished loading and the animation is ready to commence.

If the final frame of my animation has finished loading the function takes the `src` property of the current animation frame and assigns it to the `src` property of the `titleAnim` Image object. Since the `titleAnim` Image object is tied to an `<img>` tag, the new picture replaces the old one on the screen.

Note the use of the increment operator (++) in the assignment statement. This will bump up the current frame of the animation by one. The `if` statement that follows will then check to see if the end of the animation has been reached. If it has, the number of the current frame is reset to zero so that the animation can start all over again.

If you think there's something missing from this whole scenario, you're absolutely correct. Even if you understand every line of this code, you might be wondering, "Where's the next call to `setTimeout()`? How can the animation progress if the `titleAnimate()` function doesn't call `setTimeout()` again?"

Actually, there isn't any need for another call to the `setTimeout()` method, because there's one already built into the `<img>` tag! You see, when you assign a new value to an Image object's `src` property, you are starting the process of loading the image all over again. So, if that Image object is tied to an `<img>` tag, and that tag has an `onload` handler, that handler will be executed every time you assign a new value to the Image object's `src` property. This means that the simple act of switching animation frames actually kicks off the process that will cause the next frame to be loaded.

OK, I admit it ... creating an animation this way is a lot of work. However, this technique does work with any graphic file format that your browser can load. So, if you have bunch of .jpg or .png files that you want to animate, you can do so without having to convert them into a .gif animation. In fact, if you don't mind a bit of extra work, you can even create your animation using files that are stored in different graphics formats!

Loading Images Based on Screen Size

In Session 8, I briefly mentioned the `screen` property of the `window` object. This property holds information about the client's current screen settings. So you can, for example, use this information to determine if your graphics will fit on the client's screen. If your default graphics won't fit the screen properly, you can either load a set of correctly sized graphics (which will require you to actually *have* a set of correctly sized graphics), or you can dynamically reset the `width` and `height` properties of your Image objects. An example of the first approach is shown in the following code:

```
for (x=0; x < titleNumFrames; x++) {
    titleFrames[ x] = new Image();
    if (screen.availWidth < 800) {
        titleFrames[ x].src = "titleAnim" + x + "-small.jpg";
        }
    else {
        titleFrames[ x].src = "titleAnim" + x + ".jpg";
        }
    }
```

Here, I'm checking the `availWidth` property of the `window.screen` object. If it is less than 800 pixels, I'm loading an equivalent, but smaller, version of my animation frame.

The other approach relies on the fact that, if you resize an image along one axis, the browser will automatically scale it properly along the other axis.

```
<img name='titleAnim' src='titleAnim0.jpg' border='0'
onload="setTimeout('titleAnimate()', titleAnimSpeed)" />
<script language= "javascript">
if (screen.availWidth < 800) {
    document.titleAnim.width = document.titleAnim.width / 2;
    }
</script>
```

Done!

REVIEW

In this session, you learned all about how JavaScript interacts with images on the HTML page. You saw how to create a rollover button and how event handlers can be used as triggers for changing the images that are displayed in the Web browser. You also learned how to create a JavaScript-based animation and how to dynamically resize the images in the browser to fit the available space in the client's browser window. With all of this under your belt, it's time to begin dressing up the shopping cart. On your CD-ROM, you'll find new versions of the index.htm and babyPalooza.js files. These new versions incorporate just about everything you've learned from this session to add an animated title and rollover buttons to the basic product display. (To see the new look of the shopping cart, load the index.htm file from the Session14 folder.) Take a few moments to study these files and you'll have a good idea of how the information from this session can be combined with the knowledge you already have.

QUIZ YOURSELF

1. What does the `complete` property of an Image object tell you? (See "The complete property.")

2. What happens when you assign the Web address of an image file to the `src` property of an Image object? (See "The src and lowsrc properties.")

3. How can you create an Image object without a corresponding HTML `<img>` tag? (See "Images without the <img> tag.")

4. Which events allow you to create a rollover graphic button? (See "Creating Rollovers with JavaScript.")

5. How do you determine the time between the frames of a JavaScript-based animation? (See "Timing your animation.")

Validating Form Data

Session Checklist

✔ Learning how to validate the data in a form using JavaScript

✔ Understanding the value of defensive programming

**30 Min.
To Go**

One of the most popular uses of JavaScript is to validate the data in a form before that data is sent to the server. As the Web has become more and more popular, this ability has become increasingly important. After all, if thousands of people are hitting the same Web site every second, it's much easier for the Web server to cope if most of the data validation chores can be performed on the client.

Another reason to perform data validation on the client is so your users will get immediate feedback. When you validate form data with JavaScript, you can instantly tell users that there is a problem and get it corrected. If you send the data to the server for validation, the user has to sit there and wait for the data to be sent, processed, and a result page returned. If the data was bad, the user then has to back up a page, fix it, and send it off again. This can be incredibly frustrating, especially if the error message that comes back from the server is cryptic or incomplete.

Program Defensively

The key to data validation is to assume, right from the beginning, that users will be entering bad data. Yes, this is a pessimistic view, and it does mean more work for you, the programmer, but adopting it will save you a lot of heartache in the long run. Actually, there isn't really that much extra work involved; all you have to do is look for ways to remove the possibility of bad data being entered. A few ways to do this include:

- Set up default values that make sense. If you supply good default values in your form fields, the user may never even touch most of the fields, which means they won't enter bad data in them. (Another advantage is that if the user resets the form, the default values will be reloaded. If this isn't the behavior that you want, you can create an onreset event handler to reset the form the way you want.)

- Protect fields that you don't want changed. Very few people realize that JavaScript makes it easy to set up a field so that users can't mess with it. As you'll see later in this session, an onfocus handler is all you need to make this happen.

- Use select lists whenever possible. If you present users with a list of possible values for a form field, it's impossible for them to enter bad data into that field. For example, instead entering a two-character state code (AL, AK, and so forth) into a text box, give them a select list with all of the states already in it. Like this:

  ```
  <select name="state" size="1">
      <option value="AL">Alabama</option>
      <option value="AK">Alaska</option>
      <!-- other states follow -->
  </select>
  ```

- Provide an interface that controls how the user can make changes to the form. For example, provide buttons that increase or decrease a value by a certain amount.

Setting up default values

If you are using JavaScript to dynamically generate your HTML page (as seen in Session 11), it's very simple to set up controls with appropriate default values. As an example of this, let me return to the shopping cart I've been building. To create an informative shopping cart display, it's a good idea to include a count of how many units of an item are available along with a count of how many units the user has put in her cart. One way to display this information on screen would be to put each value in its own text field. To implement this in my shopping cart, I need to add two slots to my product arrays: one for the quantity on hand and another for the number of units the user has in her shopping cart. So, my product array definition would now look like this (note that all of the code you'll be seeing in this session can be found in the index.htm and babyPalooza.js files in the Session15 folder on your CD-ROM):

```
var index = 0;
var strollerInfo = new Array();
strollerInfo[index++] = 199.95;
strollerInfo[index++] = "Rock & Stroll - Deluxe";
strollerInfo[index++] = "st-001";
strollerInfo[index++] = 20;
strollerInfo[index++] = 10; // Quantity on hand
strollerInfo[index++] = 0; // Number in cart
```

Now, assuming that I want to display each of these new values in a text field, it's a fairly simple matter to come up with the JavaScript code that will generate the appropriate HTML. For example, the following shows the code I'll add to the showProductInfo() function to create the needed text fields.

```
var onHandBox = "<input type='text' name='quan_" + pInfo[2] + "'";
    onHandBox += " value='" + pInfo[4] + "' size='6' />";
var inCartBox = "<input type='text' name='inCart_" + pInfo[2]+
"'";
inCartBox += " value='" + pInfo[5] + "' size='6' />";
```

As you can see, this code will create two text field definitions. Each of these definitions will have a default value attribute that's taken directly from my product information array. The tags created by this code will look like this:

```
<input type='text' name='quan_st-001' value='10' size='6' />
<input type='text' name='inCart_st-001' value='0' size='6' />
```

(Another simple defensive trick is to use the maxlength= attribute of your text fields to restrict the amount of data that can be entered into a field. For example, if a field will hold a 5-digit postal code, you would set the maxlength= attribute to 5.)

Protecting fields with an onfocus handler

Now that I have these text fields defined, I need to determine exactly how I want the user to interact with them. The `inCart` field is pretty simple: I want the user to be able to type a number directly into it so that they can specify exactly how many units of an item that they want. It would also be nice if there were a button or two that would increase or decrease the number in this field by one. I'll show you how to do that in just a moment, but first I need to talk about the quantity on hand field.

The quantity on hand field poses a bit of a problem: I want to be able to update it myself (to reflect how many units of an item remain), but I don't want the user to be able to change the value in the field. Fortunately, the solution to this problem is incredibly simple, as shown here:

```
<input type='text' name='quan_st-001'
onfocus="document.cart.elements['inCart_st-001'].focus()"
value='10' size='6' />
```

In this code, I've added an `onfocus` event handler to the definition of my quantity on hand text field. All the handler does is call the `focus()` method for the corresponding `inCart` text field. As I've mentioned before, the `onfocus` event is generated when a control becomes the target of the user's keystrokes. So, if the user clicks in this field or tabs to it, the `onfocus` handler will be called. The handler will then call the `focus()` method for the `inCart` field. This method then makes the `inCart` control the target of the user's keystrokes. The overall effect is that when the user tries to type something into the quantity on hand field, the insertion point will actually jump to the `inCart` field! The upshot of this is that with this event handler in place, the user can never type anything into my quantity on hand field. (If your site is based on HTML v4.0 or XHTML, a simpler approach is to create your controls with the `readonly` attribute. As the name implies, this attribute makes a control read-only, so that the user cannot edit its contents. For example, `<input type="text" readonly />` would create a read-only text box. However, this attribute is not available in older versions of HTML, while the JavaScript-based approach shown above should work in most JavaScript-capable browsers.)

**20 Min.
To Go**

Controlling user input

With the quantity on hand field protected, I can now turn my attention to the `inCart` field. As I said before, I'd like the user to be able to type a number into this field to immediately specify how many units of an item they want. However, in addition to that ability, I'd like to provide users with a set of buttons that will allow them to add or subtract one unit at a time. These buttons (along with the rest of the new shopping cart design) are shown at the end of each row in Figure 15-1.

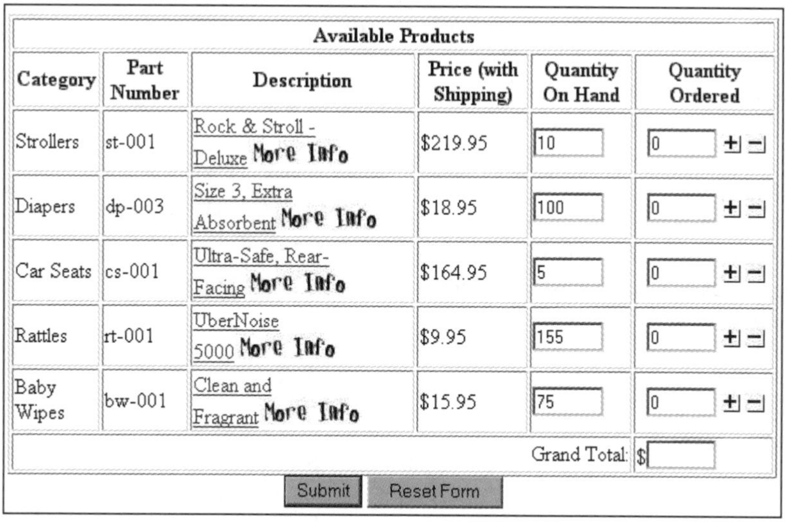

Available Products					
Category	Part Number	Description	Price (with Shipping)	Quantity On Hand	Quantity Ordered
Strollers	st-001	Rock & Stroll - Deluxe More Info	$219.95	10	0 ± =
Diapers	dp-003	Size 3, Extra Absorbent More Info	$18.95	100	0 ± =
Car Seats	cs-001	Ultra-Safe, Rear-Facing More Info	$164.95	5	0 ± =
Rattles	rt-001	UberNoise 5000 More Info	$9.95	155	0 ± =
Baby Wipes	bw-001	Clean and Fragrant More Info	$15.95	75	0 ± =
				Grand Total:	$

Submit   Reset Form

Figure 15-1
Shopping cart with text fields and other controls added

As you can see, these are simple plus and minus buttons. When the user clicks one, I want the buttons to react with an appropriate animation — that is, the buttons should appear to depress and then pop back up — and to either add or subtract one unit to the appropriate inCart text field. The HTML that sets this up looks like this:

```
<img name='plus_st-001' src='plus.jpg'
onmousedown="document.images['plus_st-001'].src='plusOn.jpg'"
onmouseout="document.images['plus_st-001'].src='plus.jpg'"
    onmouseup="document.images['plus_st-001'].src='plus.jpg'" />
<img name='minus_st-001' src='minus.jpg'
onmousedown="document.images['minus_st-001'].src='minusOn.jpg'"
onmouseout="document.images['minus_st-001'].src='minus.jpg'"
onmouseup="document.images['minus_st-001'].src='minus.jpg'" />
```

In this code, I'm using three mouse-related event handlers to control the animation for my buttons. (The onmouseout handler is necessary to handle the case where the user clicks the button, but moves the mouse away from the button before they let go of the mouse button.) As shown here, this code only creates a couple of animated buttons. If I actually want to react to clicks on these buttons, I have to change the `onmouseup` handlers to call a function that will update the values in my text fields.

```
onmouseup="doPlus('st-001');document.images['plus_st-
001'].src='plus.jpg'"
onmouseup="doMinus('st-001');document.images['minus_st-
001'].src='minus.jpg'"
```

Here I've defined a couple of new functions: `doPlus()` and `doMinus()`. These functions add one and subtract one unit of an item from the user's shopping cart. To specify which item is being added or removed, I pass each function an appropriate part number. Since these functions are so similar, I'll just go over the first one, `doPlus()`:

```
function findPartNo( partNo) {
    var result = "";
    for (x=0; x < productInfo.length; x++) {
        if (productInfo[x][2] == partNo) {
            result = productInfo[x];
            break;
            }
        }
    return result;
    }
function doPlus( partNo) {
    var prodInfo = findPartNo( partNo);
    // Do we have enough on hand to do this?
     if (prodInfo[ 4] > 0) {
        // Update the quantities in the array
        prodInfo[ 4]--;
        prodInfo[ 5]++;
        // Copy these new values to the form
        document.cart.elements[ "quan_" + partNo].value =
        prodInfo[ 4];
        document.cart.elements[ "inCart_" + partNo].value =
        prodInfo[ 5];
        }
    else {
        alert( "There are no more of this item in stock!");
        }
    }
```

When `doPlus()` is called, the first thing it does is use the `findPartNo()` function to search for the array that contains the selected product information. As you can see, the `findPartNo()` function is just a simple `for` loop that moves through the `productInfo` array until it finds a match for the part number that was specified. At that point, the entire sub array is returned to the caller (in this case, the `doPlus()` function).

Once the `doPlus()` function has the correct product information, it checks to see if there are any units remaining in stock. If there aren't, an alert window is displayed to alert the user to this fact. If however, there is at least one more unit in stock, the function subtracts one from the quantity on hand field and adds one to the number in cart field.

After this, all that's left is to copy these new values to the text fields on-screen. To do this, the function takes the part number it was passed and uses it to access the text fields via the `elements` array in the form. (Remember, the `elements` array in a `form` object lets you access a control in the form by supplying a string containing the control's name. Instead of hard-coding that string, I'm simply building it on the fly.) This updates the text fields on the screen and lets the user know that the item has been added to the cart.

Validating Text Fields

At this point, all that's left is to make sure the user doesn't type something invalid into one of the `inCart` text fields. This is easily accomplished using an `onchange` event handler. The following HTML shows how to set this up.

```
<input type='text' name='inCart_st-001'
onchange='enterQuantity("st-001")' value='0' size='6' />
```

As mentioned before, an `onchange` event fires when the user changes the value in a control and the control loses the focus. So, this is a great time to make sure the user has typed in a value that's appropriate for the control. In this case, I need to check to see if the control is empty and, if not, does it contain a number?

Checking for blank text fields

Checking for a blank text field is one of the simplest, and most common, data validation tasks in programming. After all, it's very hard to give your users what they want if they don't supply you with all the information you need. So, it's very important to have a function handy that can check for a blank string in a field.

```
function isBlank( theString) {
    var result = true;
    if (theString != "") {
        for (x=0; x < theString.length; x++) {
            var theChar = theString.charAt( x);
            if (theChar != " ") {
                result = false;
                break;
                }
            }
        }
    return result;
    }
```

This function takes a very simplistic approach to checking for a blank string. First it compares the string to the empty string. If the string is not empty, it then checks each character in the string to see if any of them are not space characters. If even one character is not a space, the string is not blank and so the function returns a false. Otherwise, the function returns a true. (You might have noticed that this function checks a string and not a text field. I'll show you how to use this function with a text field in just a moment.)

Checking for numeric values

Another common task is checking user input to make sure that it contains nothing but numbers. There are lots of ways to do this, one of which looks like this:

```
function isNumeric( theString) {
    var validChars = "0123456789";
    var result = true;
    for (x=0; x < theString.length; x++) {
        var theChar = theString.charAt( x);
        // is this char in the set of validChars?
        if (validChars.indexOf( theChar) == -1) {
            result = false;
            break;
            }
        }
    return result;
    }
```

This is another fairly simple operation. I'm simply checking each character in the string to see if it is one of the characters 0 to 9. If even one character isn't in this set of valid characters, the entire string is rejected.

Using data validation in a program

**10 Min.
To Go**

Now that I've got functions to check for blank and numeric values, I can use these functions to create my enterQuantity() function. This function is quite lengthy, so instead of presenting it here, I'll ask you to find it in the babyPalooza.js file (in the Session15 folder on your CD-ROM) and follow along in your HTML editor.

As you saw a bit earlier, an onchange event in one of my inCart text fields will cause this function to execute. The first thing the enterQuantity() function does is grab the product information array that the user is trying to update. Then, it retrieves the value that is typed into the text field and checks to see if that value is blank. If it is, we set the value to a "0" string and proceed. (It seems reasonable to me that someone would empty a field to zero it out, so that is what this code assumes.)

Once the function has retrieved the string from the text box, it needs to make sure that it is actually a number. If the isNumeric() function says the string is not a number, the function puts up an alert window to that effect and resets the value in the inCart text field to the value that is saved in the product information array. If however, the value is a number, things get a little more interesting. First, the function uses a JavaScript function named parseInt() to convert the string into an actual number. The parseInt() function can take up to two parameters, the first is the string you want to convert and the second is the base of the number that the string represents. In this case, my number is a decimal value, so I pass a base value of 10. (Note that you don't have to supply base information to the parseInt() function. If you don't however, parseInt() will look at the string itself for a hint as to what the base of the number is. If the number starts with a 0 character, it will assume that the number is octal (base 8). If the number starts with 0x it will assume that it is hexadecimal (base 16). So, just to be on the safe side, I always specify the base of the number I'm converting.)

Once the conversion is done, the function makes sure that there are enough units to cover the request. If not, it will display an alert window and reset the value in the inCart text field to the value saved in the product information array.

If there are enough units to cover the request, the function performs the necessary math to update the product information array and then puts those new values into the appropriate fields in the form. (If you are wondering why this function is returning a Boolean result, see the "Validating Data When a Form Is Submitted" section later in this Session.)

Validating Other Types of Controls

Of course, not every form is made up of nothing but text fields. However, text fields are probably the most difficult to validate. After all, text fields can contain just about any type of data and that data can have all sorts of restrictions on it. The techniques I've just shown you are intended to give you an idea of how to go about writing your own data validation routines for your own text fields. The other types of fields you can include in a form are, for the most part, self-validating. For example, if you set it up correctly, a select list should contain nothing but valid values. As for check boxes and radio buttons, if you need to require that one or more of them be turned on or off, you can check them simply by looking at the checked property of each control and reacting accordingly.

About the only other type of control that really requires any sort of data validation is the file upload field. (For an example of how to validate one of these fields, see "Working with the File Upload Control" in Session 13.)

Validating Data When a Form Is Submitted

The examples I've shown so far try to validate the data in a form as the user is entering that data. However, you can wait until a form is submitted before you validate its data. As you saw in Session 10, you do this by creating an event handler for the onsubmit event. When the user clicks a Submit button it generates an onsubmit event. Your onsubmit handler can then check each field in the form for valid data. If you find something wrong with the form, your event handler can return a false and the form will not be submitted. If the data is good, you can simply return a true and the form will be submitted.

Actually, it's usually a good idea to do both kinds of data validation. In other words, check the data as it's being entered and then again when the user clicks the Submit button. This gives you an extra bit of protection against those users that like to kill time by finding ways to break Web sites. With that in mind, here's the doSubmit() function that I'm using to check my data one last time before submitting it.

```
function doSubmit() {
    var partNo = "";
    var result = true;
    // Look at each product in the inventory
    for (y=0; y < productInfo.length; y++) {
        partNo = productInfo[ y][ 2]; // Get the part number
        // And use that to check each field
```

```
        if (!enterQuantity( partNo)) {
            result = false;
            break;
            }
        }
    return result;
    }
```

Done!

You might have noticed earlier that the enterQuantity() function returns a Boolean result. Here is why: By returning a Boolean result, I can reuse the enterQuantity() function to automatically validate each field from the doSubmit() function. If any field has bad data in it, the enterQuantity() will report that fact and the doSubmit() function can then return a false value to cancel the submission of the form.

REVIEW

In this session, you saw several different techniques for data validation. You learned how to validate data on the fly, as well as how to validate data when the user clicks the Submit button. You saw how programming defensively and using default values could help reduce the amount of data validation you actually have to do. I also showed you how to protect a text field from user input by using an onfocus handler. You even learned how to create a set of custom graphics-based controls that limit the range of user input to a form.

QUIZ YOURSELF

---

1. Can select lists reduce your data validation chores? (See "Program Defensively.")

2. How can your JavaScript program generate custom controls with default values? (See "Setting up default values.")

3. How can you use an onfocus event handler to protect a field? (See "Protecting fields with an onfocus handler.")

4. Why would you check for blank text fields? (See "Checking for blank text fields.")

5. How does the onsubmit handler allow you to validate your form data? (See "Validating Data When a Form Is Submitted.")

Cooking up Cookies with JavaScript

Session Checklist

✔ Learning about the internal structure of cookies and how to manipulate them

✔ Learning how to determine if cookies are active

30 Min. To Go

As of now, my shopping cart has almost all of the basic functionality that it needs. One glaring exception is that if the user leaves the site and returns later, the contents of the shopping cart will be forgotten and the user will have to make her selections all over again. To fix this, I need some mechanism that will allow the shopping cart to remember its contents and rebuild itself accordingly. Browser cookies were invented to solve exactly this sort of problem.

What Is a Cookie?

A cookie is a tiny chunk of data that the Web browser stores on the client's machine. When I say "tiny," I mean about 4 KB (4,096 bytes), though the exact size depends on the browser that's being used. (Just keep your cookies under 4,000 bytes in length and you shouldn't have any problems.) While cookies are usually thought of as a strictly client-side affair, they are actually managed by both the Web browser and Web server working together. The Web browser can send a cookie to the server, which will store it for later use. Then, when a Web browser requests an HTML document, the server looks at all of the cookies it has available and determines which of these should be sent along with the requested document. These cookies are sent as headers that precede the actual HTML document. As these cookie headers reach the browser, they are parsed and incorporated into the Browser Object Model representation for that HTML document.

As you may remember from Session 9, so far as JavaScript is concerned, a cookie is just another property of the document object. This makes reading and writing cookies simple:

```
var theCookie = document.cookie; // read the cookie
document.cookie = theCookie; // write the cookie
```

However, actually *using* the contents of a cookie can be much trickier. But to understand why, you have to understand how cookies are structured.

Ingredients of a cookie

When you reduce it down to its simplest terms, a cookie is simply a name string, followed by an equal sign, followed by a string that represents the value of the cookie. A semicolon marks the end of this value string. So, the simplest cookie you could cook up might look like this: name=value; The name you give to a cookie can be just about anything. However, it can't contain white space characters (blank spaces, tabs, and such), commas, or semicolons. The value part of a cookie has the same restrictions.

While cookie names can be just about anything, you'll probably want to give your cookie a name that describes exactly what the cookie contains. For example, since my cookie will eventually hold shopping cart information, I might want to call it "bpShopCart" (for "baby-palooza shopping cart") or something similar. So, without actually knowing what's in the shopping cart, my basic cookie might look something like this:

```
bpShopCart=shopcartcontents;
```

Cookie attributes

After the initial name and value pair, you can add any or all of the following four attributes to gain more control over how your cookie will be used.

- `expires`: This attribute is followed by a value that specifies an expiration date for the cookie. This date tells you when the Web browser should delete the cookie from the client's machine. If no expiration date is specified, the cookie will be deleted when the user exits the Web browser. I'll be discussing the `expires` attribute in much greater detail a bit later in this session.

- `domain`: By default, cookies are only available to the HTML documents that are on the same server as the document that created the cookie. For example, if a cookie is created by a document on the "www.baby-palooza.com" server, that cookie will not be available to a document on the "orders.baby-palooza.com" server. You can change this by adding a `domain` specification to your cookie:

  `bpShopcart=shopcartcontents;domain=baby-palooza.com`

  Here the domain I've specified means that this cookie will be made available to any HTML document requested from "www.baby-palooza.com," "orders.baby-palooza.com," or any other server in the "baby-palooza.com" domain.

- `path`: Normally, a cookie is only available to the HTML documents that are in the same folder as the document that created the cookie. (In other words, if a cookie is created by a document in the Session16 folder, it isn't available to a document in the Session15 folder.) However, by adding a `path` specification to your cookie, you can make it available to the documents in other folders. For example, if I wanted my cookie to be available to all documents in all of the "Session" folders that are at the root of my Web server, I could specify:

  `bpShopcart=shopcartcontents;path=/Session`

  With this `path` specification in place, the Web server will supply this cookie along with any HTML document that comes from any root-level folder whose name begins with "Session." (Note that the `path` and `domain` attributes you specify are case sensitive only if your Web server is case sensitive.) If you want your cookie to be sent along with every HTML document on the server, you would specify a path of `/`. (Which specifies the root and everything under it!)

- `secure`: If this attribute is specified, the cookie will only be sent if the client and server are joined by a secure connection (that is, "https" or some other secure connection). `bpShopcart=shopcartcontents;secure`

Cookie values

At this point, you might be thinking that cookies look pretty simple. Well, they are pretty simple. However, I've yet to consider what the value of my cookie will actually be. Remember, I've got to somehow store the entire contents of my shopping cart inside my cookie. How can I do this? Well, I *could* create a separate cookie for each item in my product inventory and then check each cookie in turn. However, the cookie specification states that no client may store more than 300 cookies total, and that no more than 20 cookies can come from the same domain. So, if my product inventory has more than 20 products, this restriction will make a "one cookie per product" approach unworkable.

A much better approach is to store all of my shopping cart information inside a single cookie. I can accomplish this by encoding the part number and quantity for each item in my shopping cart and placing all of this information into a single value string.

Remember, a cookie value can contain almost anything you wish, with the exception of white space characters, commas, and semicolons. Fortunately, I don't need to use any of these characters to create my cookie value. (Of course, if you do ever need to use one of the characters that aren't allowed in a cookie, you can use the JavaScript escape() function to encode those characters into a form that you can safely keep in a cookie. To decode these characters, you can use the unescape() function to return them to their original state. I'll be discussing these functions in greater detail in Session 28.) So, what will my cookie actually look like? Consider the following sample cookie:

```
bpShopCart=3st-0015dp-003;
```

Given what you know about the way the Baby-Palooza product inventory is set up, you might be able to discern that, according to this cookie, there are three units of part number st-001 and five units of part number dp-003 in the shopping cart. However, you are only able to make this determination because you are familiar with the way the inventory is set up and because the human brain is the best pattern-matching machine in the known universe. A JavaScript program, on the other hand, will have no earthly idea what this string signifies. Worse yet, it will find it almost impossible to extract any meaningful information from it at all. So, let me refine the design of my cookie so that it's easier to see how my data is actually arranged:

```
bpShopCart=3:st-001|5:dp-003;
```

In this version, I've added two different separator characters that break up the value in the cookie and give it a bit of structure. The vertical bar (also sometimes called a "pipe") character is used to separate the information for each product in the shopping cart (that is, to separate the diapers from the strollers). Inside each of these divisions, a colon character is used to separate the quantity in the cart from the product number it is applied to. So, with a mere glance, a human can tell that this shopping cart holds three units of part number st-001 and five units of part number dp-003. And, as I'll show you shortly, it's now child's play for a JavaScript program to extract useful information from this cookie.

So, why did I pick the vertical bar and colon characters for my separators? Honestly, I did it because, for me, they provide the best visual cues as to how this data is arranged. When you design the cookies you'll be using in your own projects, you can use whatever separator characters you want. The only restrictions are that you can't use white space characters, commas, or semicolons and that your separators shouldn't be something that might appear as data inside your cookie. (For example, since my part numbers contain dashes, I wouldn't want to use a dash for one of my separators.)

At this point, it's important that you realize that the cookie string I'm building here is unique to this shopping cart. In all likelihood, each project that you work on will require a completely different cookie structure (if the project even uses cookies at all). The point of this session is to introduce you to the issues that you will confront when working with cookies, not to make you think that there is only one correct way to build and use them.

Cookie Usage Guidelines

20 Min. To Go

Over the years, cookies have received a fair amount of bad press. This is because several clever companies figured out that, because a cookie can hold just about anything, they could just as easily hold personal information as well as what's in a shopping cart. This can include credit card numbers, passwords, and, perhaps most disturbing of all, information about a person's Web browsing habits. When privacy advocates got wind of this, there was a general outcry against the use of cookies. As you might imagine, the ability to use cookies is far too useful to go away completely, so Web browser manufacturers responded by allowing individual users to set up their browsers to notify them when a cookie was being saved or to reject all cookies automatically. This means that, if you build a site that depends on cookies being enabled, you have to be prepared for the inevitable case where a user has turned them off and they simply aren't available.

As you'll see a bit later, it's not that hard to tell if cookies are turned off or not, but it's much more difficult to persuade cookie-haters to even use your site. Your best bet is to tell visitors that you are using cookies and explain to them exactly what you are tracking with those cookies. This can usually be accomplished with a simple disclaimer or privacy guidelines information page. If, after reading your disclaimer the user still doesn't want your cookies on her machine, there's very little you can do about it. While this may be a victory for privacy advocates, it can be a real pain for the JavaScript programmer. If cookies aren't available, you can either lock the user out of your site (which is not the best way to keep a customer if you are building an online business) or you can provide the user with as much functionality as possible without using cookies. (For the Baby-Palooza site, I'll be trying to provide my users with as much functionality as possible.)

Building and Saving Cookies

As you've seen, the act of saving a cookie is really very simple. All you have to do is build your cookie string and then issue a statement similar to this:

```
document.cookie = theCookie;
```

The tricky part is the actual building of the cookie string. However, once you've decided what your cookie value will actually look like, this isn't too difficult to do. As you'll remember from earlier in this session, my cookie string is going to look like this:

```
bpShopCart=quantity:partNumber|quantity:partNumber|etc. . .;
```

So, really, all I need is a simple loop that will go through my product information array and add each product's information to my final cookie string. Here is a simple function that will do the job quite nicely.

```
function saveCart() {
    var theCookieName = "bpShopCart=";
    var theCookieValue = "";
    for (x=0; x<productInfo.length; x++) {
        // Only include if this item has
        // been placed in the shopping cart
        if (productInfo[x][5] > 0) {
            // if this is the first item we've found
            // do not add a separator
            if (theCookieValue != "") {
                theCookieValue += "|";
                }
            // add the quantity to the cookie
            theCookieValue += productInfo[x][5] + ":";
```

```
                    // add the part number to the cookie
                    theCookieValue += productInfo[x][2];
                    }
            }
    document.cookie = theCookieName + theCookieValue + ";";
    alert( document.cookie);
    }
```

As you can see, this code isn't terribly complex. I'm simply moving through my product information array and, if a product has been placed in the shopping cart, I add its information to my cookie value string. After I've built my cookie value, I simply concatenate it with the cookie's name and a semicolon and assign it to the document.cookie property. The call to the alert() method simply allows me to check the contents of my cookie so I can tell if I've built it properly.

At this point, the question becomes, "When do I build and save my cookie?" Well, if you glance back at Session 10, you might notice an event called the onunload event. This event is fired whenever the browser unloads the current Web page. This happens when the user moves to another page, or when the Reload button is clicked. You trap the onunload event by specifying your handler in the <body> tag of your HTML document. So, if I change my <body> tag to look like this:

```
<body bgcolor="white" onunload="saveCart()">
```

The saveCart() function will be called whenever the page containing my shopping cart is unloaded. So, if I place three strollers and two rattles in my shopping cart and then reload the page, I'll get an alert window with a cookie string that looks like this:

```
bpShopCart=3:st-001|2:rt-001.
```

Hopefully, this is almost exactly what you expected the cookie to look like. However, if you look closely, you'll notice something missing: the ending semicolon. Even though the saveCart() function adds a semicolon to the end of the cookie when it saves it, that semicolon is not a part of the cookie string that you get when you later examine the document.cookie property. While this might be unexpected, it actually makes processing cookies easier, simply because you don't have to worry about stripping off the semicolon.

Adding an expiration date

As it stands now, my cookie is ready to use. However, one little thing is missing: an expiration date. Without an expiration date, this cookie will only exist for as long as the user has her Web browser open. This is because, as I mentioned earlier, a cookie saved without an expiration date will be deleted as soon as the user ends her browser session.

You see, when you close your Web browser, part of its shutdown process is to look at the expiration dates of all of the cookies it has gathered. If the expiration date of a cookie has passed, or if the cookie simply doesn't have an expiration date, the browser will delete the cookie from the client's machine. So, in its current form, my cookie will only be good until the user closes her Web browser. While this might sound good enough, consider the poor user that spends an hour shopping at your site, filling her cart with all sorts of goodies, only to realize that her credit card has expired. Having renewed her credit card a few days later, she returns to your site only to find that everything she has selected has disappeared! How likely is she to repeat all of that work just to give you money?

Again, you specify a cookie expiration date by adding an `expires=` attribute to the end of your cookie. This will give you a cookie that looks something like this:

```
bpShopCart=shopcartcontents;expires=expirationdate;
```

The catch here is that you have to format the expiration date in a very specific way. Fortunately, JavaScript contains an object that makes creating a properly formatted expiration date very simple.

Using the Date object with a cookie

As the name suggests, the JavaScript Date object is used to hold information about a date. As with the other built-in JavaScript objects you've seen, you create a new Date object by using the new keyword, like this: `var currentDate = new Date();`

In this example, I've not passed any parameters to the Date constructor method. Because of this, the constructor will return a Date object that contains information about the current time and date that are contained in the client's system clock. Once you've got a Date object created, there are lots of different things you can do with it. However, at this point, I'm only interested in using it to create an expiration date for my cookie. (I'll be discussing the Date object in detail in Session 27. For now, I'm just going to discuss the parts of the Date object that are useful for the creation of cookies.)

I can do this by adding a time interval to my Date object and then using the resulting date to tack an expiration date onto the end of my cookie. For example, if I want my cookie to expire in two weeks, I create a Date object representing the current time, add two weeks to that, and then use this new date (which is two weeks into the future) to generate the expiration date for my cookie. In order to accomplish this, you need to know about three methods of the JavaScript Date object.

- The getTime() method. This method returns the date as the number of milliseconds that have passed since midnight on January 1, 1970.

- The setTime() method. This method accepts a single parameter: an integer number of milliseconds that have passed since midnight on January 1, 1970. This number will be used to reset the Date object to that date.

- The toGMTString() Method. A cookie's expiration date must follow a certain format. Specifically, it must be formatted as a Greenwich Mean Time (GMT) date string. This method returns the contents of a Date object in exactly that format.

Now that you know about these methods of the Date object, take a look at the revised saveCart() function.

```
function saveCart() {
    var theCookieName = "bpShopCart=";
    var theCookieValue = "";
    for (x=0; x<productInfo.length; x++) {
        // Only include if this item has
        // been placed in the shopping cart
        if (productInfo[x][5] > 0) {
            // if this is the first item we've found
            // do not add a separator
            if (theCookieValue != "") {
                theCookieValue += "|";
                }
            // add the quantity to the cookie
            theCookieValue += productInfo[x][5] + ":";
            // add the part number to the cookie
            theCookieValue += productInfo[x][2];
            }
        }
    var expireTime = new Date(); // add the expiration date
    // How many milliseconds are there in two weeks?
    var twoWeeks = 14 * 24 * 60 * 60 * 1000;
    expireTime.setTime( expireTime.getTime() + twoWeeks);
    document.cookie = theCookieName + theCookieValue + ";expires="
    + expireTime.toGMTString() + ";";
    alert( document.cookie);
    }
```

As you can see, there really isn't that much to this. The first new step is to create a Date object that contains the current time and date from the client's system clock. After this, a simple calculation yields the number of milliseconds that make up a two-week interval. (Remember, there are 1,000 milliseconds in a second.) I then use the getTime() method to extract the number of milliseconds that constitute the current date and add my two week interval to that. I then pass this result to the setTime() method and my expireTime Date object will then contain a date that is two weeks into the future.

The only thing left to do is extract this information in the form of a GMT formatted string and add it onto the end of my cookie string. When it's all over, the cookie string that's generated might look something like this:

```
bpShopCart=2:rt-001;expires=Tue, 12 Dec 2000 19:38:17 UTC;
```

Loading and Decoding Cookies

Now that I've got my cookie saved out and I know that it's going to be around for a while, I have to turn my attention to loading it back in when the user returns to my site.

As you've probably guessed, if the onunload event is a good time for saving a cookie, the onload event is a perfect signal for loading a cookie back in. If you'll remember, loading the actual cookie is a snap: var theCookie = document. cookie;

As with saving a cookie, the real work comes from decoding the information that is contained in the value portion of the cookie string. Fortunately, the Array and String handling methods you saw in Session 5 and Session 6 make this very easy to do.

```
function loadCart() {
    var myCookieName = "bpShopCart";
    var theCookie = document.cookie;
    // Remember, there can be multiple name=value pairs!
    // So, break the cookie up along the semi-colons
       var allCookies = theCookie.split( ";");
    // Now, take each of those name=value pairs and split them
    for (a=0; a<allCookies.length; a++) {
        var thisCookie = allCookies[a].split( "=");
        // Does the name in this cookie match?
        if (thisCookie[0] == myCookieName) {
```

```
                // break out the products in the cart
                if (thisCookie.length > 1) {
                    var products = thisCookie[1].split( "|");
                    if (products.length > 0) {
                        // Split out the part numbers and quantities
                        // for each product
                        for (b=0; b<products.length; b++) {
                            var detailInfo = products[b].split( ":");
                            // Store the new value in the
                            // on-screen text box
                            document.cart.elements[ 'inCart_' +
                                detailInfo[1]].value = detailInfo[0];
                            // Finally, use the enterQuantity function
                            // to validate the value and update the
                            // main productInfo array
                            enterQuantity( detailInfo[1]);
                        }
                    }
                else {
                    // If there is nothing in the cookie,
                    // do nothing
                    break;
                    }
                }
            }
        }
    }
```

As you can see, I'm using the String object's split() method to break the cookie apart into smaller and smaller units of information. The first call to split() breaks up any name=value pairs that are in the cookie. I then loop through these pairs and use a second call to split() to break them into their constituent parts (that is, the name and the value). I then search each pair for the name I used for my cookie ("bpShopCart").

If the names match, and the cookie is not empty, I know that this is the value I'm interested in. So, I then split that value into yet another array that contains the information about all of the products that were in my shopping cart when the cookie was saved. One last loop splits each chunk of product information into an array containing the part number and quantity.

At this point, it's a simple matter to assign the quantity to the appropriate text box on screen. A final call to the enterQuantity() function ensures that the value is valid and updates the values in the actual productInfo array. With all of this code in place, my shopping cart will automatically rebuild itself whenever the user returns to it. (As long as they come back within two weeks!)

Deleting a Cookie

While it's nice to be able to make cookies hang around, there are times when you want to get rid of them completely. One such time might be when the user actually places an order. After all, once they've ordered the products in their shopping cart, they'll hardly want to see those items pop up in their cart again.

The only way to really delete a cookie is to save a cookie with the same name, but with an empty value and no expiration date. This will force the browser to delete the cookie when the user finishes using the Web browser. For the Baby-Palooza site, this can be accomplished fairly simply. All I need to do is create a new global variable called clearCookie. Then, when the order form is successfully submitted, clearCookie will be set to true. All that remains is to modify the last few lines of the saveCart() function to look like this:

```
if (clearCookie) {
    document.cookie = theCookieName + ";expires=;";
    }
else {
    document.cookie = theCookieName + theCookieValue +
    ";expires=" + expireTime.toGMTString() + ";";
    }
```

Telling if Cookies Are Turned Off

Finally, I need to address how you can determine if cookies have been disabled in the user's browser. In the case of the shopping cart I've been building here, not having access to cookies really won't be that much of a tragedy. If the user leaves or resets the page with the shopping cart on it, she'll simply lose all of the items she had previously added to her cart. While this isn't that big a deal for the Baby-Palooza site, it can be a real headache for some other sites. So, it's a good idea to have a way to determine if cookies are available or not. The function shown here can do just that:

```
function cookiesActive() {
    var result = false;
    if (document.cookie != "") { //Handle the simple case first
        result = true;
        }
    else {
        document.cookie = "active=yes;";
        // Try to save and reload it
        if (document.cookie == "active=yes") {
            result = true; // now trash it...
            document.cookie = "active=;expires=;";
            }
        }
    return result;
    }
```

As you can see, this function takes a very simple approach to the problem. If the document.cookie property is not empty, cookies must be active. If it is empty, it checks to see if it can save and reload a simple cookie. If it can, cookies are active. If not, cookies must be turned off. That's about all there is to it!

Done!

> **If your browser is Internet Explorer version 5 or Netscape Navigator version 6, you can also check the** navigator. cookieEnabled **property. You'll learn more about this property in Session 26.**

REVIEW

In this session, you learned all about cookies and how they can be used from JavaScript. You learned that cookies are stored as name=value pairs. You also found out about the four cookie attributes that you can specify (expires, domain, path, and secure) for your cookies. You learned how to use the value portion of a cookie to store multiple chunks of information, rather than breaking that information up among multiple cookies. I also told you about some of the privacy concerns surrounding cookies and how you might address those on your Web site. You learned how to use the onunload and onload events to trigger the saving and loading of cookie information. I showed you how to build a cookie complete with an expiration date (using the JavaScript Date object). You also saw how to delete a cookie and how to determine if cookies are active in the client browser.

QUIZ YOURSELF

1. What can you store in a cookie? (See "Ingredients of a cookie.")

2. How does the browser know when to delete a cookie? (See "Adding an expiration date.")

3. How do you delete a cookie? (See "Deleting a Cookie.")

4. What statement will load a cookie? (See "What Is a Cookie?")

5. How can you determine if cookies are active in the client's browser? (See "Telling if Cookies Are Turned Off.")

PART

III

Saturday Afternoon

1. Create a simple HTML document that uses JavaScript to dynamically create a new JavaScript code block. This new code block should execute the following `alert()` call: `alert("Welcome to Babies-A'Plenty!")`

2. What does the `elements` array inside a `form` object represent?

3. What does the `reset()` method of a `form` object do?

4. What does the following JavaScript represent? `document.forms[2]`

5. How can you use JavaScript to check or uncheck a check box in a form?

6. What does the `options` array inside a Select object represent?

7. If you extract the `value` from a password field, what will you actually get?

8. What is the difference between a Submit or Reset button and a generic button?

9. What does the `src` property of an Image object represent?

10. What does the `onload` event signify for an `<img>` tag?

11. What does the `onerror` event signify for an `<img>` tag?

12. In your own words, how does a JavaScript-based *rollover* work?

13. What does the `parseInt()` function do?

14. Why should you try to validate data as it's being entered and when the user submits a form?

15. Why should you assume that users would enter bad data into your forms?

16. In your own words, why is data validation so important?

17. How much data can a cookie hold?

18. When are the ideal times to save and load your cookies?

19. What does a cookie's expiration date signify?

20. You might have noticed that a "Grand Total" text box appeared on the baby-palooza.com Web site in Session 15. However, no code was added to actually place a grand total here. Take the final source code from Session 16 and update it to calculate and display the grand total whenever the user changes a quantity elsewhere in the shopping cart. Also, be sure to protect the grand total text box so that the user cannot type anything into it. (Note that when you have this code completed, you might find that the values calculated for the grand total contain more decimal places than you expect. You'll learn how to solve this problem in Session 25.)

PART

IV

Saturday
Evening

Understanding JavaScript Objects

Session Checklist

✔ Learning how to create your own objects

✔ Understanding constructor functions

✔ Learning how to define properties for your objects

✔ Understanding what "this" is

**30 Min.
To Go**

As of this moment, you've actually seen everything you need to create a JavaScript-based Web site. However, if you want to tap the real power of JavaScript, you need to learn how to create and use your own JavaScript objects.

What Is an Object?

I've been throwing around the word "object" for quite a while now, but I've not yet really explained what an object is. Of course, you know what an object is in the real world: It's simply something that is an entity unto itself. For example, a golf ball is an object, as is a human being.

In the real world, objects have physical properties as well as actions that can be performed by, on, or with them. A golf ball, for example, has physical properties including its size (4.27 centimeters in diameter), its shape (the good ones are usually spherical), and its texture (it's got all those cute dimples). There are lots of things you can do with golf balls too: You can roll them, bounce them, or even play golf with them.

One interesting thing about real world objects is that they can contain other objects. A golf ball contains a rubber ball surrounded by a tightly wound rubber band. (Well, that's what was in the one my grandfather cut open when I was seven!) Each of these is an object in its own right, but they've been packaged together to create a new type of object.

Computer-based objects are very similar in concept. The main difference is that instead of dealing with chunks of physical matter, computer objects deal with chunks of computer data. So, computer-based objects have *properties* as well as a set of *actions* that they can perform. (As you've guessed by now, these actions are called *methods* for a computer-based object.) Finally, as with real-world objects, computer-based objects can be combined to create completely new types of objects.

You've seen examples of each of these things throughout the first half of this book. For example, a JavaScript String object has a `length` property that tells you how many characters are in the string. It also has lots of different methods (actions) that it can perform. For example, the `toUpperCase()` method will return all of the characters in the string in their uppercase equivalents.

You've also seen how objects can be combined to create totally new entities. For example, the `document` object is just a collection of a bunch of different types of objects — forms, controls, a few strings — each with its own set of properties and methods. All of these objects work together to create something much more interesting and useful.

Compare this to, say, a human being from the real world. A human being is really just a collection of objects — kidneys, lungs, the odd brain or two — each with its own properties and "methods," all working together to create something much more interesting and useful.

Why Bother Creating Your Own Objects?

At the start of this session, I mentioned that you know all you need to know to create a JavaScript-based Web site. So, why should you even bother learning how to create and use objects? Actually, for most Web sites, you won't need to use objects (other than the ones that are built into JavaScript) at all! However, as you'll see in the next few sessions, you'll need to use objects if you want to build really cool, complex, and useful Web sites.

Of course, there are other reasons to use objects. One of the best is reusability. When you define a new type of object, you end up with a complete, self-contained entity that describes the properties and methods of a particular type of data. (This is called *encapsulation*.) You can then take that object definition and drop it into any new project that you work on. This is much nicer than having to rebuild everything from scratch. (If you don't think reusability is a big deal, just ask your doctor which would be easier: transplanting a kidney or building a new one from scratch.)

Imagine if you will, a shopping cart object. Now imagine that your quite-mad employer has ordered you to put together 50 e-commerce sites. Wouldn't it be nice if you could take your shopping cart object and reuse it in each site with almost no modification?

How to Define and Create JavaScript Objects

Every programming language that supports objects has a slightly different way of creating those objects. However, those differences are usually just a matter of syntax; the steps you go through are almost always exactly the same.

The first thing you have to do is decide what type of data your object will represent. Is it a string, an array, or a sales detail? For the purposes of this discussion, I'll be defining an object to represent an individual product in my product information array.

Next, you have to decide what kinds of properties and methods your object should have. To do this, stop and think about the data you are trying to encapsulate in your object. What sorts of information will you need to store in the object? What sorts of actions do you need to be able to perform on that data?

Once you've got all of this nailed down, you can begin to write the program code that will actually define your object. In JavaScript you do this by defining a constructor function along with one or more functions that will implement the methods of your object.

I've already got a definition for a product information array, which looks like this:

```
First slot = Price
Second slot = Description
Third slot = Part Number
Fourth slot = Shipping cost
Fifth slot = Quantity on Hand
Sixth slot = Quantity Ordered
```

With this definition in place, I was able to write a bunch of assignment statements that created a product information array. Like this:

```
var index = 0;
var strollerInfo = new Array();
strollerInfo[index++] = 199.95;
strollerInfo[index++] = "Rock & Stroll - Deluxe";
strollerInfo[index++] = "st-001";
strollerInfo[index++] = 20;
strollerInfo[index++] = 5;
strollerInfo[index++] = 0;
```

This is pretty simple, but it does mean that I have to repeat the same basic statements over and over again for each product in my inventory. (See the discussion in Session 6 for a reminder of just how much code this is.)

The question then is how do I rework this as an object? Well, first I need to create a constructor function, like this one:

```
function itemInfo( oPrice, oDesc, oPartNum, oShipping, oInStock) {
    this.price = oPrice;
    this.description = oDesc;
    this.partNumber = oPartNum;
    this.shipping = oShipping;
    this.inStock = oInStock;
    this.inCart = 0;
    }
```

As you look at this listing, I'm pretty sure you're wondering what the heck this is. Before I address that question, let me point out a few other things. First of all, notice that this constructor function is defined using the function keyword that you are already familiar with. In JavaScript, constructor functions are defined almost exactly like other functions. The main difference is how and when they are used. Specifically, they are only used to create new objects; you don't call them for any other reason.

Second, just like a regular function, you can pass parameters to constructor functions. These parameters can be used for anything you like, but the most common use is to pass default or original values that you want placed into your object when it is first created. In the itemInfo constructor, I'm allowing the passage of parameters that will specify the original price, description, and so forth for the product I want to store information about.

What the heck is this?

Which brings us neatly to the subject of the this keyword. In the simplest terms, whenever you see the this keyword, it is referring to the current object. So, what is this doing in a constructor function?

To answer that, remember what a constructor function does: It actually builds an object and fills it with data. Now, if you are in the middle of constructing an object, that object won't actually have a name yet, so the JavaScript interpreter needs some way to differentiate it from any other objects that might be floating around in memory. The this keyword is just what the doctor ordered: When used inside a constructor function, it refers to the object that is being built right at that moment. (Note that you can use the this keyword outside of constructor functions. It's a very handy keyword!)

How is an object constructed?

Now that I have my constructor function, let me show you how it's used. With this constructor function in place, instead of coding this:

```
var index = 0;
var strollerInfo = new Array();
strollerInfo[index++] = 199.95;
strollerInfo[index++] = "Rock & Stroll - Deluxe";
strollerInfo[index++] = "st-001";
strollerInfo[index++] = 20;
strollerInfo[index++] = 5;
strollerInfo[index++] = 0;
```

I can now code this:

```
function itemInfo( oPrice, oDesc, oPartNum, oShipping, oInStock) {
    this.price = oPrice;
    this.description = oDesc;
    this.partNumber = oPartNum;
    this.shipping = oShipping;
    this.inStock = oInStock;
    this.inCart = 0;
    }
var strollerInfo = new itemInfo( 199.95, "Rock & Stroll - Deluxe",
"st-001", 20, 5);
```

So, what's going on here? Well, as with the array-based version, I'm using the new keyword to invoke a constructor function. In this case however, I'm invoking a constructor that I've written myself (the itemInfo() constructor function) and *not* one that's built into the JavaScript interpreter.

When the constructor function is invoked, it's passed five parameters. The first of these parameters goes into the parameter variable named oPrice. Then the following statement is executed: this.price = oPrice;

Remember, at this point, the JavaScript interpreter is in the middle of creating a new object. Given that circumstance, this statement tells the JavaScript interpreter that this new object should have a property named "price." Furthermore, the value of the price property should be the value that was passed via the oPrice parameter. So, since it's being executed in the context of object creation, this statement actually does a couple of things:

- It creates a property in the new object.
- It assigns an initial value to the newly created property.

When the constructor finishes, you'll have a new object stored in the strollerInfo variable. That object will have the structure and contents shown in Table 17-1.

Table 17-1
Contents of the strollerInfo Object

Property Name	Value
price	199.95
description	"Rock & Stroll – Deluxe"
partNumber	"st-001"
shipping	20
inStock	5
inCart	0

One thing to note here is that I didn't use a parameter value to fill in my inCart property. Instead I simply assigned it a default value that makes sense. (After all, when my shopping cart is first created, it will be empty.) Again, constructor functions are, at heart, functions. This means that you can make them as complex or as simple as you like. Just remember: The purpose of a constructor function is to create a new object, *not* to make something happen elsewhere in your program. (At this point, you might be wondering how to define the methods that belong to this object. It isn't that hard to do, but, because it is a bit more complex than defining properties, I'm going to leave the discussion of how to define and use methods until the next session.) So, with that said, I can now replace my product information arrays with objects, as shown by the following code:

```
var strollerInfo = new itemInfo( 199.95, "Rock & Stroll - Deluxe",
"st-001", 20, 5);
var diaperInfo = new itemInfo( 13.95, "Size 3, Extra Absorbent",
"dp-003", 5, 100);
var carSeatInfo = new itemInfo( 149.95, "Ultra-Safe, Rear-Facing",
"cs-001", 15, 5);
var rattleInfo = new itemInfo( 4.95, "UberNoise 5000", "rt-001",
5, 155);
var babyWipeInfo = new itemInfo( 9.95, "Clean and Fragrant", "bw-
001", 6, 75);
```

You might have heard other programmers use the terms *class* **and** *instance* **when talking about objects. What do these terms mean? Well, when the above code finishes executing, I'll have five different objects, each of which holds information about a different product in my inventory. However, since each object was created by the same constructor function, they are all said to be of the same class, specifically, the** itemInfo **class. (A class gets its name from its constructor function.) Each individual object, however, is called an instance of that class. In the real world, a class could be thought of as a group of people, for example, American citizens. An instance of that class of people would be an individual citizen, like the former American president Gerald Ford.**

When this code has executed, I'll have five itemInfo objects. Each of these will have exactly the same properties, but the values in those properties will be different, depending on the values I passed to the constructor function. Table 17-2 shows exactly what I mean.

Table 17-2
Contents of the Five itemInfo Objects

			Object		
Properties	**strollerInfo**	**diaperInfo**	**carSeatInfo**	**rattleInfo**	**babyWipeInfo**
price	199.95	13.95	149.95	4.95	9.95
description	"Rock & Stroll – Deluxe"	"Size 3, Extra Absorbent"	"Ultra-Safe, Rear-Facing"	"UberNoise 5000"	"Clean and Fragrant"
partNumber	"st-001"	"dp-003"	"cs-001"	"rt-001"	"bw-001"
shipping	20	5	15	5	6
inStock	5	100	5	155	75
inCart	0	0	0	0	0

Using the Objects You Create

Now, if I simply leave my code in this state, I've got a big problem: Every bit of the code I've created so far has used arrays to manipulate my product information. Of course, I'm still going to need an easy way to loop through all of my inventory items, so it's probably a good idea to leave the main productInfo array as it is for now. This means that the following code can stay exactly the way it is:

```
index = 0;
var productInfo = new Array();
productInfo[index++] = strollerInfo;
productInfo[index++] = diaperInfo;
productInfo[index++] = carSeatInfo;
productInfo[index++] = rattleInfo;
productInfo[index++] = babyWipeInfo;
```

What remains then, is to change all of the functions that treat productInfo as if it was a multidimensional array. One such function is the function you wrote to calculate the grand total of everything in the shopping cart. (You wrote this function as the answer to one of the Saturday Afternoon Part Review questions.) My version is shown here:

```
function calcGrandTotal() {
    var grandTotal = 0;
    for (x=0; x<productInfo.length; x++) {
        // Are there any of this item in the cart?
        if (productInfo[x][5] > 0) {
            grandTotal += calcFinalCost( productInfo[x][0],
            productInfo[x][3]) * productInfo[x][5];
            }
        }
    document.cart.elements['grandTotal'].value = grandTotal;
    }
```

**10 Min.
To Go**

So, what I've got to do here is rewrite this, and the other functions in babyPalooza.js so that they no longer try to access a second dimension in the `productInfo` array. There are a lot of functions to consider in the babyPalooza.js file, but the approach to fixing each one is pretty much the same, so I'll just go over the changes that are required for the `calcGrandTotal()` function.

```
function calcGrandTotal() {
    var grandTotal = 0;
    for (x=0; x<productInfo.length; x++) {
        var thisItem = productInfo[x];
        // Are there any of this item in the cart?
        if (thisItem.inCart > 0) {
            grandTotal += calcFinalCost( thisItem.price,
            thisItem.shipping) * thisItem.inCart;
            }
        }
    document.cart.elements['grandTotal'].value = grandTotal;
    }
```

As you can see, this isn't too different from the previous version. The main difference is that as I move through the `productInfo` array, I extract the `itemInfo` object and place it in a local variable called `thisItem`. Like this: `var thisItem = productInfo[x]`; I can then access the appropriate properties in the object to carry out the needed calculations. Like so:

```
grandTotal += calcFinalCost( thisItem.price, thisItem.shipping) *
thisItem.inCart;
```

As another example, let's see how the `findPartNo()` and `doPlus()` functions look like after they've been changed to support objects.

```
function findPartNo( partNo) {
    var result = "";
    for (x=0; x < productInfo.length; x++) {
        var thisItem = productInfo[x];
        if (thisItem.partNumber == partNo) {
            result = thisItem;
            break;
            }
        }
    return result;
    }
function doPlus( partNo) {
    var prodInfo = findPartNo( partNo);
    // Do we have enough on hand to do this?
    if (prodInfo.inStock > 0) {
        // Update the quantities in the array
        prodInfo.inStock--;
        prodInfo.inCart++;
        // Copy these new values to the form
        document.cart.elements[ "quan_" + partNo].value =
        prodInfo.inStock;
        document.cart.elements[ "inCart_" + partNo].value =
        prodInfo.inCart;
        calcGrandTotal()
        }
    else {
        alert( "There are no more of this item in stock!");
        }
    }
```

As you can see, there really isn't that big a difference here. All I've done is switch from array slot numbers to object property names. (To compare these new functions with their old counterparts, see the babyPalooza.js file in the Session16 folder on your CD-ROM.) You should find that the baby-palooza.com site behaves exactly the same way as it did before. (For a challenge, take the code from the PartReview03 folder and change it to use objects. Be sure not to cheat by looking at the code in the Session17 folder!)

Done!

REVIEW

In this session, you learned the basics of creating your own JavaScript objects. You learned what objects are and how they have many of the same qualities as objects from the real world. You learned how to create a simple constructor function and how to call it to create a new object. You also learned about the `this` keyword and saw how it is used in a constructor function. (Don't worry, I'll be telling you how to use `this` in other places in upcoming sessions.) Finally, you saw how to use the objects you create in your JavaScript code. Of course, at this point, I really haven't shown you much to recommend objects over arrays. I'll be taking care of this in the next session when I show you how to define and use methods with your objects.

QUIZ YOURSELF

1. What is the difference between an object you define in your JavaScript program and an object in the real world? (See "What Is an Object?")

2. What does a constructor function do? (See "How is an object constructed?")

3. What does the `this` keyword represent? (See "What the heck is this?")

4. What's the difference between a constructor function and a regular function? (See "How is an object constructed?")

5. How do you access the properties in the objects you create? (See "Using the Objects You Create.")

Creating and Using Methods

Session Checklist

✔ Adding methods to your JavaScript objects

**30 Min.
To Go**

As you saw in the last session, creating your own JavaScript objects really isn't too difficult. However, really simple objects that just have properties in them (like the itemInfo object from the last session) don't really give you all that much bang for your buck. Objects become really interesting and *much* more useful, when you add methods to them.

What Is a Method?

As I said earlier, a method is sort of like a function that belongs to an object. Actually, methods belong to an entire class of objects. For example, every object that's a member of a String class has a toUpperCase() method. So, it's a bit more precise to say that a method is a function that belongs to an entire class of objects.

The upshot of this is that — as with properties — when you define a new class (by creating a constructor function), any methods that you define in your class will be available to each and every object that you create with that constructor function.

Defining a method

In JavaScript, adding a method to a class is a two-part process.

- Define the method in the constructor function. This requires a single line of code. In this line of code, you give the method a name, and you associate it with a function that will actually carry out the processes of the method.
- Write the function that implements the method. When you call a method, an actual JavaScript function is executed. The catch is, when you create your own objects, you have to write these functions yourself. Fortunately, these functions are just like every other function you've seen so far. The only difference is that you should never execute them directly; they should only be called as a result of a method being called.

If this is a bit confusing, don't worry. It should become clear once you see an example.

But, before I can show you an example, I need to back up a bit and decide exactly what I want to write a method for. To do this, I'll return to the itemInfo object I defined in the last session and see if it could benefit from a method or two.

Well, what are some operations that might make sense for this type of object? Looking at the source code I've written so far, I can see that the calcFinalCost() function is an ideal candidate for being turned into a method for this class of objects. Here's the code for calcFinalCost() as it appeared the last time you saw it:

```
function calcFinalCost( baseCost, shippingCost) {
    return baseCost + shippingCost;
    }
```

As you can see, this is a very simple function. It takes two numbers as parameters and returns the sum of those numbers. While it's a fairly simple function, using it is a bit more complex than it would be if it were a method of the itemInfo class. For example, consider the original source code for the calcGrandTotal() function:

```
function calcGrandTotal() {
    var grandTotal = 0;
    for (x=0; x<productInfo.length; x++) {
        var thisItem = productInfo[x];
        // Are there any of this item in the cart?
        if (thisItem.inCart > 0) {
            grandTotal += calcFinalCost( thisItem.price,
```

```
            thisItem.shipping) * thisItem.inCart;
            }
        }
    document.cart.elements['grandTotal'].value = grandTotal;
    }
```

Looking at this, you might be wondering how in the world this could be any simpler. Well, notice that in order to call calcFinalCost(), I actually have to extract the price and shipping properties from the itemInfo object I'm working with. As you'll see in a moment, by reworking calcFinalCost() as a method, I can get rid of these two steps completely!

Specifying a method in a constructor function

Now that I've decided what to turn into a method, I can show you how to actually do it. First, I have to modify the itemInfo constructor function to actually define the method. This is shown in my updated itemInfo constructor.

```
function itemInfo( oPrice, oDesc, oPartNum, oShipping, oInStock) {
    this.price = oPrice;
    this.description = oDesc;
    this.partNumber = oPartNum;
    this.shipping = oShipping;
    this.inStock = oInStock;
    this.inCart = 0;
    this.calcFinalCost = itemInfo_doCalcFinalCost;
    }
```

In the new version of the itemInfo constructor function, only one thing has changed: I've added the following statement to the end of the function.

```
    this.calcFinalCost = itemInfo_doCalcFinalCost;
```

The left hand side of this statement works exactly like the statements above it. It tells the JavaScript interpreter that, for this object that is being created right now, I want to add a new slot that goes by the name "calcFinalCost."

What then, differentiates this from the definition of a property? Well, it's what's on the right hand side of the statement that does the trick. The right hand side of this statement is the name "itemInfo_doCalcFinalCost." Now, since this isn't the name of a local or global variable, and it isn't a numeric value or a quoted string, the JavaScript interpreter realizes that it must be something else. It is, in fact, the name of the function that will be used to implement the method whose name is given on the left hand side of the statement.

To put it another way, this line tells the JavaScript interpreter that every object created by this constructor function will have a method named "calcFinalCost." But, whenever the `calcFinalCost()` method is called, the JavaScript interpreter should actually execute the function named "itemInfo_doCalcFinalCost."

So, to sum up, the name on the left-hand side of the statement is the name I want to give my *method,* but the name on the right-hand side of the statement is the name of the *function* that will actually be executed when the method is called. (Technical types like to say that the function *implements* the method.)

Once again, there isn't anything magical about the names I'm using. I've simply adopted a standard way of naming methods and the functions that implement them. Specifically, I always prefix my implementation functions with the name of the class they belong to, followed by an underscore and the characters do. This lets me quickly see which functions are actually method implementation functions and which class they belong to. If you like, you can give your method implementation functions any valid function name you like. Lot's of programmers actually use the same name for the method and the implementation function. This is perfectly fine, but it can lead to some confusion when you revisit your source code a few months later.

Writing a function to implement a method

**20 Min.
To Go**

With my method defined in my constructor function, I need to actually create the function that will implement the method. Fortunately, in this case, all I have to do is rename and tweak the `calcFinalCost()` function, as shown here:

```
function itemInfo_doCalcFinalCost() {
    return this.price + this.shipping;
    }
```

As you can see, the only things that have changed here are the name of the function and the fact that the `this` keyword now appears in the function. Why is this necessary? Well, remember that this method will be accessible from any object that is created by the `itemInfo` constructor function. Because of this, the method needs some way to determine which `price` property and which `shipping` property to use. Here again, the `this` keyword tells the method to use the properties that belong to the current object. Of course, that begs the question, "How does an object become the 'current' object?"

Assuming that the method definitions you've just seen are in effect, consider the following code:

```
var strollerInfo = new itemInfo( 199.95, "Rock & Stroll - Deluxe",
"st-001", 20, 5);
```

```
var diaperInfo = new itemInfo( 13.95, "Size 3, Extra Absorbent",
"dp-003", 5, 100);

var strollPrice = strollerInfo.calcFinalCost();
var diaperPrice = diaperInfo.calcFinalCost();
```

In this example I've created two new itemInfo objects: strollerInfo and diaperInfo. I then proceed to call the caclFinalCost() method for each object. Now, when I call the method, I have to give the name of the object along with the name of the method. The simple act of naming the object along with the method tells the JavaScript interpreter which object should be used when the this keyword is encountered in the method. Neat, eh?

Using a custom method in your program

Now that my method and its implementation function are defined, the last thing I need to do is change the other code in my program so that any calls to the old calcFinalCost() *function* become calls to the calcFinalCost() *method*. (There are actually two or three places where this happens, so I'm just going to show you the changes in the calcGrandTotal() function.)

```
function calcGrandTotal() {
    var grandTotal = 0;
    for (x=0; x<productInfo.length; x++) {
        var thisItem = productInfo[x];
        // Are there any of this item in the cart?
        if (thisItem.inCart > 0) {
            grandTotal += thisItem.calcFinalCost() *
            thisItem.inCart;
            }
        }
    document.cart.elements['grandTotal'].value = grandTotal;
    }
```

As you can see, this actually makes my code a bit smaller and a *lot* simpler!

When I say "simpler," I don't just mean that it's easier to type; I'm also talking about maintenance and adding functionality in the future. In this example I only have to change my code in two or three places. But, what if the actual math required for calculating the final cost had changed? (For example, what if sales tax became a consideration?) Using the old setup, I might have to change each and every call to the calcFinalCost() function (perhaps to include a third or fourth parameter). However, by using the object and method approach, I only have to change the code in *one* place: the implementation function.

No parameters required

Looking at my new `itemInfo` constructor, you might have noticed that when I defined my method I didn't specify any parameters.

```
this.calcFinalCost = itemInfo_doCalcFinalCost;
```

This isn't because the `itemInfo_doCalcFinalCost()` function doesn't take any parameters, it's because you simply aren't allowed to list parameters (or even an empty set of parentheses) when you define a method. As with every other JavaScript function you create, the functions that implement your methods can accept as few or as many parameters as you want. You just can't list them inside your constructor function.

Implementing the Inventory as an Object

Since practice makes perfect, let me walk you through the process of reworking the inventory as an object. Basically, I want to take the `productInfo` array that I've been using, and make it part of a larger object that handles all of my inventory-related tasks. As things stand right now, those tasks include finding items in the inventory, adding items to the inventory, and adding and subtracting units to and from the inventory. As before, my first step is to create a constructor function for my new `inventory` class.

```
function inventory() {
    this.productList = new Array();
    this.addInventoryItem = inventory_doAddInventoryItem;
    this.findPartNo = inventory_doFindPartNo;
    this.plusOne = inventory_doPlusOne;
    this.minusOne = inventory_doMinusOne;
    }
```

The first line of this constructor creates a property called `productList`. This will end up serving the same purpose as the old `productInfo` array. (Note that I didn't have to change the name; however, since this array is now part of a larger structure, I felt this new name better described the purpose of the array.)

The second line defines a method called `addInventoryItem`. As the name implies, the purpose of this method is to add an item to my inventory. In the old scheme of things, I simply added the items to my `productInfo` array one after the other. However, now that this array is held inside an object, it makes sense to have a method for this task rather than access the array directly.

This brings up another advantage of using objects: If, at some point in the future, I decide to change the way items are stored in my inventory (that is, I want to store them in something other than an array), I don't have to hunt down and replace all of the code that adds items to my inventory. Instead, I just have to rewrite the addInventoryItem method.

The remaining statements define the other three methods that my inventory class needs at this point. The names may look familiar because these are three functions that I've already written! So, all I have to do is rework them a bit to turn them into methods. All four of these methods are pretty straightforward, so I'll just give you all of them now.

```
function inventory_doAddInventoryItem( theItem) {
    var next = this.productList.length;
    this.productList[ next] = theItem;
    }
function inventory_doFindPartNo( partNo) {
    var result = "";
    for (x=0; x < this.productList.length; x++) {
        var thisItem = this.productList[x];
        if (thisItem.partNumber == partNo) {
            result = thisItem;
            break;
            }
        }
    return result;
    }
function inventory_doPlusOne( partNo) {
    var prodInfo = this.findPartNo( partNo);
    // Do we have enough on hand to do this?
    if (prodInfo.inStock > 0) {
        // Update the quantities in the array
        prodInfo.inStock--;
        prodInfo.inCart++;
        // Copy these new values to the form
        document.cart.elements[ "quan_" + partNo].value =
        prodInfo.inStock;
        document.cart.elements[ "inCart_" + partNo].value =
        prodInfo.inCart;
        calcGrandTotal()
        }
    else {
```

```
            alert( "There are no more of this item in stock!");
            }
        }
function inventory_doMinusOne( partNo) {
    var prodInfo = this.findPartNo( partNo);
    // Do we have enough on hand to do this?
    if (prodInfo.inCart > 0) {
        // Update the quantities in the array
        prodInfo.inStock++;
        prodInfo.inCart--;
        // Copy these new values to the form
        document.cart.elements[ "quan_" + partNo].value =
        prodInfo.inStock;
        document.cart.elements[ "inCart_" + partNo].value =
        prodInfo.inCart;
        calcGrandTotal()
        }
    else {
        alert( "You have no more in your shopping cart!");
        }
    }
```

**10 Min.
To Go**

If you compare these methods with the functions they were derived from, you can see that there really isn't much difference. Of course, all of the references to the old productInfo array have been replaced with references to productList, but that's probably the most obvious change. What's less obvious is that the this keyword has snuck its way into all of these methods. Why? Well, remember that these are methods now, so they belong to an object. Until now, there's only been the possibility of having one shopping cart with only one inventory. But, now that everything is being rewritten as an object, there's the very real possibility of multiple shopping carts, each with one or more inventory objects inside it! Because of this, these methods must use the this keyword in order to know which inventory object they are actually working with when they are called.

The only truly new method here is the addInventoryItem() method. As you can see though, there really isn't that much to it. You simply pass it an itemInfo object, and it adds it to the end of the productList array.

The only thing left to do now is to actually put the new inventory object to use. The code that does this is shown here.

```
// create the inventory object
var bpInventory = new inventory();
```

```
// now, load it with items
var strollerInfo = new itemInfo( 199.95, "Rock & Stroll - Deluxe",
"st-001", 20, 5);
var diaperInfo = new itemInfo( 13.95, "Size 3, Extra Absorbent",
"dp-003", 5, 100);
var carSeatInfo = new itemInfo( 149.95, "Ultra-Safe, Rear-Facing",
"cs-001", 15, 5);
var rattleInfo = new itemInfo( 4.95, "UberNoise 5000", "rt-001",
5, 155);
var babyWipeInfo = new itemInfo( 9.95, "Clean and Fragrant",
"bw-001", 6, 75);


bpInventory.addInventoryItem( strollerInfo);
bpInventory.addInventoryItem( diaperInfo);
bpInventory.addInventoryItem( carSeatInfo);
bpInventory.addInventoryItem( rattleInfo);
bpInventory.addInventoryItem( babyWipeInfo);
```

That's pretty much all there is to it! Of course, the other chunks of code that need to access the productList array will need to be rewritten a bit. The changes that are required, however, are trivial. The following code shows how the calcGrandTotal() function has to change to accommodate the inventory object. (Be sure to compare this to the original code for calcGrandTotal(), shown earlier in this session.)

```
function calcGrandTotal() {
    var grandTotal = 0;
    for (x=0; x<bpInventory.productList.length; x++) {
        var thisItem = bpInventory.productList[x];
        // Are there any of this item in the cart?
        if (thisItem.inCart > 0) {
            grandTotal += thisItem.calcFinalCost() *
            thisItem.inCart;
            }
        }
    document.cart.elements['grandTotal'].value = grandTotal;
    }
```

Done!

REVIEW

In this session, you learned how to add methods to your JavaScript objects. As part of this, you learned how a method differs from a function and what an implementation function is. You also saw several examples of how to turn "ordinary" JavaScript code into a set of objects with properties and methods.

QUIZ YOURSELF

1. How does a method differ from a function? (See "What Is a Method?")

2. What are the steps for adding a method to a class? (See "Defining a method.")

3. What is the implementation function of a method? (See "Defining a method.")

4. How do you actually specify that an object will contain a particular method? (See "Specifying a method in a constructor function.")

5. How should you name your methods and implementation functions? (See "Specifying a method in a constructor function.")

Enhancing HTML with JavaScript Objects

Session Checklist

✔ Using JavaScript objects to enhance HTML controls

✔ Understanding how JavaScript objects can make data validation easier

✔ Adding your own properties and methods to predefined JavaScript objects

**30 Min.
To Go**

At this point, you know how to create and use your own objects. You also know how to use JavaScript to work with the various parts of the HTML page. So, you might be thinking that it would be really neat if you could create custom objects that would make working with an HTML document even easier. Well, you can!

Enhancing HTML Controls

Probably the most useful thing you can do is to create custom JavaScript objects that enhance the HTML controls on your Web pages. As you'll recall from Session 13, all of the various HTML controls already have equivalent JavaScript objects, complete with a slew of properties and methods. However, these objects really only provide the most basic functionality. For example, why is there no `getValue()` method to return the value of the selected radio button in a family? Sure, you can figure out which radio button is selected and get its value by yourself, but the omission is puzzling. Of course, just because one method is missing, that doesn't mean that you'll want to throw away a perfectly good object. An ideal solution would be to take the JavaScript objects that already exist (like the String object or the object that represents a radio button) and add the new properties and methods to them that you want.

In other programming languages, this sort of thing is very easy to do. You take a preexisting class of objects, add some new properties and methods to it, and you've got a new class. This new class is called a *subclass;* and it can contain all of the properties and methods of the old class (which is called the "super class") along with all of the new properties and methods that you've added. This process doesn't affect the old class in any way, so the two classes will actually coexist inside your program at the same time. Unfortunately, in JavaScript, this isn't as easy as it should be. JavaScript *does* offer a way to add new properties and methods to a predefined class, but it doesn't really allow you to create subclasses, and it doesn't seem to work at all with the classes that are in the Browser Object Model. (I'll be discussing this aspect of JavaScript a bit later in this session, in the section titled, "Extending Preexisting JavaScript Objects.")

Creating an object wrapper

Since you can't modify the properties and methods of a control object directly, I'll show you how to do the next best thing: create a wrapper object. As the name implies, a *wrapper object* is an object that wraps around another object. Since the wrapper is itself an object, you can give it whatever properties and methods you want. Now, before this gets too confusing, let me walk you through an example to show you exactly what I'm talking about.

For this example, I'll try to address my earlier complaint about radio buttons. Specifically, why isn't there a `getValue()` method associated with radio button objects? In the code that follows, I'm going to create a wrapper object that will add this method, along with a few others, to radio buttons. As with any other object you create, you need to decide exactly what functionality you want your wrapper object to have. A quick look at the constructor for my wrapper should give you an idea of what sort of functionality I want. (This source code can be found in the Session19 folder on your CD-ROM.)

```
function radioObj( radioFamilyObject) {
    this.control = radioFamilyObject;
```

```
this.getLength = radioObj_doGetLength;
this.getSelected = radioObj_doGetSelected;
this.setSelected = radioObj_doSetSelected;
this.channelUp = radioObj_doChannelUp;
this.channelDown = radioObj_doChannelDown;
this.getValue = radioObj_doGetValue;
}
```

In this constructor, I've defined one property (`control`) and six new methods. You'll also notice that this constructor accepts a parameter, `radioFamilyObject`. This parameter is assigned to the `control` property as the object is being created. So, what *is* the `control` property? Well, remember that this is a *wrapper* object. What it's wrapping is, in fact, another object. In this case, it's wrapping around a preexisting JavaScript radio button object. If that's still not clear, consider the following code.

```
<form name="delivery">
    Select a Delivery Method<br />
    <input type="radio" name="dMethod" value="standard" checked />
    Standard Shipping<br />
    <input type="radio" name="dMethod" value="overnight" />
    Overnight Shipping<br />
    <input type="radio" name="dMethod" value="snail mail" />
    Slowest Possible<br />
    <script language="javascript">
    // 'wrap' my custom object around the JavaScript object
    var dMethodRadio = new radioObj( document.delivery.dMethod);
    </script>
</form>
```

In this listing, I've created a very simple form with one radio button family inside it. In the script block that follows, I'm calling the `radioObj` constructor and passing it the JavaScript object that represents that radio button family. This object is what's assigned to the `control` property inside the wrapper object. So, after this code executes, my wrapper object will have access to this control object and all of the properties and methods that come with it. For example, if I were to code

```
alert( dMethodRadio.control.length);
```

an alert window containing a "3" would appear.

The only trick to creating the methods for a wrapper object is to remember to use the `control` property to actually retrieve information about your JavaScript control object. While the code to do this isn't difficult, it *is* fairly lengthy! So, open up the radioObj.htm file from the Session19 folder on your CD-ROM and give it a quick look over. Then use it to follow along with the rest of the discussion.

**20 Min.
To Go**

The first method for my wrapper, getLength(), is the simplest of them all. Like the short example I gave earlier, it simply looks at the length property of the control object and returns it. Note also the presence of the this keyword. Remember that since this is an object, there could actually be dozens or hundreds of radio button families (and radioObj objects) defined in this HTML document. Again, the this keyword tells the JavaScript interpreter which of the radioObj objects I'm actually working with at that moment.

The remaining methods work much the same way. However, you'll also notice that each of the other methods has a tendency to call one another. For example, the getValue() method calls the getSelected() method to determine which radio button to return the value from.

Tying your objects to your HTML

The last piece of this puzzle is the way you actually tie your custom objects to your HTML page. As you've already seen, your custom objects can actually include a preexisting JavaScript object as a property. But, how do you actually get these objects to interact with other parts of the HTML page? As always, the answer is event handlers. Take a look at the <form> at the end of the radioObj.htm file and you'll see what I mean.

This is basically the same as first form you saw in this session, but I've added onclick handlers to my radio buttons. I've also added several simple buttons, each with an onclick handler that calls a different method of the dMethodRadio object.

Don't forget that just about *any* nonempty HTML tag (that is, any HTML tag with a beginning and ending tag) can trigger events. So, if you need to, you can hook your custom objects (or even your plain old functions) to just about any HTML tag in your document.

Extending Preexisting JavaScript Objects

As I mentioned at the start of this session, JavaScript contains a mechanism that will allow you to add properties and methods to some preexisting JavaScript objects. This is done by adding properties and/or methods to an object's *prototype*.

You can think of an object's prototype as its blueprint. If you change the prototype, you change the structure of the object. It's sort of like making a change to an object's constructor function, except that you can do it while your program is running.

Now, before I go further, I need to tell you a bit more about how JavaScript objects work. In addition to the String and Array objects that you've already learned about, JavaScript has several other built-in objects. (You'll learn about most of these other objects in subsequent sessions.) All of these objects however, are based upon a single *parent* object that is named simply, Object. The Object class is the basis of almost every object in JavaScript, including the objects you create yourself.

The point of all this is that you can only change the prototype for a class if that class is built into the JavaScript language or if that class is one that you define yourself. So, while you can change the prototype for, say, the String class, you can't change it for something like a radio button object. This is because radio button objects are a part of the Browser Object Model and *not* a part of the JavaScript language.

Enhancing the String class

So, with that in mind, what sorts of enhancements would be nice for something like the String class? Well, as you'll remember, one of the more common data validation tasks for strings is to check and see if the string is blank. So, let's add a method to the string class that does just that. The following line of code shows how you actually add a new method to the String class.

```
String.prototype.isBlank = String_doIsBlank;
```

Pretty simple, eh? On the left-hand side of my statement is my class (String in this case), followed by the `prototype` keyword, followed by the name of the new method (`isBlank`). On the right-hand side of the statement is the name of the function that will implement the new method. The only thing left to do is to actually write the implementation function and test it out.

```
function String_doIsBlank() {
    var result = true;
    if (this != "") {
        for (x=0; x < this.length; x++) {
            var theChar = this.charAt( x);
            if (theChar != " ") {
                result = false;
                break;
            }
        }
    }
```

```
        return result;
        }
var oldAndBlank = "   ";
// Add the new method to the String prototype
String.prototype.isBlank = String_doIsBlank;

var blank = "";
var notBlank = "Not blank!";
var alsoBlank = "     ";
alert( blank.isBlank());
alert( notBlank.isBlank());
alert( alsoBlank.isBlank());
// Even 'old' strings get the new method!
alert( oldAndBlank.isBlank());
```

If you are thinking that the code for the isBlank() method looks familiar, you are right. This is simply the code for the isBlank() function that I've been using all along. Of course, it's been modified a little: The parameter that was passed (which told the function which string to check) has been replaced by the this keyword.

As you can see from this code, after I modify the prototype for the String class, *every* String object I create immediately has access to the new method. However, something you might not have expected is that even the String objects I created *before* I added the new method (the oldAndBlank variable in this example) have access to it! As far as I know, this rather surprising behavior is unique to JavaScript and it makes the prototype a "retroactive blueprint" for all of your objects, rather than a simple blueprint for any new objects you create.

Adding properties via the prototype

Of course, you can add properties in exactly the same way as you add methods. The values you assign to these properties will be immediately available in all objects of that class. For example, if I wanted to add a language property to all of my String objects, I would simply code:

```
String.prototype.language = "English";
var greeting = "Bonjour!";
greeting.language = "French";
```

I can then use this property just like any other property of the String class; I could even create methods to work with the property. Of course, if you want to use the prototype approach to extend a class of objects, be sure to place all of your prototype-modifying statements at the start of your HTML document. This way, you'll be sure that all of your modifications have been made before the main part of your code begins to execute.

**10 Min.
To Go**

Adding Data Validation to HTML Controls

If you put all of this together in your mind, I think you might begin to see that a natural use for these techniques would be to add enhanced data validation methods to the controls in your HTML forms. For example, wouldn't it be neat if your text boxes could validate themselves? Of course it would!

```
function textObj( textControl, validChars) {
    this.control = textControl;
    this.allowedChars = validChars;
    this.isValid = textObj_doIsValid;
    this.getText = textObj_doGetText;
    this.setText = textObj_doSetText;
    this.isBlank = textObj_doIsBlank;
    }
```

Here I have a fairly simple object that I'll be able to wrap around a JavaScript text box control object. The control property is the same as what you've seen before, and I'm pretty sure you can guess what the getText(), setText(), and isBlank() methods do. But, the allowedChars property and the isValid() method are entirely new.

Basically, the allowedChars property lets you specify which characters can be typed into the control, and the isValid() method makes sure that only those characters are actually in the control. For example, if I wanted to create a control that only accepted numeric characters, my HTML might look like this:

```
<input type="text" size="30" name="NumText" />
```

And my JavaScript code would look like this:

```
var numText = new textObj( document.formName.NumText,
"0123456789");
```

The code in the textOjb.htm file shows one way to implement all of these methods. (Again, this code isn't too difficult, but it is pretty long, so open the file in your HTML editor so you can follow along.)

For the most part, these methods defined in this file are all very straightforward. (You'll notice, however, that the isBlank() method simply calls the isBlank() method that I added to the String class. To see exactly how this is done, see the textObj.htm file on your CD-ROM.) The only tricky method in the bunch is the isValid() method. This method examines the characters that have been typed into the control and compares them with the characters that are in the allowedChars property for the object. If any of those characters are not in the set of allowedChars, an alert window is displayed telling the user which characters actually are allowed.

By taking this approach, I can set up a text box that can validate its own contents against any set of characters that I define. Better still, I don't have to write a custom validation routine for each different type of data. The example file on your CD-ROM creates text boxes that check for numeric characters, alphanumeric characters, hexadecimal characters, octal characters and more. However, if you really wanted, you could set up a text box that only allowed consonants or just vowels. It's totally up to you.

Of course, I still have to tie this validation routine to my control. As usual, all this requires is an appropriate event handler.

Done!

```
<input type="text" size="30" name="NumText"
onchange="numText.isValid()" />
```

REVIEW

In this session, you saw how JavaScript objects can be used to enhance the abilities of your HTML documents. You learned how to create a wrapper object to add new properties and methods to the JavaScript objects that represent the controls in your HTML forms. You also learned about how to change the prototype for any of JavaScript's built-in objects to add new properties and methods to those objects. Finally, you saw an example of how to use these new techniques to create a text box object that "knows" how to validate its own contents.

QUIZ YOURSELF

1. What is a wrapper object? (See "Creating an object wrapper.")
2. How do you "hook" your JavaScript objects to your HTML? (See "Tying your objects to your HTML.")

3. What is an object's prototype? (See "Extending Preexisting JavaScript Objects.")

4. When you add a property or method via the prototype of a class, which objects can use the new property or method? (See "Enhancing the String class.")

5. Why might you want to create self-validating controls? (See "Adding Data Validation to HTML Controls.")

Dynamically Creating and Executing JavaScript

Session Checklist

✔ Learning about the eval() function

✔ Understanding how setTimeout() and setInterval() work with JavaScript objects

**30 Min.
To Go**

I n Session 11, you learned how to use JavaScript to create HTML tags on the fly. You also saw how to dynamically create blocks of JavaScript code. The idea behind both of these tricks was that you could build a customized Web page before the browser even shows the page. But what if you need to create and execute a JavaScript statement after your Web page has finished loading? As you saw in Session 9, trying to generate new content for a page after it's loaded will actually wipe out the page as it currently exists. So, what you need is some way to dynamically create and execute new JavaScript statements without harming the current contents of your HTML document. Fortunately, JavaScript provides a function that lets you do exactly that.

Using the eval() Function

The eval() function is probably the coolest, and most powerful, function in all of JavaScript. Simply put, the eval() function takes a string and passes it to the

JavaScript interpreter for execution. So, this line of code: eval("alert('Hello World!')"); has exactly the same effect as this line of code: alert('Hello World!"); in both cases, an alert window containing the words "Hello World!" will appear.

As I said, you pass the eval() function a string for it to pass along to the JavaScript interpreter. In the example above, I passed it a hard-coded string. However, I could have passed it a variable that contained a string

```
var myCommand = "alert( 'Hello World!')";
eval( myCommand);
```

and the result would be the same. In fact, you can mix variables and hard-coded strings.

```
var myCommand = "alert";
eval( myCommand + "( 'Hello World!')");
```

As long as the end result is a string, the eval() function will dutifully pass it to the JavaScript interpreter for execution.

While the eval() function is very cool, it isn't magical. So, once your string gets to the JavaScript interpreter, it still has to be a valid JavaScript statement. For example, the following eval() call will generate an error just as it would if you had hard-coded the statement into your program: eval("allert('Hello World!')");

Variables and the eval() function

When the eval() function passes a string to the JavaScript interpreter for execution, the interpreter executes the command just as if it were a part of your program. This means that the command has access to all of your global variables and any local variables that a normal statement would at that point in your program. For example:

```
var who = "World!";
var greeting = "Hello ";
eval( "alert( greeting + who )");
function greet() {
    var who = "Everybody!";
    eval( "alert( greeting + who )");
    }
greet();
```

Here, the first eval() call will produce an alert window that says, "Hello World!" Inside the function however, I've declared a local variable named who that will be used by the second `eval()` call. This will result in an alert window that says, "Hello Everybody!"

In the above example, you'll notice that the string I'm passing to the `eval()` function contains the names of my variables that I want the `alert()` method to display.

```
eval( "alert( greeting + who )");
```

In other words, the contents of the `greeting` and `who` variables won't be evaluated until after this command string has been passed to the JavaScript interpreter. However, I could have written this statement in a slightly different fashion:

```
eval( "alert( '" + greeting + who + "')");
```

Do you see the difference here? In this second version, the contents of my variables are being extracted and placed into the command string *before* it's passed to the JavaScript interpreter. This is the same as coding:

```
eval( "alert( 'Hello World!')");
```

So, the question as to whether you should pass variables or hard-coded strings is pretty much a matter of personal preference. However, as you can see from these simple statements, from a coding point of view, it's certainly easier to just pass your variable names and let the JavaScript interpreter sort everything out for you.

What kinds of statements can you eval()?

Thus far, all the examples I've shown you have been of very simple statements being passed to the `eval()` function. However, the `eval()` function can handle even the most complex JavaScript statements. The following example, while not the most complex possible, should give you an idea of what I'm talking about:

```
<form name="myForm">
<input type="text" name="result" />
</form>
<script language="javascript">
var theForm = "myForm";
var theControl = "result";
var val = "Hello World!";
eval( "document." + theForm + "." + theControl + ".value = val");
</script>
```

Back in Session 11, I said that one of the most powerful things about using JavaScript to create HTML was that you could store entire HTML structures in

JavaScript variables and then rearrange them programmatically to get the output you wanted. In this example, I've applied that same idea to JavaScript structures. By placing the names of these structures (that is, the names of my form and my text box) into JavaScript variables, I can use them to build commands that can be passed to the eval() function for execution.

**20 Min.
To Go**

The setTimeout() and setInterval() Methods

You might be thinking that the eval() function seems very similar to the window.setTimeout() and window.setInterval() methods that you learned about in Session 8. Well, it is! These methods of the window object do pretty much exactly the same thing as the eval() function, they simply do it after a specified delay. (For detailed examples of these methods, refer back to Session 8.)

Using objects with setTimeOut() and setInterval()

As I said, the main difference between these methods and the eval() function is that the eval() function executes your command immediately. The setTimeOut() and setInterval() methods, however, wait until a specified number of milliseconds have passed before they will execute your command. Due to the speed at which today's computers run, even a few milliseconds can make a *big* difference in the state of your program. So, if you want to use either of these methods with an object, you have to be a little more careful about how you structure the command you pass to the method. For example, consider this:

```
function annoying_doAnnoy() {
    alert( this.msg);
    setTimeout( 'this.annoy()', 5000);
    }
function annoying( message) {
    this.msg = message;
    this.annoy = annoying_doAnnoy;
    }
var annoyEM = new annoying( "Hello!");
annoyEM.annoy();
```

Looking at this, you might think that this code will repeatedly display an alert window with the message "Hello!" in it. Well, that's what it's intended to do, but there is a flaw in the code that will cause it to fail after the first alert window is displayed. The flaw is in the setTimeout() statement: setTimeout('this.annoy()', 5000);

This statement is telling the JavaScript interpreter to wait five seconds and then call the annoy() method of this object. The problem with this is that, in five seconds the value of this will almost certainly be undefined, simply because our method will have finished executing five seconds ago. Actually, during those five seconds, this will probably have taken on several new values. Unfortunately, none of them are likely to be the same as when the setTimeout() method was called. The end result is that the annoy() method won't be found and you'll get an error message.

The only way around this is to specify the name of the object whose method you want to be called. Of course, all of the Browser Object Model objects are smart enough to keep their names hidden away inside themselves. You can do the same thing with your custom objects, but it does require a bit of extra work when you define your objects. The following short program will show you what I'm talking about.

```
function annoying_doAnnoy() {
    alert( this.msg);
    setTimeout( this.name + '.annoy()', 5000);
    }
function annoying( name, message) {
    this.name = name;
    this.msg = message;
    this.annoy = annoying_doAnnoy;
    }
var annoyEM = new annoying( "annoyEM", "Hello!");
annoyEM.annoy();
```

In this listing, I've added a name property to my object definition. It's important to note that the value I assign to this property is the same as the name I'm giving to the JavaScript variable that will hold the object I'm creating. In other words, the name property in my object is the same as the name of the JavaScript variable that is holding the object. In this case, that name is "annoyEM."

Why bother? Well, by giving my object knowledge of its own JavaScript variable name, I can create a setTimeou() call like this one:

```
setTimeout( this.name + '.annoy()', 5000);
```

In this case, this is the same as coding:

```
setTimeout( 'annoyEM.annoy()', 5000);
```

When this statement executes five seconds later, the correct object will be referenced and the call will be successful. (Note that everything I've told you here about setTimeout() can be applied to setInterval() also.)

Using setTimeout() creating an animation object

Don't be fooled by the simplicity of this concept. Keeping an object's JavaScript variable name inside it is an incredibly powerful technique that can allow you to perform all sorts of tasks that would otherwise be quite a bit more difficult. For example, in Session 14, I showed you how to create a simple animation. While the code involved was fairly simple, it really doesn't lend itself to multiple animations on the same page. However, if this code could be rewritten as an object, it would be a simple matter to sprinkle JavaScript-based animations throughout your pages. Here's one way to create an animation object.

```
function animation_doPreLoad() {
    for (x=0; x < this.numFrames; x++) {
        this.animFrames[ x] = new Image();
        this.animFrames[ x].src = this.imgPath + this.name + x +
        ".jpg";
        }
    }
function animation_doAnimate() {
    if (this.animFrames[ this.numFrames - 1].complete) {
        eval( "document." + this.imgName + ".src =
        this.animFrames[ this.currentFrame++].src");
        if (this.currentFrame == this.numFrames) {
            this.currentFrame = 0;
            }
        }
    else {
        setTimeout( this.name + '.animate()', this.animSpeed);
        }
    }
function animation( name, path, numFrames, speed) {
    this.name = name;
    this.imgName = name + "_img";
    this.imgPath = path;
    this.animFrames = new Array();
    this.numFrames = numFrames;
    this.animSpeed = speed;
    this.currentFrame = 1;
    this.preLoad = animation_doPreLoad;
    this.animate = animation_doAnimate;
    this.preLoad();
    }
```

**10 Min.
To Go**

Here I've taken the animation code from Session 14 and turned it into a simple object. The first parameter to the `animation` constructor function is the name of the JavaScript variable that will hold the object. I've also decided that the names of my graphics files will be based on this name as well. (So, if my JavaScript variable is `titleAnim`, the names of the graphics files on disk will be `titleAnim0.jpg`, `titleAnim1.jpg`, etc.) This is an arbitrary decision, but it makes the design of the object much simpler and establishes a logical relation between my graphics and the JavaScript code that will work with them.

The second parameter is the path that must be followed on the server to actually get to the graphics for my animation. Note that this is only a partial path, up to, but not including, the actual file name.

The remaining parameters specify the number of frames in the animation as well as the speed the animation should be replayed at. With this object defined, all that's needed to create and play an animation is a simple JavaScript statement, like this:

```
var titleAnim = new animation( 'titleAnim', "../images/", 16, 250);
```

Along with a corresponding `<img>` tag in your HTML document:

```
<img name='titleAnim_img'
src='../images/titleAnim0.jpg' border='0'
onload="setTimeout('titleAnim.animate()', titleAnim.animSpeed)" />
```

Looking at the `animate()` method, you can see that both the `eval()` function and the `setTimeout()` method play a role in making this animation work. The `eval()` function is needed (along with the name of the `<img>` tag) to load the next frame. But, before the animation can start, the `setTimeout()` method (along with the name of the JavaScript variable) is needed to check if all of the frames are loaded. It's easy to perform these tasks when you are working with simple functions, but when you move to an object-based animation, you need access to the names involved to make things run smoothly.

Creating the Shopping Cart Object

At last! You've finally seen all of the techniques that are needed to create the shopping cart object. So, without further delay, let me show you the constructor for the shipping cart object. (Note that, since there's so much code involved, I'm just going to show you the most important parts. Of course, you'll find all of the source code for the shopping cart object on your CD-ROM in the Session20 folder.)

```
function shopCart( cartName) {
    this.name = cartName;
    this.cartForm = cartName + "_form";
    this.cookieName = cartName + "_cookie";
    this.clearCookie = false;
    this.inven = new inventory();
    this.initCart = shopCart_doInitCart;
    this.calcGrandTotal = shopCart_doCalcGrandTotal;
    this.plusOne = shopCart_doPlusOne;
    this.minusOne = shopCart_doMinusOne;
    this.enterQuantity = shopCart_doEnterQuantity;
    this.showProductInfo = shopCart_doShowProductInfo;
    this.drawCart = shopCart_doDrawCart;
    this.saveCart = shopCart_doSaveCart;
    this.loadCart = shopCart_doLoadCart;
        this.submitCart = shopCart_doSubmitCart;
    this.initCart();
    }
```

As you've probably guessed, I've simply retooled my old functions to become methods of the shopCart class. Since the methods are, for the most part, things you've already seen, let me go over the properties that are defined here.

The first property is name. As with the other examples you've seen in this session, the name property is used to dynamically create JavaScript statements. However, these statements aren't used with the eval() function. Consider this excerpt from the showProductInfo() method.

```
var inCartBox = "<input type='text' name='inCart_" +
pInfo.partNumber + "'";
inCartBox += "onchange='" + this.name + ".enterQuantity(\"" +
pInfo.partNumber + "\")'";
inCartBox += " value='" + pInfo.inCart + "' size='6' />";
```

For each item in my inventory, I create a text box that shows how many of that item the user has in her shopping cart. This code defines that text box. Now, if the user changes the value in this text box, I need to call an onchange handler to verify that the value typed in is valid. This job falls to the enterQuantity() method, but I also need to specify which object this method belongs to. (Remember, there *could* be multiple shopping cart objects, so I can't hard-code the name of my JavaScript variable here.) This is where the name property becomes invaluable. Assuming that the name of my shopping cart variable is "bpCart", this code will generate the following HTML for the first item in my inventory:

```
<input type='text' name='inCart_st-001'
onchange='bpCart.enterQuantity("st-001")' value='0' size='6' />
```

As you can see, the `onchange` handler that's generated is exactly what's needed to invoke the `enterQuantity()` method for the `bpCart` variable.

The second property is `cartForm`. This is simply the name followed by "_form". One of the advantages of objects is that they let you "encapsulate" everything that something can do. One of the things that I want my shopping cart to do is to create and output the form that it will display its information in. So, this is the name that I'll use to create that form. This name is used in lots of different places in the `shopCart` methods, but the simplest is the `calcGrandTotal()` method, as shown here:

```
function shopCart_doCalcGrandTotal() {
    var grandTotal = 0;
    for (x=0; x<this.inven.productList.length; x++) {
        var thisItem = this.inven.productList[x];
        // Are there any of this item in the cart?
        if (thisItem.inCart > 0) {
            grandTotal += thisItem.calcFinalCost() *
            thisItem.inCart;
            }
        }
    eval( "document." + this.cartForm +
    ".elements['grandTotal'].value = grandTotal");
    }
```

The statement of interest here is the last statement in the method. Here I'm using the `cartForm` property to create a command string that is then passed to the `eval()` function. Once the JavaScript interpreter executes this statement, the text box showing the grand total of items ordered will be updated with the new total. The remainder of the properties and methods in the `shopCart` class work in much the same way. The `cookieName` property lets each shopping cart maintain its own cookie and all of the other methods have been reworked to use the `cartForm` property to communicate with the HTML form that is associated with each `shopCart` object.

Take a minute to load the index.htm file that's in the Session20 folder into your Web browser. As you'll see, it works exactly like the last version you saw. The only difference is that almost all of the underlying JavaScript has been converted to make use of objects.

Done!

REVIEW

In this session, you learned how to use the eval() function to dynamically create and execute JavaScript statements. You also learned how this function works with global and local variables. Next, you learned about how using the setTimeout() and setInterval() methods with JavaScript objects can lead to problems. I showed you that one way around this problem is to give your JavaScript objects a name property to hold the name of the JavaScript variable the object is kept in. This name can then be used to build setTimeout() and setInterval() statements that access the proper object and work correctly. Finally, you saw how all of these techniques can be used together to create a complex object like a shopping cart object.

QUIZ YOURSELF

1. What does the eval() function do? (See "Using the eval() Function.")

2. How does eval() differ from setTimeout() or setInterval()? (See "The setTimeout() and setInterval() Methods.")

3. Why should you not use the this keyword with the setTimeout() and setInterval() methods? (See "Using objects with setTimeout() and setInterval().")

4. Should you pass strings or variable names to the eval() function? (See "Variables and the eval() function.")

5. What kind of statements should you not pass to the eval() function? (See "What kinds of statements can you eval()?")

PART

IV

Saturday Evening

1. When speaking about objects, what is the difference between a class and an instance?

2. When used inside a constructor function, what does the `this` keyword refer to?

3. What steps do you go through to create a custom class of objects?

4. What kinds of data can you store in the properties of an object?

5. How many parameters can you pass to a constructor function?

6. How are the parameters of methods shown inside a constructor function?

7. In your own words, what is a method?

8. What is the difference between a method and an implementation function?

9. When used inside a method, what does the `this` keyword refer to?

10. Assuming that the following statement appears inside a constructor function, what does it signify?

    ```
    this.action = doAction;
    ```

11. How can you enhance HTML controls with JavaScript objects?

12. How do you connect a wrapper object to the object it wraps around?

13. What happens when you add a property or method to an object's prototype?

14. What statement would you use to add a new property called "languageDirection" to the String class?

15. What is the Object class?

16. When you pass a statement to the `eval()` function, when is that statement executed?

17. What will happen when the following statement is executed?

    ```
    eval('documint.write( "Hello World!")');
    ```

18. What advantage is there to storing an object's JavaScript variable name with the object?

19. Which of the following statements is more likely to succeed?

    ```
    setTimeout( "myObject.myMethod()", 1000);

    setTimeout( "this.myMethod()", 1000);
    ```

20. In Session 20, I created an animation class. As written, this class will only work with JPEG graphics. Take the animationObject.js source code from the Session20 folder and change it so that the type of graphic to be used in the animation can be specified when you create a new animation object.

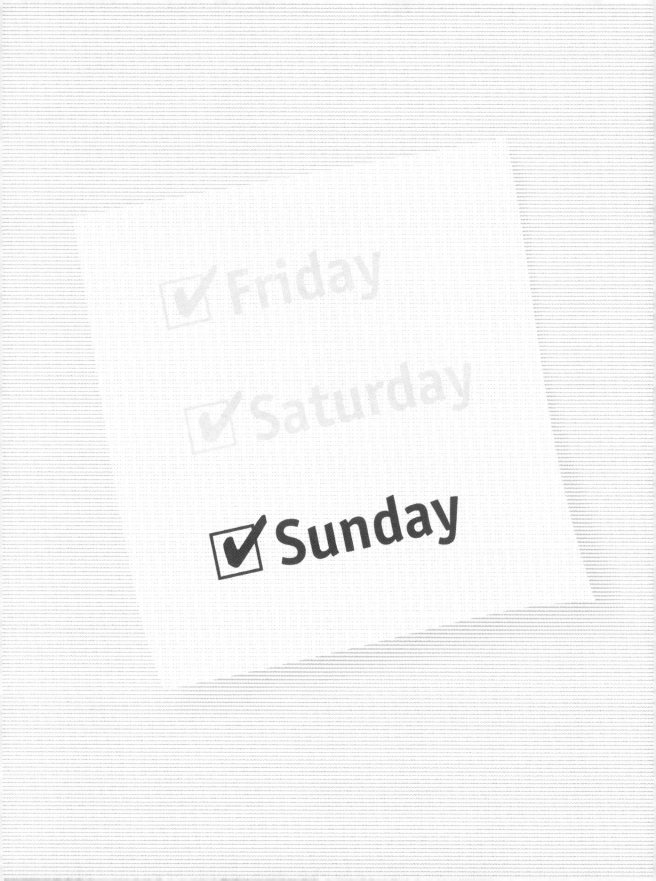

PART

V

Sunday Morning

Working with Cascading Style Sheets

Session Checklist

✔ Learning the basics of Cascading Style Sheets

✔ Understanding how JavaScript works with Cascading Style Sheets

✔ Learning about the Document Object Model

30 Min.
To Go

Over the past few years, there's been a big push to try to separate Web content (the words and pictures on a Web page) from the style in which that content is presented (the text fonts, sizes, and so forth). The idea is that if you can separate the content from the styles, you can present the same content on a wide variety of devices (such as Macintoshes, Palm PDAs, Windows PCs, televisions, and the like) simply by changing the styles that are used. To make this dream a reality, the World Wide Web Consortium (usually referred to as the W3C) created a standard called Cascading Style Sheets or simply CSS. By using CSS, you can control the appearance of just about every element on your HTML page, including the font family, size, color, transparency, and position. Best of all, you can use JavaScript to modify these styles after your page has been loaded and drawn in the Web browser. But, before I can tell you how to use JavaScript to work with your style sheets, I need to tell you a little about how style sheets themselves work. (By the way, since this book's primary concern is JavaScript, I'm not going to go into the CSS standard in detail. For everything you need to know about CSS, visit the official CSS information site at www.w3.org/TR/REC-CSS2.)

The Basics of CSS

The first thing to know is that if you are going to use style sheets, you should make the commitment to use them for all of the styles that you use in your Web pages. This means no <font> tags of any sort and no color or bgcolor attributes in your tables! While this might sound like a big sacrifice, believe me, once you use style sheets a few times, you'll *never* want to go back to using the <font> tag! (If you just can't let go of the <font> tag, you *can* mix style sheets with older styling options. However, I *strongly* recommend that you move entirely to style sheets as soon as you are comfortable with them.)

What are style sheets?

Simply put, style sheets are lists of rules that tell the browser how to style various elements in your HTML document. These style rules are then applied to your HTML document as the Web browser is loading and drawing it in the browser window. For example, I might define a style rule that says, "I want anything inside a set of <address></address> tags to be shown in green." With this information in hand, the Web browser will scan my document and whenever it finds a set of <address></address> tags, it will color the text inside green.

The <style> tag

Now that you know what style sheets are, the question becomes, "How do I put them in my HTML document?" There are actually several ways to insert styles into your HTML document, but the easiest way is to use the HTML <style> tag. For example, here's the <style> tag that would tell the browser to color all of my <address> tags green:

```
<style type="text/css">
address { color:green }
</style>
```

The tag itself tells the browser that a list of style rules will be coming next. The type= attribute tells the browser what standard these rules follow. The type specified here tells the browser that these rules are plain text and that they follow the Cascading Style Sheet standard. (Note that there is at least one other style sheet "standard." Ironically, it's the JavaScript Style Sheets standard that was developed by Netscape. However, even though this is a book about JavaScript, we won't be talking about this standard, simply because it is not the official standard of the

W3C, and because only Netscape browsers support it.) Of course, you can have more than one rule in a style block, as shown here:

```
<style type="text/css">
address { color:green }
p { color:red }
</style>
```

About the only other thing you need to remember about the <style> tag is that you should include it at the top of your HTML document (preferably inside the <head></head> tags) so that the browser will know about your rules before it tries to render your document.

Anatomy of a style rule

OK, so what exactly does the rule address { color:green } mean, and how does it work? Well, at the most basic level, CSS rules are intended to be applied to HTML tags. So, the first part of a rule is simply the name of the HTML tag that you want the rule applied to; in this case, that's the <address> tag.

The rest of the rule is enclosed in curly braces ({}) and tells the browser exactly how you want it to style the contents of the specified tag. In this case, I've specified that I want the color of the contents of this tag to be green.

Knowing this, it's pretty easy to see that the second rule in my example, p { color:red } tells the browser that I want to color all of the text in all of my <p> tags red.

This brings up an important point: When you specify a style rule in this fashion, you are requesting that *every* occurrence of the specified tag should be styled in exactly the same way. While this can be useful, it's more common to want to apply styles to individual parts of a document. To allow for this, the CSS standard also allows for *classes* and *IDs*.

**20 Min.
To Go**

Using CSS classes

CSS classes aren't the same as the object classes you learned about last night, but they are similar in concept. You define a CSS class when you want a group of elements on your HTML page to use the same style. For example, consider the following style sheet.

```
<style type="text/css">
p { font-weight:bold }
p.alert { font-style:italic }
</style>
```

The first rule says that all <p> blocks should be boldface. The second rule defines a class of <p> blocks that go by the name alert. This rule states that any <p> blocks in the alert class should be styled in italics. (You can list more than one style specification in the curly braces.) The trick now is simply creating a <p> block that is in the "alert" class. This is done simply by adding an appropriate class= attribute to a <p> tag:

```
<p>Write to us at:</p>
<p class="alert">
Hungry Minds<br />
909 Third Avenue<br />
New York, NY 10022<br />
</p>
<p>Thank You!</p>
```

If you apply the style sheet defined earlier to this, you'll see something like Figure 21-1.

Figure 21-1
The effect of our style sheet when applied to our HTML

As you can see, the first line is in boldface, the address is in italics and the last line is back to just being boldface. What you might not also notice is that the italic section is in boldface as well. This is the "cascading" part of CSS. When two or more rules match an element, they all apply to the element. If there is a conflict between rules, the rule that more precisely matches the element wins. If two or more rules precisely match the element, the last rule that was defined is the one that wins. As an example of this, consider the following:

```
<style type="text/css">
p { font-weight:bold }
p.alert { font-weight:normal; font-style:italic }
</style>
<p>Write to us at:</p>
<p class="alert">
Hungry Minds<br />
909 Third Avenue<br />
New York, NY 10022<br />
</p>
<p>Thank You!</p>
```

If you load this code into your browser, you'll see something like Figure 21-2.

Figure 21-2
An example of cascading and conflicting style rules

Both rules define a setting for font-weight, but the second rule is the one that wins because it more precisely matches the HTML tag that surrounds the address.

In each of these examples, I've shown a class being defined for a particular tag. While this is perfectly valid, you don't have to tie a class to any one type of tag. The following code shows how to define a class for use with just about *any* HTML tag.

```
<style type="text/css">
p { font-weight:bold }
.alert { font-weight:normal; font-style:italic }
</style>
<p>Write to us at:</p>
```

```
<p class="alert">
Hungry Minds<br />
909 Third Avenue<br />
New York, NY 10022<br />
</p>Or, send us an
<a class="alert"
href="mailto:custserdum@hungryminds.com">e-mail!</a>
<p>Thank You!</p>
```

Notice that in this example, I've defined my class without a tag simply by creating a rule that begins with a period. This is followed by the class name I want to use and then the styles that should be applied to elements of that class. I can then use this class inside both my <p> and my <a> tag.

Using CSS IDs

OK, so you can create document-wide styles and styles that are applied to a group of tags that you specify. What if you want a style to apply to a single element and no others? In that case, you can create a style that is associated with a CSS ID. This is an ID that should be unique inside a given type of HTML tag. In other words, you can have a <p> tag with an ID of contactInfo and you can have an <h1> tag with an ID of contactInfo, but you can't have two <p> tags (or two <h1> tags) with an ID of contactInfo. The following shows how to declare and use a style rule using an ID.

```
<style type="text/css">
p { font-weight:bold }
#contactInfo { font-weight:normal; font-style:italic }
a#contactInfo { font-weight:bold; font-style:italic }
</style>
<p>Write to us at:</p>
<p id="contactInfo">
Hungry Minds<br />
909 Third Avenue<br />
New York, NY 10022<br />
</p>Or, send us an
<a id="contactInfo"
href="mailto:custserdum@hungryminds.com">e-mail!</a>
<p>Thank You!</p>
```

As you can see, ID definitions are preceded with a pound sign (#) character. Here I've defined two ID-oriented rules: The first will match any element with an id= attribute of contactInfo and the second will match only the <a> tag that has an id= attribute of contactInfo.

Styles can also be applied to individual tags by using the style= attribute. You simply list the style specifications you want applied to the tag and separate them with semicolons. For example, if I only wanted one set of <p></p> tags to be red and boldface, and I didn't want to bother with an ID definition, I could code:

```
<p style="color:red;font-weight:bold">I'll be red and bold!</p>
```

The problem with this approach is that it scatters your style definitions throughout your HTML document, making them difficult to update if and when a change is necessary.

The <span> tag

Most HTML tags that enclose text have side effects. For instance, the <a></a> tags create a link and the <p></p> tags create the look of a paragraph by adding white space above and below the text in the tags. So, what tag can you use if all you want is to apply a style to a chunk of text without any visual side effects? You can use the <span> tag!

The <span> tag is a recent addition to HTML that exists for no purpose other than to allow you to demarcate a chunk of text. This makes it perfect for applying styles without any HTML-related side effects. Here's an example of the <span> tag in action.

```
<style type="text/css">
p { font-weight:bold }
#contactInfo { font-weight:normal; font-style:italic }
a#contactInfo { font-weight:bold; font-style:italic;
text-decoration:none }
.noticeMe { text-decoration:underline }
</style>
<p>Write to us at:</p>
<p id="contactInfo">
Hungry Minds<br />
909 Third Avenue<br />
New York, NY 10022<br />
</p><span class="noticeMe">Or, send us an</span>
<a id="contactInfo"
href="mailto:custserdum@hungryminds.com">e-mail!</a>
<p>Thank You!</p>
```

Using the `<span>` tag, along with an appropriate style rule, allows me to underline the text I want without any other visual side effects.

Using external style sheets

While the `<style>` tag makes it easy to create styles for a document, you don't really begin to tap the power of style sheets until you use them to style all of the documents on your Web site. You can do this by storing your style rules in an external file and then linking that file to each of the HTML documents that you want to use those rules. There is one huge advantage to keeping your styles in external files: If you need to change a style on your Web site, you simply change the external style sheet and all of the pages that use that external style sheet will reflect the change immediately. This might not seem to important if your site only has a few pages, but if your site is several hundred or several thousand pages in size, it can save you hours or even days of work! There are two basic ways to use an external style sheet with your HTML documents: the `<link>` tag and the `@import` rule. (Note that any rules that are specified in an external style sheet can be overridden by the rules you specify in your document's `<style>` block. Simply define the styles you want to take precedence *after* you link in your external style sheet.)

Using the <link> tag

The `<link>` tag is an HTML tag that lets you establish a link between your HTML document and an external document of some sort. Using it to create a link with an external style sheet is actually very simple. All you do is code something like this:

```
<link rel="stylesheet" type="text/css" href="babyPalooza.css"
title="bpStyles" />
```

This tag is pretty simple. The `rel=` attribute tells the browser what type of document we are linking to while the `type=` attribute tells the browser what type of style sheet it is. The `href=` attribute tells the browser the Web address of the external file. Finally, the `title=` attribute gives the external file a name that the browser can use to reference the file.

The @import rule

Another way to bring in an external style sheet is to use the `@import` rule at the start of your `<style>` block. It looks like this.

```
<style type="text/css">
@import "babyPalooza.css";
p { font-weight:bold }
</style>
```

You simply create a new rule that starts with @import and then follow that with the Web address of the style sheet you want to import. (You can specify styles using any or all of these methods. However, if you are going to use the @import rule, be sure to use it before you define any other styles. If you don't, the @import rule will be ignored by the browser.)

That's pretty much the basics of what you need to know about CSS in order to be able to use them. Of course, there are *tons* of other styling options that you can specify. In order to find out about all of these other details, I once again recommend that you visit the official CSS documentation page at www.w3.org/TR/ REC-CSS2. So, with all of that out of the way, it's time to show you how you can use CSS and JavaScript together.

Using JavaScript with CSS

**10 Min.
To Go**

The key to using JavaScript with your style sheets is the Document Object Model. Now, I've already told you about the Browser Object Model, but the Document Object Model is slightly different. The Browser Object Model is the set of objects that allows a programming language (in our case, JavaScript) to interact with the Web browser and everything in it, including the document loaded into the browser. The Document Object Model (DOM for short) is a standardized set of objects that can be used to represent an HTML or XML document in any environment. (Like CSS, the DOM standard is maintained by the W3C.) Fortunately, the document object that's included in the Browser Object Model is based on the DOM and that's what allows your JavaScript programs to interact with the styles that you apply to the elements in your HTML document.

In Session 9, you got a pretty thorough tour of the document object. However, to save space (and avoid confusion) I did leave out many of the methods that are specified in the DOM standard. At this point however, it's necessary to tell you about one of those methods: the getElementById() method. You see, when an HTML document is turned into a DOM-compliant object, every element (that is, each set of tags) in the document has a corresponding object created to represent it. These objects are called *element objects* and they contain an unbelievable amount of information about the element and what's inside it. But, before you can inspect or change any of that information, you have to get hold of the element object itself. That's where the getElementById() method comes in. If you pass the ID of an element to this method, it will return the corresponding element object. You can then do pretty much what you want to the element and the changes will show up in the browser window.

As an example of this, I'll create a CSS-based script that will hide and show a control simply by changing the style rule that's associated with the control. To make this example both interesting and useful, the control I'll do this to will be the debug information text box on the Baby-Palooza.com home page. First, I need to define a couple of styles that will make hiding and showing the control possible.

```
body { background-color:white; font-family:arial; font-size:8pt }
td { font-size:8pt }
textarea.debug { visibility:visible }
textarea.debugHidden { visibility:hidden }
```

Next, I need to slightly change the tag that defines the text area control that will display my debug information. (This is in the index.htm file.)

```
<textarea id='debugCtl' name='debug' rows='20' cols='70'>
```

All that's left at this point is to define a button to trigger the change and the JavaScript function that will actually make it happen. Here's the definition of that new button from the index.htm file:

```
<input type='button' name='toggle' value='Hide Debug Info'
onclick='doShowHideDebug()' />
```

And the JavaScript function is shown here:

```
function doShowHideDebug() {
    var debugText = document.getElementById( "debugCtl");
    if (document.forms[1].toggle.value == "Hide Debug Info") {
        debugText.className = "debugHidden";
        document.forms[1].toggle.value = "Show Debug Info";
        }
    else {
        debugText.className = "debug";
        document.forms[1].toggle.value = "Hide Debug Info";
        }
    }
```

The first thing this function does is call the document.getElementById() method and pass it an ID of debugCtl. This returns an element object that represents my text area control. I then use an `if` statement to determine whether I should hide or show the control. This decision is based on the `value` that's inside my button. (Remember, the `value` property of a button is the string that actually shows up in the button on screen.) If the value in the button is `Hide Debug Info` the control must be visible. So, I change the `className` property of the text area to `debugHidden`. This immediately switches the style rule that is applied to the control and removes it from the screen. The final step is to change the value property of my button so that the button reads `Show Debug Info`. (Showing the control again is done in much the same way. To see all of this code in action, load the index.htm file from the Session21 folder on your CD-ROM.)

As I said earlier, the object returned by the `getElementById()` method exposes a lot of information about the element in question. However, anything else you might do with this information lies in the realm of Dynamic-HTML. This is a large topic with so much neat stuff to cover, I'll leave it for now so that I can discuss it in depth in the next session.

Deciding Which Style Sheet to Use

Remember at the start of this session, I said that style sheets were intended to help separate the content in a Web page from the style in which it was presented. So, you can define one set of styles for use with a Windows PC, another for a Macintosh, and so on. The trick is deciding which set of styles to use.

Of course, you can specify styles inside a set of `<style></style>` tags, so you could just use JavaScript to dynamically generate all of your rules right there inside your page as it's loaded. However, this would be incredibly inefficient because you'd have to keep all of your styles for all the platforms you support right there in your JavaScript code. So, using external style sheets and dynamically deciding which one to link is the way to go. The only problem is how do you determine which platform the browser is running on so that you can dynamically generate the appropriate `<link>` tag?

In Session 26, I'll be telling you all about the `navigator` object and how it can help you write cross-browser scripts. Until then, one property of the `navigator` object provides a perfect solution to this problem. This property, named *platform*, tells you exactly what you think it does: which computer platform the browser is running on. Table 21-1 shows the value of `navigator.platform` for several browsers and platforms.

Table 21-1
Values of navigator.platform

Platform	Browser	Value of navigator.platform
Windows Me	Netscape/Internet Explorer	Win32
Macintosh OS 9.0.4	Netscape/Internet Explorer	MacPPC
Linux (Mandrake 7.1)	Netscape	LinuxELF2.0

As you can see, finding out which computer you are running on is pretty simple. The following code will show you how you can use this information (and a couple of String methods) to dynamically generate the appropriate <link> tag.

```
var styleLink = '<link rel="stylesheet" type="text/css"
title="bpStyles" ';
var platform = navigator.platform.substring(0, 3).toUpperCase();
if (platform == "WIN") {
    styleLink += 'href="babyPalooza-Win.css" />';
    }
if (platform == "MAC") {
    styleLink += 'href="babyPalooza-Mac.css" />';
    }
if (platform == "LIN") {
    styleLink += 'href="babyPalooza-Linux.css" />';
    }
document.writeln( styleLink);
```

Done!

Of course, to work properly, this code should appear at the top of your HTML document.

REVIEW

In this session, you learned about Cascading Style Sheets. You saw how to create a style sheet inside your HTML document and how to load an external style sheet. You saw how JavaScript can extract an object that represents an individual element (tag) from the document object. You also learned that, once you've got that element object in hand, you can do all sorts of neat things to it. Finally, you learned how the platform property of the navigator object can help you create a JavaScript program that lets you dynamically load the style sheet that's best suited for the platform that the browser is running on. In the next session, I'll be delving even further into these topics as I show you how to use Dynamic HTML to create all sorts of neat effects on your Web pages.

QUIZ YOURSELF

1. What is the purpose of a style sheet? (See the opening paragraphs of this session.)

2. What are the two ways of linking to an external style sheet? (See "Using external style sheets.")

3. What is the difference between a CSS class and a CSS ID? (See "Using CSS classes" and "Using CSS IDs.")

4. What does the `document.getElementById()` method do? (See "Using JavaScript with CSS.")

5. What information does the `navigator.platform` property contain? (See "Deciding Which Style Sheet to Use.")

Creating Dynamic HTML with JavaScript

Session Checklist

✔ Learning how JavaScript can manipulate HTML dynamically

✔ Learning about DHTML properties

✔ Moving elements around the screen with CSS and JavaScript

✔ Changing the text on screen after the page has loaded

**30 Min.
To Go**

In Session 11, you learned how to dynamically create HTML in order to present your users with customized Web pages. In this session, you'll be learning how you can use JavaScript to dynamically change the appearance and content of an HTML page *after* it's already loaded into the Web browser. This process is called Dynamic-HTML or DHTML for short.

In the past, creating DHTML was a rather arcane art. Each of the major browsers had a different underlying object model and, as a result, you had to write completely different blocks of DHTML and JavaScript to accomplish the same things in each browser. Fortunately, with the adoption of the latest Document Object Model (DOM) standard, and the release of the latest versions of Internet Explorer and Netscape Navigator, that's beginning to change for the better. Unfortunately, however, DOM support isn't yet complete in both browsers so it's still necessary to use a trick or two to create a DHTML script that will run without modification. But it can be done, and it's actually *very* simple to do!

As I write this, the latest version of the DOM is Level 2. As noted above, the major browsers have incorporated a large part of the functionality of the Level 2 DOM, but some pieces are still missing. I'll be focusing on the parts that work in the latest versions of both Internet Explorer and Netscape Navigator. (In other words, what you'll be learning in this session is *not* guaranteed to work in older browsers.) For more information on the DOM Level 2 standard, visit www.w3.org/TR/DOM-Level-2-Core/.

Dynamically Changing Styles

Cascading Style Sheets (CSS), which you studied in the last session, are the basis of all style manipulation under the DOM. So, to make styles easy to manipulate, the DOM makes provisions for browsers to define style objects that contain all the information needed to apply various style information to an element on the HTML page. The latest versions of both Internet Explorer and Netscape Navigator make this information available to your JavaScript program in the form of an object named *style* that's a property of an element object.

When working in the realm of the DOM, the term *element* refers to a set of opening and closing HTML tags and their contents or a single empty HTML tag. For example:

```
<p>This is an element</p>
```

In the line above, everything (including the <p></p> tags) is one element. In addition, elements (and element objects) can be nested one inside the other. In the line

```
<p>This is a <b>bunch</b> of elements</p>
```

there are actually several elements: one for the <p></p> tags, one for the <b></b> tags. And each of these chunks of text:

```
This is a
bunch
of elements
```

Is an element all it's own, regardless of how many lines it may take. Finally, an empty tag like <hr /> is an element as well.

Obtaining an element object

If you'll remember from the last session, you can obtain an element object simply by calling the `document.getElementById()` method and passing it the `id=` attribute of the element you are interested in. So, if I have the following HTML defined:

```
<p id="welcome">Welcome to Baby-Palooza.com!</p>
```

You can obtain the element object that represents this set of `<p></p>` tags (including all the subelements) with the following JavaScript:

```
var welcomeElement = document.getElementById( "welcome");
```

Once you have the element object in your possession, things begin to get *very* interesting.

Examining the style object

In the previous session, I showed you how to show or hide an element by changing the CSS class that it was associated with. While this is a neat trick, it's also a fairly inelegant way to do things. After all, when you change an element's CSS class, you are basically changing *all* of the style information for that element. It would be much nicer if you could only change a particular aspect of an element's style without affecting its class or other style attributes. This is exactly what a style object allows you to do.

Getting at the style object for an element is easy: Simply extract the element in question using the `getElementById()` method and then you can examine any property of the style object that you are interested in. For example, to see the `color` property of the `welcomeElement` defined earlier, I could code:

```
alert( welcomeElement.style.color);
```

By now, you're probably very curious as to the names of all the properties inside the style object. Well, unfortunately, there are a *lot* of them. No really, I mean a *lot!*

Because of this, I'm not going to go over each property in detail. Instead, I'm going to give you a quick JavaScript program to list all of the properties and their contents. I will be going over some of the more useful properties, but for the full list (along with valid values for each) you should check out the CSS information page at www.w3.org/TR/REC-CSS2.

```
<p id="welcome">Welcome to Baby-Palooza.com</p>
<script language="javascript">
```

```
// Get the element that represents our test paragraph
var welcomeElement = document.getElementById( "welcome");
// List all the properties of the element's style object
for (x in welcomeElement.style) {
    document.write( x + " = ");
    document.write( eval( 'welcomeElement.style.' + x));
    document.write( "<br />");
    }
```

If you load this program (it's in the Session22 folder on your CD-ROM), you'll see the welcoming text followed by a list of properties that come straight from the style object.

Changing a style property

The nice thing about the style object is that all of its properties are changeable. So, if I want to make my welcoming text red, all I have to code is:

```
welcomeElement.style.color = "red";
```

and the text will immediately become red on the screen. Of course, while you can assign values to the various properties of the style object, you need to make sure that the value you assign is valid for that property. Again, you'll find a complete list of valid values for each style property at www.w3.org/TR/REC-CSS2. But, in the interest of getting you going right away, here's a list of some of the more useful style properties along with their valid values. (As usual, you'll find a program demonstrating each of these properties on your CD-ROM. As you play with the example programs on the CD-ROM, don't worry too much about entering an invalid value. Usually, the DOM will reject an invalid value and use an applicable default without any trouble. About the worst you might run into is a simple JavaScript error dialog.)

When you compare the list of style properties on the W3C Web site with the list here, the W3C properties will have names like "background-color" rather than "backgroundColor." Since the W3C names are not valid JavaScript variable names, the browser makers removed the hyphens and capitalized the first letter of the second word in order to make them usable from JavaScript. However, when you are using these properties in your CSS style rules, you must use the hyphenated form.

The backgroundColor property

This property controls the background color of the element. Valid values include any of the standard color names from Session 9 or any six-digit RGB hexadecimal color value. (See Table 9-1 for a partial list.)

```
welcomeElement.style.backgroundColor = "yellow";
```

The backgroundImage property

This property lets you specify an image to be placed in the background of the element (above the background color but behind the text). You must specify the Web address of the image in a very specific format, as shown in the example below. (Note that no quotes are necessary inside the parentheses.)

```
welcomeElement.style.backgroundImage =
"url(../images/happyBaby.jpg)";
```

The backgroundRepeat property

If you specify a background image, you can also specify if that image should be repeated in the element by setting this property. Valid values are repeat (the default), repeat-x (repeats the image across the page), repeat-y (repeats the image down the page), and no-repeat. (For some really nifty background image effects, be sure to check out the background-attachment and background-position properties at www.w3.org/TR/REC-CSS2.)

```
welcomeElement.style.backgroundRepeat = "no-repeat";
```

The borderColor property

If you have created a border around an element (see the borderStyle property later in this session), this property can be used to set its color. Valid values are the same as for the color property.

```
welcomeElement.style.borderColor = "green";
```

You can also pass multiple values to specify a different color for each edge of the border.

```
welcomeElement.style.borderColor = "green red black blue";
```

**20 Min.
To Go**

The borderStyle property

This property lets you specify style of the border around the element. Valid values
are dashed, dotted, double, groove, inset, none, outset, ridge, and solid.
You can specify a single value and it will be used for all four edges of the border.
Or, you can specify a value for two, three, or all four edges. For example, the following statement will create a double border around the element.

```
welcomeElement.style.borderStyle = "double";
```

The following statement will create a border that is solid on the top and bottom
and dashed down the sides.

```
welcomeElement.style.borderStyle = "solid dashed";
```

(For more precise control over the border around an element, you can set the bor-
der-top, border-left, border-right, and border-bottom properties individually.)

The borderWidth property

If you have created a border around an element (see the borderStyle property,
above), this property can be used to set the width of the line used to draw it. Valid
values are medium, thin, thick, or a number of pixels. (Note that you cannot
specify a negative number.)

```
welcomeElement.style.borderWidth = "10px";
```

You can also pass multiple values to specify a different width for each edge of
the border.

```
welcomeElement.style.borderWidth = "thin thick medium 20px";
```

The color property

This property controls the color that the element's text is drawn in. Valid values
include any of the standard color names from Session 9 or any six-digit RGB hexadecimal color value. (See Table 9-1 for a partial list.)

```
welcomeElement.style.color = "brown";
```

The display property

This property controls how the element is laid out and displayed in the Web
browser. Valid values are block, inline, list-item, and none. Elements that

"block out" areas on the screen (like the `<p></p>` tags) should have a value of `block`, while elements that exist inside other elements (like the `<b></b>` tags) should have a display value of `inline`. The `list-item` setting is similar to the block setting with the addition of a list item marker. (In other words, a bullet. Note that not all browsers support this setting.) To remove an element from the screen and cause the other elements on the screen to fill in where the element was, set the element's `display` property to `none`.

```
welcomeElement.style.display = "none";
```

The fontFamily property

This property controls the font family (Helvetica, Arial, Times, to name a few) used to draw the text inside the element. You can, theoretically, specify any font family installed on the client. If you specify a font family that isn't installed on the client, the browser's default font will be used.

```
welcomeElement.style.fontFamily = "symbol";
```

The fontSize property

This property controls the font size of the text inside the element. Any number from zero up is valid, but you also need to supply a unit measurement for the size specified. Table 22-1 presents valid units.

Table 22-1
Valid Units of Measurement to Specify Font Size of an Element

Unit	Usage
%	The font should be scaled to the given percentage of the default font size for the element. (For example, if the default height is 10pt and a 120% `fontSize` is specified, the font would be scaled to 12pt.)
cm	Centimeters — the size is supplied in centimeters.
em	ems — this means that the number is expressed in ems.
ex	x-height — this scales the font relative to the height of the character x in the font.
mm	Millimeters — the size is supplied in millimeters.

Continued

Table 22-1 *Continued*

Unit	Usage
pc	Picas — the number supplied is a number of picas.
pt	Points — this is a traditional font point size. (Approximately 1/72 of an inch.)
px	Pixels — this means that the number supplied is a number of pixels. (Note that if you don't supply a unit designation, px will be used by default.)

So, any of the following statements would be a valid assignment to the `fontSize` property:

```
welcomeElement.style.fontSize = "10px";
welcomeElement.style.fontSize = "45%";
welcomeElement.style.fontSize = "10cm"; // yikes!
```

The fontStyle property

This property controls the style applied to the text inside the element. Valid values are `normal`, `italic`, and `oblique`. (Most browsers render `italic` and `oblique` the same way.)

```
welcomeElement.style.fontStyle = "italic";
```

The fontWeight property

This property controls the weight (density) of the text inside the element. Valid values are `normal`, `bold`, `bolder`, `lighter`, 100, 200, 300, 400, 500, 600, 700, 800, and 900. The `normal` setting is equivalent to 400 and the `bold` setting is equivalent to 700.

```
welcomeElement.style.weight = "900"; // as bold as it gets!
```

The height property

This property specifies the height of the element on the screen. You can assign this property any positive number and the element will be resized. (Note that you can use the same measurement units specified in Table 22-1, in the discussion of the `fontSize` property earlier in this section. Note also that a percentage value is interpreted to mean a percentage of the vertical space visible in the browser window.)

```
welcomeElement.style.height = "50%";
```

The margin property

This property lets you specify the margins surrounding the element. Valid values include positive and negative numbers. (Note that all browsers may not support specifying negative values. You can use the same measurement units specified in Table 22-1.)

```
welcomeElement.style.margin = "50px";
```

You can also pass multiple values to specify a different margin size for each side of the element.

```
welcomeElement.style.margin = "20px 50pt 10px 35mm";
```

(For more precise control over the margin around an element, you can set the margin-top, margin-left, margin-right, and margin-bottom properties individually.)

The padding property

This property lets you specify the padding on the inside of the element (that is, the space between the outside edges of the element and the text inside). Valid values include positive numbers from zero on up. (You can use the same measurement units specified in Table 22-1.)

```
welcomeElement.style.padding = "50px";
```

You can also pass multiple values to specify a different padding width for each side of the element.

```
welcomeElement.style.padding = "20px 50pt 10px 35mm";
```

(For more precise control over the padding inside an element, you can set the padding-top, padding-left, padding-right, and padding-bottom properties individually.)

The textAlign property

This property specifies the alignment of the text in the element. Valid values are `left`, `right`, and `center`.

```
welcomeElement.style.textAlign = "center";
```

The visibility property

This property determines if the element is visible or not. Valid values are visible and hidden.

```
welcomeElement.style.visbility = "hidden";
```

Note that even if you hide an element it will still take up space on the page. To remove an element from the layout of a page, set its display property to none. (See the discussion of the display property earlier in this session for more information on this.)

The width property

This property specifies the width of the element on the screen. You can assign this property any positive number and the element will be resized. (Note that you can use the same measurement units specified in Table 22-1. Note also that a percentage value is interpreted to mean a percentage of the horizontal space visible in the browser window.)

```
welcomeElement.style.width = "25px";
```

**10 Min.
To Go**

Moving Elements Around

One of the nice things about CSS is that it lets you *precisely* position elements on the screen. Simply by specifying the appropriate values for the position, top, left, bottom, and right properties of the style object, you can tell the browser exactly how and where you want something to appear on the screen. The really cool part however, is that you can also take an element and, simply by repeatedly *changing* one or more of these position-related properties, move stuff around the browser window. (There are loads of other neat things you can do with the position-related properties of the style object. Unfortunately, there just isn't room to cover them all in this book. So, I'll just be focusing on how to move things around the screen. For the scoop on all the other capabilities these properties give you, be sure to visit the official CSS documentation site at www.w3.org/TR/DOM-Level-2-Core/.)

The position property

The key to CSS-based animations is the position property. This property lets you tell the browser *how* you want an element positioned on the page as opposed to exactly where you want it positioned. There are several different values you can assign to the position property, but for the purpose of animation, you want to specify a value of absolute. This value tells the browser that you, the programmer, will let the browser know exactly where to position the element on the page. It's then up to you to specify a physical position and shape for the element by setting the top, left, bottom, right, height, and width properties to the appropriate values. You already know about the height and width properties, so let me tell you a bit about the others.

The top, left, bottom, and right properties let you determine where on screen an element is drawn, relative to the parent element that it's inside. For example, if you have a <span></span> inside a <p></p>, and you reset the top, left, bottom, or right properties of the <span></span> element, the values you specify will be taken as being relative to the position of the <p></p> element.

For example, if I assign a value of 50 to the bottom property of the <span></span> element, the bottom of that element will be moved so that it's 50 pixels away from the bottom of the <p></p> element.

If an element has no parent (or if the parent element isn't positioned itself), these properties specify the position of the element relative to the <body></body> element (in other words, the browser window).

If you found that a bit confusing, don't worry... it's really not that hard once you've seen it in action. So, with that in mind, crank up your HTML editor and open the movingThings.htm file from the Session22 folder on your CD-ROM. This is a rather simple (if lengthy) program that takes a paragraph element and moves it back and forth across the top of the browser window. I've thrown in a background image so that you can watch the paragraph float over it.

Looking at this code, you see that after specifying my styles, I create a simple paragraph element that holds my usual greeting. When my JavaScript begins executing, the first thing it does is retrieve the element object for my paragraph. Next I assign a value of "absolute" to this element's position property. This removes the element from the layout flow of the page and gives me the ability to move it around.

Skipping to the end, you'll see that a simple call to the setInterval() method is what kicks off the animation and keeps it going. Every 10/1000 of a second, it calls the moveit() function, which slides the paragraph back and forth across the page. While the concept behind the moveit() function is fairly simple, the way the styles work in today's browsers make it a little trickier than you might expect.

The first problem is that, unless you specify a nonzero value for the top, left, bottom, or right style properties, they will contain empty strings until you put something in them. So, the moveit() function checks for that, and sets the curPos variable to zero if the left property actually is empty.

If the `left` property isn't empty, we've actually got an even stickier problem to deal with. You see, all four of the position-related properties are actually stored as strings, complete with unit information at the end! So, if you assign a zero to the `left` property, what you'll actually get back later is `0px`. This makes performing math with these properties rather difficult. So, rather than fooling around with a bunch of intermediate String method calls, the `moveit()` function splits the contents of the `left` property into an array (using the p in px as the separator) and then converts the numeric part into an actual number. (Remember, px are the default units for all of the numeric style properties. So, if you use a different set of units, you'll have to modify your code accordingly to extract the numbers you need.) Once I've secured the value I need, I check to see which direction I'm moving and incrementally increase or decrease the `left` property accordingly.

Finally, you'll notice that in order to change directions, I'm forced to compare the `left` position of my element with the width of the screen minus a hard-coded value (470). This is necessary because, unless you set the `width` property of an element, there's no way to tell how wide it is. So, if you'll look at the style rule I defined for my paragraph, you'll see that I set it to be 450 pixels wide, just enough to get all my message text on one line. (The 20 extra pixels account for the scroll bar on the right-hand side of the window.)

While this is a very simple program, it actually contains all the tricks you need to create your own CSS-based animations. Remember, with this technique, you can move *any* element: a paragraph, a list, an image, whatever you want.

Changing Text in the Browser Window

The last DHTML trick I want to share with you is how to change the text you see in your browser window. As you've seen before, if you try to do this with `document.write()` calls, you'll just end up erasing the contents of your browser window. Fortunately, DHTML makes what seems impossible, incredibly easy.

The innerHTML property

The key to this trick is a wonderfully nonstandard property of the element object named innerHTML. That's right, I said it was nonstandard. Unfortunately, there really isn't a simple equivalent to the `innerHTML` property in the DOM. That's too bad, because the `innerHTML` property is incredibly easy to use and incredibly powerful too. Even though `innerHTML` isn't a part of the DOM, I'm telling you about it here for two reasons:

1. As I've said before, DOM compliance in the major browsers isn't yet 100%. So, while there might be a multistep way to accomplish the same thing via the DOM, not all versions of the major browsers support the DOM fully enough to allow it.

2. Amazingly, all current browser versions on all platforms (that I've been able to test) support the innerHTML property. This combined with its usefulness and popularity, have me convinced that the innerHTML property is here to stay.

So, what does the innerHTML property do? Well, it allows you to change the HTML that's inside an element. It's that simple and that powerful. For example, consider the following code.

```
<p id="welcome">Welcome to Baby-Palooza.com</p>
<script language="javascript">
    var welcomeElement = document.getElementById( "welcome");
welcomeElement.innerHTML = "<b>Thanks for your business!</b>";
</script>
```

As usual, this code defines a paragraph element and then a call to the getElementById() method retrieves the object that represents that element. The final statement however, is what makes the innerHTML property so special. You'll notice that I'm assigning a new string to the innerHTML property. Part of this string is a set of <b></b> tags. Immediately after this statement executes, the text in my paragraph will change to the text "Thanks for your business!" and it will be in boldface! (If you don't believe it, give the innerHTMLProperty.htm file a try and see for yourself.) If that seems simple, it is! Fortunately, the innerHTML property is just as powerful as it is simple. So, make sure you know exactly what you are changing when you use the innerHTML property and remember that the key is to assign each of your elements a unique ID. Once you've done that, creating your DHTML JavaScript code becomes incredibly simple.

Done!

REVIEW

In this session, you learned how to create JavaScript code that will dynamically manipulate the HTML elements in your Web pages. You learned how an element's style object contains everything you need to manipulate the appearance of an element on the page. In addition, you found out how JavaScript can move an HTML element around the browser window. Finally, you learned how the innerHTML property of an element can be changed to place new text on the screen.

Since there's been so much concept and theory in this session, I didn't have room to show you a neat little JavaScript program that allows you to investigate all of the properties of the style object at your leisure. You'll find this program in the dhtmlStyle.htm file on your CD-ROM. Load it into your favorite browser and start changing style properties. After you've played with it a bit, take a look at the source code. It incorporates almost everything we've discussed in this session and more than a few concepts from the other parts of the book. Plus, it's a very useful investigative tool in its own right!

Quiz Yourself

1. Where is the style information for an element kept? (See "Dynamically Changing Styles.")
2. What exactly is an element? (See "Dynamically Changing Styles.")
3. How do you format a Web address when you assign it to the backgroundImage property of the style object? (See "The backgroundImage property.")
4. What are the different units of measurement used by CSS and the properties of the style object? (See "The fontSize property.")
5. What do you need to watch out for when working with the position-related top, left, bottom, and right properties? (See "The position property.")

Working with Frames

Session Checklist

✔ Understanding how JavaScript can communicate between frames

✔ Dynamically creating new content for a frame

✔ Handling frame-based documents loaded without their frameset

✔ Resizing frames with JavaScript

**30 Min.
To Go**

Whether you love them or hate them, frames-based Web sites are here to stay. Fortunately, from a JavaScript programmer's point of view, working with a frames-based site is almost as easy as working with a nonframes-based site.

How JavaScript Views Frames

To create a frames-based site, you first have to define an HTML frameset document. This is just an HTML document that has a set of <frameset></frameset> tags rather than a set of <body></body> tags. Inside the <frameset></frameset> tags you define one or more <frame> tags that tell the browser which file to load for each frame along with how the frame should appear in the browser window. The following code shows a simple frameset document. (Note that this code is in the listing23-1.htm file in the Session23 folder.)

```
<html>
<head><title>Welcome to Baby-Palooza.com!</title></head>
<frameset rows="70%,*" frameborder="0">
    <frame name="prodInfo" src="welcome.htm" scrolling="yes"
    frameborder="no"></frame>
    <frame name="cart" src="cart.htm" scrolling="yes"
    frameborder="no"></frame>
</frameset>
</html>
```

In Session 8, I mentioned that, as far as JavaScript is concerned, a frame is just another window object. So, when you load this document into a Web browser, it actually creates three window objects: one to represent the frameset document itself and one for each of the <frame> tags. The window object representing the frameset document becomes the parent object, and the others become entries in the parent.frames array.

If you look closely at the preceding code, you'll see that, in addition to specifying which HTML file should be loaded into each frame (the src= attribute), I've also given each of my frames a name= attribute. As you might expect, these will end up being used as the names of the JavaScript window objects that represent each frame.

Communicating between frames

If you have a bit of JavaScript in one frame that needs to talk to a bit of JavaScript in another frame, it's very simple to do. For example, let's assume that the frameset shown earlier is loaded and that the following code is defined in the welcome.htm file:

```
function welcome() {
    alert( "Welcome to Baby-Palooza.com!");
    }
```

If I wanted to call this function from the cart.htm file, any one of the following statements would do the trick.

```
parent.prodInfo.welcome();
parent.frames[0].welcome();
parent.frames['prodInfo'].welcome();
```

How does this work? Well, consider the first of these statements:

```
parent.prodInfo.welcome();
```

The first thing to remember is that this statement is being executed from inside a frame (the `cart` frame to be exact). So, in order to reach the `prodInfo` frame, the code has to have a reference point in common with the `prodInfo` frame. That's where the `parent` object comes in. Since both of these frames were created from the same frameset document, they both have the same `parent`. So this code says, "Look inside my `parent` object. Inside this, you should find another object named `prodInfo`. Look inside this object and call the function named `welcome`." The other two statements work in almost exactly the same way. The only difference is that they go through the `parent` object's frames array rather than addressing the frame directly by name.

Frame-to-frame communication isn't restricted to making function calls. You can access any variables, functions, or objects that you might have defined in another frame.

Working with nested frames

As you can see, using JavaScript to work with frames is pretty simple. However, it's entirely possible to create a frames-based site that has multiple framesets nested one within the other. Consider the following frameset document:

```
<html>
<head><title>Welcome to Baby-Palooza.com!</title></head>
<frameset rows="70%,*" frameborder="0">
    <frame name="prodInfo" src="welcome.htm" scrolling="yes"
    frameborder="no"></frame>
    <frameset cols="50%,50%" frameborder="0">
        <frame name="cart" src="cart.htm" scrolling="yes"
        frameborder="no"></frame>
        <frame name="ads" src="ads.htm" scrolling="yes"
        frameborder="no"></frame>
    </frameset>
</frameset>
</html>
```

Here, my first frameset defines two rows while my second splits the bottom rows into two columns. Assuming that my `welcome()` function is still defined in the welcome.htm file, how could code in the `ads` frame call it? Either of these statements would work.

```
parent.parent.prodInfo.welcome();
top.prodInfo.welcome();
```

When you nest frames, each set of `<frameset></frameset>` tags becomes the `parent` object of the frames defined inside it. So, because my `ads` frame is inside two sets of `<frameset></frameset>` tags, I have to back up through two `parent` objects to reach the `prodInfo` frame.

Of course, if you have a *lot* of nested frames, traipsing through all of these `parent` objects can quickly become tedious. So, JavaScript provides the `top` object. The `top` object represents the actual frameset document that was loaded into the browser. A special feature of the `top` object is that, instead of using a multidimensional array to hold nested frames, each frame's `window` object is turned into a property of the `top` object. So, even though the `ads` frame is nested two levels deep, you can access it simply by coding `top.ads`. The same holds true for `top.prodInfo` and `top.cart`. So, assuming that the following function is defined in the ads.htm file:

```
function showAd() {
    alert("Please support our sponsors!");
    }
```

You could call this function from the welcome.htm file simply by coding:

```
top.ads.showAd();
```

The timing problem

For the most part, communicating between frames is very simple. However, this assumes that the contents of all of your frames are completely loaded. What if, as it's being loaded, the JavaScript code in your first frame tries to call a function in your last frame? If the HTML document in your last frame hasn't finished loading and that function doesn't exist, you'll get an error message and your JavaScript program will halt. How can you get around this problem? The only real solution to this is to check and see if the contents of a given frame are fully loaded before you try to access anything in that frame.

For example, assume that the code from our second frameset document is being loaded. The first thing the browser will do is load the contents of the first frame (the welcome.htm) file and execute any JavaScript it finds there. If one of the JavaScript statements in this file attempts to call the `showAds()` function that's in the ads.htm file, the statement will very likely fail because the ads.htm file simply hasn't had time to be loaded into the `ads` frame yet.

You might think that you could simply put an `onload` event handler into the ads.htm file. This handler could send some sort of message to the `prodInfo` frame telling it that it was loaded and that it was safe to call the `showAds()` function. While this will work for a very simple HTML file, it might not work for a complex HTML file with a lot of forms and controls. The reason is that the `onload` handler simply fires when all of the data for a page has been loaded. Unfortunately, this doesn't always correspond to the time when all of the data on a page has been loaded and then *parsed* into all of the JavaScript objects that make up the Browser Object Model. So, even though the data for a page has been loaded into the browser, the JavaScript objects that represent that data might not be available yet. The solution to this problem is actually quite simple, but not incredibly obvious.

```
<html>
<head>
<script language="javascript">
function showAd() {
    alert("Please support our sponsors!");
    }
</script>
</head>
<body>
This is the advertising frame!
<form name="dummy">
<input type="hidden" name="dummy" />
</form>
</body>
</html>
```

Here you'll notice that I've defined a dummy form. It has no purpose other than to simply sit there and take up space. To see why, consider this version of the welcome.htm file.

```
<html>
<head>
<script language="javascript">
function welcome() {
    alert( "Welcome to Baby-Palooza.com!");
    }
function doAdShow() {
    var tryAgain = true;
    if (top.ads != null) {
```

```
            if (top.ads.document != null) {
                if (top.ads.document.forms.length > 0) {
                    top.ads.showAd();
                    tryAgain = false;
                    }
                }
            }
        if (tryAgain) {
            setTimeout( 'doAdShow()', 1000);
            }
        }
</script>
</head>
<body onload="doAdShow()">
Welcome to Baby-Palooza.com!<br />
</body>
</html>
```

Rather than calling the showAd() function directly, I've defined an onload handler that calls the doAdShow() function. This function begins by setting up a local variable called tryAgain and assigns it a value of true. With this out of the way, the function uses three if statements to check and see if the contents of the ads frame have been completely loaded and parsed. First, it checks to see if the top.ads object exists. The existence of this object tells the function that, at the very least, the <frame> tag that will load the ads.htm file has been parsed. The function then checks to see if the top.ads.document object exists. If this object exists, you can be sure that the ads.htm file has begun to load. Finally, the function checks to see if the length property of the top.ads.document.forms array is greater than zero. If this value *is* greater than zero, the function knows for sure that the dummy form has been loaded, parsed, and is available for JavaScript to use.

Why check the length of the forms array? Remember that the JavaScript interpreter loads and parses the information in an HTML document from the top to the bottom as it comes to it. By placing a an empty form at the end of my document and then checking to see if that form is loaded and parsed, I can tell if everything *before* that form has been loaded and parsed! So, if all of these tests are successful, the function can call the showAd() function with complete confidence and set the tryAgain variable to false. However, if any of these if statements fails, the value of tryAgain will remain true and a call to the setTimeout() method will tell the JavaScript interpreter to try again in one second.

Dynamically Creating Frame Content

In Session 11, you saw how document.write() and document.writeln() could be used to dynamically create HTML and JavaScript code in a window. Well, it's also possible to use these calls to dynamically create HTML and JavaScript code in a different frame.

Actually, the process for writing HTML or JavaScript out to a different frame is almost exactly the same as for writing HTML out to the current frame. The only difference is that you have to specify the name of the frame you want to write to. For example, consider this slightly different version of the nested.htm file.

```
<html>
<head><title>Welcome to Baby-Palooza.com!</title>
<script language="javascript">
function loadProdInfo() {
    top.prodInfo.document.open();
    top.prodInfo.document.writeln( "<html><body
bgcolor='white'>");
    top.prodInfo.document.writeln( "Welcome to Baby-
Palooza.com!");
    top.prodInfo.document.writeln( "</body></html>");
    top.prodInfo.document.close();
    }
</script>
</head>
<frameset onload="loadProdInfo()" rows="70%,*" frameborder="0">
    <frame name="prodInfo" src="" scrolling="yes"
    frameborder="no"></frame>
    <frameset name="shopInfo" cols="50%,50%" frameborder="0">
        <frame name="cart" src="" scrolling="yes"
        frameborder="no"></frame>
        <frame name="ads" src="" scrolling="yes"
        frameborder="no"></frame>
    </frameset>
</frameset>
</html>
```

As soon as the outermost frameset finishes loading, the loadProdInfo() function is called. This function contains five simple statements that store an entirely new HTML document into the prodInfo frame. The first of these statements calls the `document.open()` method for the `prodInfo` frame. As you learned in Session 9, this clears the current contents of the frame and opens an output stream into it.

The next three statements write out the new HTML document into the frame. It's important that you realize that these statements are writing out a complete and valid HTML document! When you replace the contents of a frame in this way, you *must* output a set of valid `<html></html>` and `<body></body>` tags if you want your new document to be processed properly. This includes any additional attributes (like the `bgcolor=` attribute in the `<body>` tag) that you need for your document to be properly formatted. While it is true that today's browsers will assume that a document is an HTML document, future browsers are under no obligation to do the same! So, to get the correct results, always output as much information as possible.

The final statement calls `document.close()` for the `prodInfo` frame. This closes the output stream and tells the browser that you are finished adding text to the document. The browser will then complete the process of rendering the HTML you've sent to the frame.

Using the frameset document as a control center

On many frames-based Web sites, you'll find that all of the JavaScript code that controls the site is loaded into one frame. This JavaScript code then creates or manipulates the contents of the other frames. Oddly, this JavaScript code is almost always to be found in one of the visible frames on the site. It's a little known fact that you can actually run JavaScript code inside a frameset document. This makes it a perfect "control center" for all of the JavaScript code associated with a site. In fact, many sites actually place their JavaScript code in a "hidden" frame. For example:

```
<frameset rows="100%,0" frameborder="0">
    <frame name="prodInfo" src="welcome.htm" scrolling="yes"
    frameborder="no"></frame>
    <frame name="cart" src="cart.htm" scrolling="yes"
    frameborder="no"></frame>
</frameset>
```

The second frame has a height of zero pixels, so it will be hidden from view. The author of the site could then place all of her JavaScript code into the cart.htm file where it would be a bit safer from prying eyes.

Protecting your JavaScript source code

One of the biggest concerns professional programmers have had about JavaScript is "How can I protect my source code?" Unfortunately, this is almost impossible to do. Since JavaScript is just plain text, it's easy for users to see it simply by using the "View Source" or "View Frame Source" of their Web browser.

Even hiding your code in a hidden frame offers no real protection. A determined user could simply view the source of your frameset document and then load the file specified in the src= attribute of your hidden frame. So, if your JavaScript code is going to contain trade secrets, you should seriously consider rewriting it as a server-side process.

Dealing with Improperly Loaded Frames

10 Min. To Go

One reason some users dislike frames is that, when they bookmark a frames-based site, they often end up bookmarking an individual page from within a frame and not the site itself. However, with the addition of a few lines of JavaScript to each page of a site, this problem is fairly easy to overcome. If I add these lines to the top of the welcome.htm file:

```
if (parent == self) {
    document.location.href = "index.htm";
    }
```

When the page loads, it will check to see if the parent object is equal to the window object that the document is loaded into. If these are equal, you know that there is no frameset present, which means that the welcome.htm file was loaded all by itself. If this is the case, the statement document.location.href = "index.htm"; will force the Web browser to immediately load the index.htm file. This in turn will set the site up appropriately in the browser window.

Of course, if your site is extremely complex, users will want a bookmark to return them directly to the page they were on. They'll also want the other frames of the site to reappear containing the pages that were loaded when the site was bookmarked. This is a bit more difficult to accomplish.

Unfortunately, most browsers only store the Web address of the frameset document when a frames-based Web site is bookmarked. So, perhaps the best way to provide this functionality is to supply a button on your site that, when clicked, will create a cookie detailing which pages are visible in each frame. When the user returns to the site, this cookie can be examined and the proper pages reloaded into the appropriate frames.

Modifying Frame Sizes

The last frame-based trick I'd like to share with you is how to use JavaScript to change the size of the frames that are on the screen. (Note that this trick relies on CSS and at least one nonstandard field of the element object. As such, it only works in the latest versions of Internet Explorer and Netscape Navigator.)

When you go to an e-commerce site, there's usually a shopping cart icon that you can click to view what's in your shopping cart. This usually loads a new page showing the contents of your cart. Then, to go back to what you were doing, you have to hit the back button and wait for the page to reload. Wouldn't it be nice if the shopping cart display could be placed in a hidden frame that, when you wanted to view it, would pop up and then go away when you were through with it? Here's one way you can make this happen.

```
<script language="javascript">
function toggleCart( turnOn) {
    var frameSetElement = parent.document.getElementById(
"bpFrames");
    if (turnOn) {
        frameSetElement.rows = "40%,*";
        }
    else {
        frameSetElement.rows = "100%,*";
        }
    }
</script>
<frameset id="bpFrames" rows="100%,0" frameborder="0">
    <frame id="prodInfo" name="prodInfo" src="bpMenu.htm"
    scrolling="yes" frameborder="no"></frame>
    <frame id="cart" name="cart" src="bpCart.htm" scrolling="yes"
    frameborder="no"></frame>
</frameset>
```

Here I've defined a frameset with two frames in it. However, I've also given it an ID of bpFrames. This ID information is used by the toggleCart() function to either hide or show the second frame based on the Boolean value that's passed to the function. The toggleCart() function itself is very simple. It uses the `getElementById()` method to retrieve the element object that represents the `bpFrames` frameset. It then makes a simple assignment to the `rows` property of the element object. Changing this property actually resizes the frames in the frameset to match the new sizes specified. (Yes, there's also a `cols` property that does exactly the same thing for the columns in a frameset.)

So, if the `turnOn` parameter is `true`, the `rows` property is set to 40%,*, which shrinks the size of the top row to just 40 percent of the visible browser window and lets the second row take up the remaining space. If the `turnOn` parameter is `false`, the `rows` property is set to 100%,0, which expands the top row to completely fill the visible browser window and sets the height of the second row to zero pixels. With this code in place, all I need is a couple of buttons or links that will call the `toggleCart()` function and pass it an appropriate value for the `turnOn` parameter. Assuming that the `toggleCart()` function will be a part of the frameset document, this code might look something like this.

Done!

```
<a href="javascript:parent.toggleCart(true)">Show Cart</a><br />
<a href="javascript:parent.toggleCart(false)">Hide Cart</a>
```

REVIEW

In this session, you learned how JavaScript views frames and how JavaScript statements can be written to work across frame boundaries. You also learned how to dynamically create a new document inside a frame as well as how to make sure that the contents of a frame are completely loaded and parsed. You've also learned how to determine if a page from a frameset has been loaded outside of its frame and how to react to fix that situation. Finally, you learned how to use JavaScript and the element object to dynamically change the size of frames in a frameset.

To tie all of these concepts together I've updated the Baby-Palooza.com shopping cart to work from inside a set of frames. To see this new version, load the index.htm file from the Session23 folder on your CD-ROM. When the page loads, you should only see a single frame. Click the Show Cart link and the shopping cart frame should appear at the bottom of the browser window. After you've played with this a bit, begin browsing through the source code to see how all the concepts from this session fit together with the things you've learned in previous sessions.

QUIZ YOURSELF

1. What is the difference between the top and parent objects? (See "Working with nested frames.")

2. How do frame objects and window objects compare? (See "How JavaScript Views Frames.")

3. What happens if you try to access something in a frame that isn't fully loaded? (See "The timing problem.")

4. What methods do you use to write new content into a frame? (See "Dynamically Creating Frame Content.")

5. How can you create a "hidden" frame in which to place your JavaScript code? (See "Using the frameset document as a control center.")

Working with Windows

Session Checklist

✔ Opening and closing windows with JavaScript

✔ Understanding how JavaScript communicates between windows

✔ Creating content in a different window

**30 Min.
To Go**

A s you've seen throughout this weekend, JavaScript gives you almost complete control over the Web browser. This includes the ability to create your own browser windows and fill them with whatever content you see fit.

Opening a New Browser Window

In Session 8, I briefly introduced you to the window.open() method. This method opens a new browser window and returns the window object that represents it. As mentioned in Session 8, window.open() can take up to four parameters in the following order:

- url: This is the Web address of a Web page that you want to automatically load into the new window.

- name: This is a string that will be placed into the window.name property of the new window.

- `featuresList`: This is a string specifying what features the new window should have. With this parameter, you can specify how big the window should be, if it should have toolbars, scroll bars, and so on. (We'll be discussing these features in the "Using the window features list" section below.)

- `replace`: This is a Boolean value that specifies if the Web address specified in the first parameter should replace the current entry in the Web browser's history list.

Of course, if all you want is a new window with nothing in it, you don't have to pass any parameters to the `window.open()` method at all. For example, the following code will create an empty browser window and assign the object that represents it to a variable:

```
var blankWindow = window.open();
```

On the other hand, if you want your new window to automatically have some content appear in it, you just pass the Web address of the page you want loaded into the window.

```
var hungryMindsSite = window.open( "http://www.hungryminds.com");
```

Giving your window a name

As you saw in Session 8, `window` objects have a `name` property. The second parameter of the `window.open()` method lets you set this property as the window is being created. For example, the following creates an empty window with its `name` property set to "cartWin".

```
var cartWin = window.open( "", "cartWin");
```

Note that you aren't required to give your new window a name when you create it. If you want, you can set it later:

```
var cartWin = window.open(); cartWin.name = "cartWin";
```

In these examples, I've set the `name` property of my new `window` object to be exactly the same as the JavaScript variable name that holds the object. (As you learned in Session 20, this isn't necessary, but it can be helpful when dynamically creating JavaScript code.) Setting the `name` property of the windows you create is completely optional. But, if you plan on having several windows open at once, it's a good idea to name them all, just to help differentiate among them.

Using the window features list

If you only use the first two parameters of the `window.open()` method, the windows you open will all look exactly alike. They'll all have a toolbar, a menu bar, scroll bars, and all the other accoutrements of a standard Web browser. If you want your new window to look a bit different, you have to specify the features you want (and don't want) by using the `featuresList` parameter. The `featuresList` parameter is a string that can contain one or more feature flags. These flags are separated by commas and look something like this:

```
"feature1=yes,feature2=no,feature3=no"
```

Table 24-1, shows each feature flag along with its possible values.

Table 24-1
Feature Flags for Use With the window.open() Method

Flag Name	Possible Values	Usage
directories	yes or no	Specifies if the window should have a set of directory buttons. (In Internet Explorer, this is the Links Bar. In Netscape Navigator, it's the Personal Toolbar.)
height and width	Any positive integer value	Specifies the height and width of the new window in pixels.
location	yes or no	Specifies if the window should have a box that the user can type a Web address into. (In Internet Explorer, this is the Address Bar. In Netscape Navigator, it's the Location Toolbar.)
menubar	yes or no	Specifies if the window should have a main menu bar. (The one containing the File and Edit menus. Note that this will not apply to Macintosh Web browsers.)
resizable	yes or no	Specifies if the user should be able to resize the window or not. (Note that there is no "e" in the middle of "resizable"!)
scrollbars	yes or no	Specifies if the window should have scroll bars.

Continued

Table 24-1   *Continued*

Flag Name	Possible Values	Usage
status	yes or no	Specifies if there should be a status bar at the bottom of the window.
toolbar	yes or no	Specifies if the window should have a main toolbar. (This is the toolbar containing the Forward and Back arrows, the Reload and Stop buttons, and so on.)

So, if I want to create an empty window with a status bar and scroll bars, I would code:

```
var cartWin = window.open( "", "cartWin",
"status=yes,scrollbars=yes");
```

If you execute this code, you'll notice that the window created has *only* a status bar and a scroll bar; none of the other window controls appear at all! This is because, when you specify a featuresList parameter, any features that you don't list are automatically given a value of no. (Except, of course, for the height and width features. If you don't give values for those, the new window will be the same height and/or width as the window that creates it.) So, if you create a window using just the height and width features, like this:

```
var cartWin = window.open( "", "cartWin", "height=100,width=200");
```

All you will get is a small window with a title bar and whatever window controls are provided by the host operating system (such as a close box). This behavior might seem a bit odd at first, but it actually makes the creation of custom windows much easier. This is simply because, when it comes to customized windows, it's usually quicker to list the things you do want rather than all the things you don't want.

**20 Min.
To Go**

Creating Content in a New Window

Once you've got a new window open, you'll probably want to put some content in it. Of course, you could just use the url parameter of the window.open() call to load an HTML document into the new window when it opens. But, if you need to create a custom document in your new window, you might find it easier to rely on document.write() calls.

The process for creating content in a different window is almost exactly the same as the process for creating content in a different frame. The only difference is that instead of going through a parent or top object, you simply go through the window object that represents the new window. For example, if I wanted to create a new window that simply says "Hello World!," the code shown here will do the trick.

```
var greetWin = window.open( "", "greetWin",
"height=100,width=200");
greetWin.document.open();
greetWin.document.write( "<html><body bgcolor='white'>");
greetWin.document.write( "Hello World!");
greetWin.document.write( "</body></html>");
greetWin.document.close();
```

As you can see, this is pretty much the same thing that you saw in the last session. First, I open up my new window and store the object that represents it in the greetWin variable. Next, the greetWin.document.open() call opens a stream into the document object inside the new window. At this point, it's a simple matter of making several document.write() calls to output the content I want to appear in the new window. After that, I call document.close() to cut off the stream and force the content to be shown in the window.

As with frames, it's very important that you remember to write out *everything* that's needed to create a complete HTML document. This includes sets of <html></html> and <body></body> tags as well as any attributes that you want included with those tags.

Communicating between Windows

As you saw in the last session, frame-to-frame communication between JavaScript programs isn't all that difficult. So, given that frames are really just windows, window-to-window communication should be fairly easy as well, right? Well, yes, it is, but there is a small difference. As you've just seen, when one window (which I'll call the "Parent") opens another (which I'll call the "Child"), the Parent window can easily access the methods (and properties and functions and global variables) of the Child window simply by working through the window object it got back from the window.open() method. However, the Child window doesn't have a way to automatically access its Parent window. (In particular, it doesn't have a parent object to work with as a frame would.)

To solve this problem, every `window` object includes an `opener` property (which I briefly discussed in Session 8). If a window was opened by some other window, its `opener` property will contain a `window` object that represents its Parent. By working through the `opener` property, a Child window can access any of the objects, functions, or variables defined in the Parent window. (Of course, if a window was not opened by the `window.open()` call, its `opener` property will be `null`.) The following bit of JavaScript opens a new window and defines a simple function (this is in the listing24-2.htm file).

```
var childWin = window.open( "childWin.htm", "childWin");
function doGreeting( theGreeting) {
    alert( "The kid says: '" + theGreeting + "'");
    }
```

This new window will automatically be loaded with the childWin.htm document:

```
<html>
<head>
<title>Calling a Window's opener</title>
<script language="javascript">
if (self.opener != null) {
    self.opener.doGreeting( "Hello from the new window!");
    }
</script>
</head>
<body>
</body>
</html>
```

If you load the listing24-2.htm file into your Web browser, you'll see the Child window open and then a moment later you'll get an alert saying "The kid says: 'Hello from the new window!'". This shows that, with its `opener` in hand, a Child window can access any of the methods, properties, functions, or global variables that are defined in its Parent.

Solving the timing problem for windows

In Session 23, you learned that if the JavaScript in one frame tries to call a function in another frame and that second frame isn't fully loaded yet, an error could occur. This same timing problem can rear its head when working with multiple windows. If a Parent window tries to call a function or fill in a form field in a Child window before that Child window is fully loaded, you'll probably be rewarded with a "not defined" error. But, since windows and frames are so similar, the solution to this problem is similar as well. Again, I'll assume that there's a function that I need to call in my Child window as soon as possible after the window opens. The following shows the HTML file that will be loaded into my Child window. (This is from the ads.htm file on your CD-ROM.)

```
<html>
<head>
<title>An Ad!</title>
<style type="text/css">
body { background-color:white }
</style>
<script language="javascript">
function showAd() {
    alert("Please support our sponsors!");
    }
</script>
</head>
<body>
This might as well be a pop-up ad!
<form name="dummy">
<input type="hidden" name="dummy" />
</form>
</body>
</html>
```

As with frames, the key to solving this problem is to place a dummy form at the end of the document you are loading. This next bit of JavaScript shows the code from my Parent window that will make sure my Child window is completely loaded.

```
function doAdShow() {
    var tryAgain = true;
    if ( adWin != null) {
        if (adWin.document != null) {
            if (adWin.document.forms.length > 0) {
                adWin.showAd();
                tryAgain = false;
                }
            }
        }
```

```
if (tryAgain) {
    setTimeout( 'doAdShow()', 1000);
    }
  }
var adWin = window.open( "ads.htm", "adWin",
"height=100,width=200");
// Attempt to call a function inside the Child window
doAdShow();
```

Here again, the solution is remarkably similar to the solution for frames. After opening my Child window, I call the doAdShow() function. This function uses a series of if statements to make sure that the window and its document object exist, and that the last form in the window has been loaded and parsed by the JavaScript interpreter. Only when all of these conditions are true does the function actually call the showAd() function inside the Child window. If even one of these conditions is false, the function uses a setTimeout() call to try again one second later.

**10 Min.
To Go**

Using the document.domain property

Thus far, all of the windows you've seen have been able to communicate with one another quite easily. However, there is one situation where JavaScript actually prohibits windows from communicating. If your JavaScript code resides in two HTML documents that come from different servers, the JavaScript in these documents will not be able to communicate. This is done in order to provide a basic level of security for your JavaScript code. After all, you certainly wouldn't want a bit of JavaScript code from "evil-crackers.com" to be able to talk to the JavaScript code on your Web site! The downside to this however, is that even if your code exists in the same domain yet on different servers (such as "www.baby-palooza.com" and "support.baby-palooza.com"), communication is still prohibited. Fortunately, a solution exists in the form of the document.domain property. Initially, this property will hold the domain and subdomain name of the Web server that the HTML document came from. For example, if you were to load "http://www.baby-palooza.com/index.htm" into your Web browser, the document.domain property for this document would be "www.baby-palooza.com."

Now, if a bit of JavaScript code inside this file wanted to open and then communicate with a the contents of the file at "http://support.baby-palooza.com/problemForm. htm," both of these files would need to establish that they were in the same domain before they would be allowed to communicate. (Note that, since I don't know what kind of setup you actually have and since neither "www.baby-palooza.com" or "support.baby-palooza.com" actually exits, I'm just going to give you the code that would be required to pull this off and then you can adapt it to your own network set up.)

In the index.htm file on the "www" server, you might have some code like this:

```
var readyToTalk = false;
var probFormWin = window.open( "http://support.baby-
palooza.com/problemForm.htm", "probFormWin");
self.document.domain = "baby-palooza.com";
```

Then, in the problemForm.htm file (on the "support" server), you might have this:

```
self.document.domain = "baby-palooza.com";
// and then at the bottom of the file . . .
self.opener.readyToTalk = true;
```

The key to this entire process is in the statement

```
self.document.domain = "baby-palooza.com";
```

which appears in both files. This tells the JavaScript interpreter that both of these HTML documents belong to the same domain and should be allowed to communicate. But you're probably thinking, "What's to stop the folks at 'evil-cracker.com' from setting the domain properties of their documents to 'baby-palooza.com'?" Actually, the JavaScript interpreter is what's stopping them! You see the JavaScript interpreter will only let you set the domain property to the domain suffix that the document originated from. So, a document that comes from "www.evil-crackers.com" can only have its domain property set to "evil-crackers.com" and *not* "baby-palooza.com" (or anything else for that matter).

Closing Your Windows

Once you are done with a window, you can either allow the user to close it or you can close it yourself with a call to the window.close() method. Using the window.close() method is fairly straightforward; you call it and the window in question disappears.

- If your JavaScript code creates a Child window and then tries to close it, the Child window should disappear without a fuss.

- If your JavaScript code creates a Child window and then the Child window tries to close itself, this too should work precisely the way you expect.

- If your JavaScript code, running in *any* window, tries to close either its Parent window or the first browser window you opened, you will get a dialog asking you to confirm the closing of the window. This is a security feature designed to prevent malicious JavaScript programs from shutting down a user's Web browser (which means that there's really no way to get around it).

Done!

REVIEW

In this session, you learned how to open new windows with the `window.open()` method. You also learned about all of the different parameters that can be passed to the `window.open()` method to create a window with exactly the features that you want (a menu bar, scroll bars, etc.). You learned that dynamically creating content in a new window is done in almost exactly the same way as with frames. You saw how easy it is, using the `window.opener` property to create two-way communications between Parent and Child windows. This allows the JavaScript in one window to access the objects, functions, and global variables in another window. You learned how HTML documents from different servers are forbidden to talk to one another, unless they have the same value in their `document.domain` properties. Finally, you learned how to close windows using the `window.close()` method.

QUIZ YOURSELF

1. Why give your new windows names? (See "Giving your window a name.")
2. How do you create an empty window? (See "Opening a New Browser Window.")
3. What does the status feature flag determine about your new window? (See "Using the window features list.")
4. What is the `document.domain` property used for? (See "Using the document.domain property.")
5. What happens when a Child window tries to close its Parent window? (See "Closing Your Windows.")

Improving the User Interface

Session Checklist

✔ Using visual cues to improve your user interface

✔ "Disguising" read-only text boxes

✔ Correcting the display of floating-point numbers

**30 Min.
To Go**

The last time I fiddled with my shopping cart (at the end of Session 23), it was very close to being complete. But, even though it doesn't need much more functionality, it could use a few tweaks to make it easier to use. So, in this session, I'm going to show you several ways that you can use JavaScript, HTML, and Cascading Style Sheets (CSS) to make your Web pages easier for your users to understand and use. (As with the other CSS-based tricks I've shown you, not all of the things discussed in this session will currently work with all browsers. However, this should be corrected in future browser releases.)

Using Visual Cues

Today's Web is largely a visual medium. Because of this, and the fact that the most popular operating systems are graphics-based, users have become a bit lazy, expecting the way things work to be obvious with just a glance. (Of course, all Web pages work in pretty much the same way, but it's still quite easy to create a Web site that can confuse even the most veteran of users.)

Highlighting your links

One of the most fundamental things you can do for your users is to make sure that they can tell what is a link and what isn't. By convention, a Web browser will underline a link and draw it in a color that's different from the surrounding text. However, if you have a bit of ordinary text that you want to underline, this can still lead to some confusion on the part of the user. Fortunately, CSS makes it easy to set up your links so that they will change color when the mouse passes over them. This creates a simple visual cue for users that tells them that the text in question is a link they can click. To set this up, all you have to do is define a CSS rule like this:

```
a:hover { color:red }
```

With this rule, you're telling the browser that, when the mouse hovers over a set of <a></a> tags, it should change the color of the text inside to red. While this is fairly obvious, the :hover designation is something that you haven't seen before. It's not a class definition, and it's not an ID definition, so what is it?

Well, the : in this rule marks it as a CSS *pseudoclass*. CSS pseudoclasses can be thought of as "convenience" classes. They represent common situations where you might want to change the appearance of an element. In this case, I'm changing the appearance of a link when the mouse hovers over it. (If you think this sounds like an image rollover as seen in Session 14, you are right, except the whole thing is managed by CSS and the browser.)

There are several other CSS pseudoclasses. However, as I write this, the current crop of browsers supports only a handful of them. For more on these other pseudoclasses, be sure to visit the CSS documentation page at www.w3.org/TR/REC-CSS2/.

Emulating :hover with JavaScript

According to the CSS documentation, the :hover pseudoclass will, one day, work with any HTML element. As of right now though, it only seems to work with <a></a> tags. This is unfortunate because the hover effect is a great way to let users know that what they have the mouse over is actually a control of some sort.

In fact, it's such a good user interface tool, that it's worth a little time and JavaScript to emulate it for the other elements on a Web page. For example, in my shopping cart, it would be nice if the + and - controls became highlighted when the mouse hovered over them.

Because these controls are implemented as images, one of the few ways I can highlight them (without drawing new images and creating a rollover) is to draw a border around them as the mouse passes over. You might remember however, that I defined these images without borders in my HTML document. So, the first thing I have to do is change my <img> tags so that they have borders. Of course, if I change the <img> tag directly, I'll end up with black borders that show up all the time. So, instead of changing the <img> tag for each of my controls, I'll define a CSS class like this:

```
img.button { border-style:solid;border-color:white;border-
width:1px }
```

Then, I can change my <img> tag definitions to make use of this class, like so:

```
<img name='plus_st-001' src='../images/plus.jpg' class='button' />
```

(Note that I've omitted most of the contents of the <img> tag to save space.) This will create a class of images that all have a solid, white border that's one pixel wide. (And, because my background color is also white, this border will be effectively invisible. Of course, you *could* use DHTML to add a border on the fly. But, if you do this, your images will jump up and down on the page as the border is added and taken away by your DHTML code. You get a much nicer effect if you start with an invisible border.)

At this point, it's a simple matter of creating a rollover effect similar to the one that you saw in Session 14. However, instead of swapping images, this rollover effect will actually be changing the style applied to my element. Since this is a bit more complex than an image swap, I'm going to define a couple of new methods to handle the effect.

```
// This method highlights an element by turning its border red
function shopCart_doHilightBorder( theID) {
    var theElement = document.getElementById( theID);
    theElement.style.borderColor = "red";
    }
// This method removes the border highlight from an element
function shopCart_doDimBorder( theID) {
    var theElement = document.getElementById( theID);
    theElement.style.borderColor = "white";
    }
```

As you can see, each of these methods takes an element ID string and uses it to retrieve the element object for that ID. It then sets the borderColor property of that element's style to either red or white, depending on whether or not the element is being highlighted or dimmed. Of course, I still need to tie these methods to my image controls. As always, simply specifying the proper event handlers does this.

```
<img name='plus_st-001' src='../images/plus.jpg' class='button'
onmouseover="bpCart.hilightBorder('plus_st-001')"
onmouseout="bpCart.dimBorder('plus_st-001')" />
```

With this code in place for all of my + and - controls, moving the mouse over any of these controls will result in the control being highlighted with a red border. When the mouse moves away, the border color will become white and the highlight will disappear.

If you are using a Macintosh or Netscape 6, you might find that this code generates errors when you pass the mouse over the + and - controls. You'll learn how to work around this in the next session.

**20 Min.
To Go**

Visual cues for text boxes

While the JavaScript-based hover effect shown above can be used for any type of element, it's especially useful for text boxes. You can even use the same code that you just saw. All you have to do is define the appropriate event handlers as shown here. (Again, I've left out some of the tag's code to save space and focus on the relevant bits.)

```
<input type='text' id='inCart_st-001' name='inCart_st-001'
onmouseover="bpCart.hilightBorder('inCart_st-001')"
onmouseout="bpCart.dimBorder('inCart_st-001')"
value='0' size='6' />
```

With these handlers in place, my "inCart" text boxes will be highlighted in red as the mouse moves over them. (Remember, text boxes already have a border around them, so there's no need for a special CSS rule.)

Highlighting the active text box

Another CSS pseudoclass that doesn't seem to work at the moment is the :focus pseudoclass. This class lets you determine how an element should look when it has the focus. This is another very useful pseudoclass, so, once again, a little

JavaScript will allow me to emulate it until the browser world catches up to the standard. The next bit of code shows two new methods that I've defined for the shopping cart object. These let me change the style of a text box that currently has the focus.

```
function shopCart_doFocusInCart( partNo) {
    var tFieldElement = document.getElementById( 'inCart_' +
    partNo);
    tFieldElement.style.borderStyle = "ridge";
    tFieldElement.style.backgroundColor = "#dddddd";
    eval( "document." + this.cartForm + ".elements['inCart_" +
        partNo + "'].select()");
    }
function shopCart_doBlurInCart( partNo) {
    var tFieldElement = document.getElementById( 'inCart_' +
    partNo);
    tFieldElement.style.borderStyle = "inset";
    tFieldElement.style.backgroundColor = "white";
    }
```

And here is the definition of a text box that uses these methods, along with the highlighting methods discussed earlier.

```
<input type='text' id='inCart_st-001' name='inCart_st-001'
onfocus='bpCart.focusInCart("st-001")'
onblur='bpCart.blurInCart("st-001")'
onmouseover="bpCart.hilightBorder('inCart_st-001')"
onmouseout="bpCart.dimBorder('inCart_st-001')"
onchange='bpCart.enterQuantity("st-001")'
value='0' size='6' />
```

When this text box gets the focus, the focusInCart() method will change the border style of the text box to a value of ridge. This will give the text box a slightly raised appearance. Then it will change the background color to #dddddd. This is a fairly light gray color that will show that the box has the focus, without overpowering the text in the box.

Finally, the focusInCart() method uses the eval() function to call the select() method of the text box. This method selects all of the text in the text box. So, when the user begins to type, what she types will automatically replace the previous contents of the box.

When the text box loses the focus, the blurInCart() method will reset the border style of the text box back to inset and then change the box's background color back to white. Of course, you can modify this handler to apply whatever styles you wish to your text boxes.

Eliminating visual cues from read-only text boxes

As it stands now, there is one *very* confusing aspect to my shopping cart: Some text boxes can be typed in and some can't. Specifically, users can type into the Quantity Ordered boxes, but they can't type into the Quantity On Hand or Grand Total boxes.

As you saw in Session 22, it *is* possible to use JavaScript and DHTML to completely remove these text boxes from the screen and replace them with sets of <span></span> tags that could be updated to reflect new totals. However, this would be a lot of work to do something that text boxes already do very well: display text.

Instead of removing the text boxes, why not simply remove the visual cues that tell the user that they *are* text boxes? Thanks to years of conditioning, most users recognize a text box from three simple visual cues: a flashing insertion point (when the text box has the focus), an I-beam cursor (when the mouse is over a text box), and a distinctive border. Take these cues away, and most users will never know that they are looking at a text box.

The insertion point is already taken care of. If you'll remember, back in Session 15, you saw how the onfocus event (and the focus() method) could be used to keep the insertion point from ever landing in a text box that you wanted to write-protect.

Taking care of the last two cues is even easier. Both the I-beam cursor and the distinctive text box border can be eliminated simply by defining an appropriate CSS class and then applying it to the text boxes you want. For example, here's the CSS class definition.

```
input.noEdit { border-style:none; cursor:default }
```

And here's the definition of a text box that belongs to this class.

```
<input type='text' class='noEdit' name='quan_st-001'
onfocus="document.bpCart_form.elements['inCart_st-001'].focus()"
value='5' size='6' />
```

The only thing new here is the cursor part of my CSS class. The cursor rule tells the browser what kind of mouse pointer to display when the mouse is over an element. In this case, I've told it to use the default pointer, which, in most operating systems, is a standard arrow pointer. (Other values that you can use for cursor include: `crosshair`, `wait`, and `help`. You can even define your own cursors and have the browser use those!) So, when the browser draws text boxes of this class, they will have no border and when the mouse passes over them, the pointer won't change into an I-beam. However, since these are still text boxes, you can still change their values with a simple JavaScript statement. Figure 25-1 shows how this appears in the browser window.

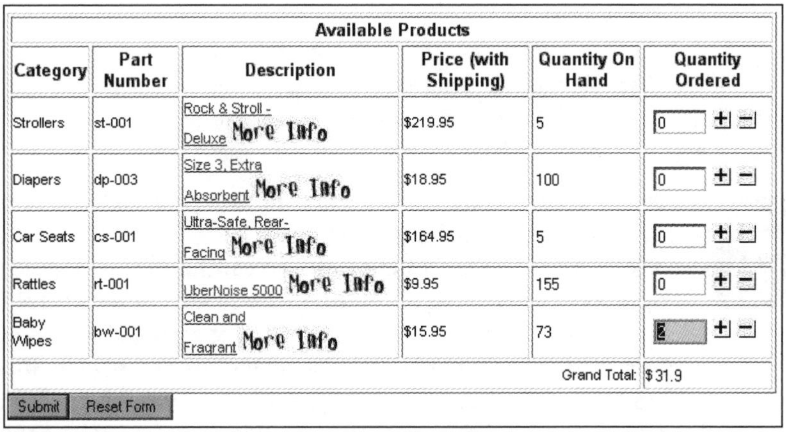

Available Products					
Category	Part Number	Description	Price (with Shipping)	Quantity On Hand	Quantity Ordered
Strollers	st-001	Rock & Stroll - Deluxe More Info	$219.95	5	0 + −
Diapers	dp-003	Size 3, Extra Absorbent More Info	$18.95	100	0 + −
Car Seats	cs-001	Ultra-Safe, Rear-Facing More Info	$164.95	5	0 + −
Rattles	rt-001	UberNoise 5000 More Info	$9.95	155	0 + −
Baby Wipes	bw-001	Clean and Fragrant More Info	$15.95	73	2 + −
				Grand Total:	$31.9

Submit Reset Form

Figure 25-1
Text boxes without borders

Using the status bar

If you have a Web page that's full of links, controls, and images, it's a good bet that even the savviest of users may have some trouble figuring out what everything does. So, it's become a fairly standard practice to give users a clue via a short message in the status bar at the bottom of the browser. (Yes, you've seen this before, but it's such an important technique, I wanted to include it here as well.) For example, in Session 23, I defined a couple of links to show and hide the frame that contains my shopping cart. Those links looked like this:

```
<a href="javascript:parent.toggleCart(true)">Show Cart</a>
<a href="javascript:parent.toggleCart(false)">Hide Cart</a>
```

If you held the mouse over one of these links, you'd see the status bar change to display the actual JavaScript statement that will be executed when the link is clicked. While this is extremely detailed information about what the link does, it isn't in the friendliest form.

The solution is to use an `onmouseover` event handler to change the contents of the status bar to something a bit more descriptive.

```
<a href="javascript:parent.toggleCart(true)"
onmouseover="window.status='View your shopping cart...';return
true;">Show Cart</a>
<a href="javascript:parent.toggleCart(false)"
onmouseover="window.status='Hide your shopping cart...';return
true;">Hide Cart</a>
```

Now, when the mouse enters one of these links, the status bar will be changed to display a nice friendly message that tells the user exactly what will happen when they click the link. (Don't forget to add the `return true;` statement to the end of your event handler. Without it, your custom message won't appear!)

One of the more annoying aspects of using a complex Web page with lots of controls is the way the tab key works. By default, the Web browser will tab from control to control in the order that the controls were defined in the HTML document. Unfortunately, this might not match the way the controls are arranged on the screen. This can lead to lots of confusion as the user repeatedly hits the tab key only to have the focus jump to a control on a completely different part of the page. To solve this problem, HTML controls can be given a `tabIndex` attribute. This attribute lets you specify the order that you want the controls on your page to be accessed via the tab key. Simply give the first control a `tabIndex` of 1, the second a `tabIndex` of 2, and so on. If there are any controls that you want the tab key to skip over, give them a `tabIndex` of 0.

**10 Min.
To Go**

Correcting the Display of Floating-Point Numbers

If you haven't noticed by now, there's something seriously wrong with the way my shopping cart displays floating-point numbers. If you haven't caught it yet, take a good look at the grand total shown in Figure 25-1. According to my calculations, the value displayed should be $50.85. However, what I've got showing is $50.8499999.

Believe it or not, this value is actually correct; at least as far as JavaScript is concerned. You see, JavaScript stores numbers internally in binary (base 2) format. While binary is great for storing integers, it's slightly less adept at representing floating-point values. Because of this, the simple act of adding a couple of float-ing-point numbers together can lead to errors like the one you see here.

It's *very* important to note that, internally, the value calculated will be correct. In other words, this problem will *not* affect any floating-point calculations that you perform in your JavaScript program. The only thing that's affected is the *display* of floating point numbers.

Unfortunately, the only real fix for this problem is to write a custom function that will truncate floating-point numbers to an appropriate number of digits before they are displayed. On the plus side, once you've got this function written, you can use it for all of the floating-point numbers you want to display. You'll find the following function in the floatingPoint.js file on your CD-ROM:

```
function twoDecimals( theNum) {
    var result = "";
    // Change the number to a string for manipulation
    var fpString = theNum + "";
    // find the decimal point
    var decimalAt = fpString.indexOf( ".");
    // if there is no decimal point, add one along with two zeroes
    if (decimalAt == -1) {
        result = fpString + ".00";
        }
    else {
        // pull off the fractional part
        var frac = fpString.substring( decimalAt);
        // multipy it by 100
        frac = parseFloat( frac) * 100;
        // Round this new number off
        frac = Math.round( frac);
        // and use it to rebuild our two decimal places
        // and return the result
        var wholeNum = fpString.substring( 0, decimalAt)
        result = wholeNum + "." + frac;
        }
    return result;
    }
```

In this listing, I've defined a simple function that accepts a floating-point num-ber and returns it rounded to two decimal places. The function starts by changing the number into a string (by concatenating it with the empty string). At that point, the indexOf( ) method is used to determine if there is already a decimal point in the string. If there isn't, the function simply appends a decimal place and two zeros to the end of the string and returns that as its result.

If there *is* a decimal point, things get a bit more interesting. First, the fractional part of the number (along with the decimal place) is stripped off and stored in the frac variable. I then use the parseFloat( ) function to convert the string in frac into an actual floating-point number. As you can see, the parseFloat( ) function does for floating-point numbers what the parseInt( ) function (discussed in Session 15) does for integer numbers. However, unlike the parseInt( ) function, there is no base parameter to worry with; the parseFloat( ) function only accepts decimal values.

This new floating-point value is then multiplied by 100. This effectively shifts the decimal place two digits to the right. So, if frac was originally ".84999999994" it will now be "84.999999994".

I can now use the Math.round( ) method to round this to the nearest whole number (in the above example that would be "85"). As you might guess, the Math object is an object that's built into JavaScript. It provides various and sundry mathematical constants and methods that you can use to manipulate numbers in your JavaScript program. (I'll be discussing this object in more detail in Session 27.) Unfortunately, the Math object does not include a method that lets you round a floating-point number to a certain number of decimal places. So, you have to resort to trickery like what's shown here to get a properly rounded floating-point number.

Once I have my fractional part correctly rounded, I simply reattach it to the whole number portion of my original number and return this result to whoever called the function. In the case of my shopping cart, the who that will call this function will be the shopCart.calcGrandTotal( ) method. Fortunately, only one line has to change in this method to support this function:

```
eval( "document." + this.cartForm + ".elements['grandTotal'].value
= twoDecimals( grandTotal)");
```

Done!

With this code in place, my shopping cart will now calculate and display all of its floating-point values correctly.

REVIEW

In this session, you saw how easy it is to use JavaScript and CSS to add visual cues to your Web site. If used properly, these cues can help visitors to your Web site understand and use it more effectively. One group of visual cues you learned about was the CSS pseudoclasses. While these don't yet work in all browsers, you saw that JavaScript can be used to emulate some of the more useful of these pseudo-classes. You also learned how CSS can be used to remove visual cues from certain elements on the page (in this case, text boxes) to keep your users focused on only those elements that they can actually interact with. You revisited the process of displaying helpful information in the browser's status bar. Finally, you learned about the problem JavaScript has with displaying certain floating-point numbers and how to correct it.

As you can see, learning to use JavaScript effectively in your Web pages isn't just about learning JavaScript. More often than not, you need to be able to mix and match various technologies to achieve the effect you want. So, take a few moments to review all of the source code in the Session25 folder of your CD-ROM to see how all of these different things come together to create what you've seen in this session.

QUIZ YOURSELF

1. What does :hover represent? (See "Highlighting your links.")

2. How can you emulate the :hover pseudoclass with JavaScript? (See "Emulating :hover with JavaScript.")

3. What does :focus do? (See "Highlighting the active text box.")

4. What does the CSS cursor rule allow you to change? (See "Eliminating visual cues from read-only text boxes.")

5. How do you correct JavaScript's floating-point display problem? (See "Correcting the Display of Floating-Point Numbers.")

Working with Different Browsers

Session Checklist

✔ Detecting different browser brands and versions

✔ Requiring a specific version of JavaScript from the client web browser

✔ Hiding JavaScript code from incompatible browsers

**30 Min.
To Go**

Almost everything I've shown you thus far has been "browser agnostic." That is to say, it should work in both of the major Web browsers without modification. (Everything you've seen so far should work in *any* browser that supports the ECMAScript, DOM Level 2, and CSS Level 2 standards.) While this is the way life *should* be, it hasn't always been so nice. Until recently, writing JavaScript that did something useful, worked in both browsers, and only required one version of your code was nearly impossible. Although this has changed dramatically for the better, there still may be an occasion when you need to create a JavaScript program that's tailored to one browser or another.

Properties of the navigator Object

The key to creating a JavaScript program that targets one browser or another is the window.navigator object. This object (which takes its name from the original

Netscape Navigator product) contains everything you need to determine which browser brand and version your program is executing in. Using the `navigator` object is actually pretty simple. You just look at the contents of one or more of the `navigator` object's properties to determine the browser brand and version. Then, based on that information, you execute the code that you know will work in that browser.

The catch to this rather simple process is that, rather than following a strict format for storing information in the `navigator` object, each browser vendor stores its data in a slightly different format. So, while you *know* that you can determine the browser version from the `navigator` object, *how* you make that determination is different for each browser. Before I actually show you how to pull this information from the `navigator` object, let me give you a quick rundown of its more useful properties. (Yes, there are other properties in the `navigator` object, but they are usually specific to one browser or another.)

The appCodeName property

Programmers love code names. I suppose it's because they make us feel like secret agents instead of the geeks we really are. Regardless of why, almost every computer program ever developed has had a code name. So, the `navigator` object contains an `appCodeName` property that is supposed to contain the code name that the browser was developed under. This is a simple String object, so it's very easy to examine and use.

While this property might seem to be a great way to determine which browser you are using, it isn't. You see, when Microsoft entered the browser market, they wanted to make sure their browser was as compatible as possible with Netscape Navigator (then the market leader). Unfortunately, a lot of scripts at the time relied on the value that they found in the `appCodeName` property. So, in order to break as few scripts as possible, all versions of Internet Explorer return exactly the same `appCodeName` as Netscape Navigator does: Mozilla. (Mozilla is the name of the original graphical Web browser. Almost every Web browser that has followed is based on it in one way or another. Mozilla is still being worked on to this day, and a great many people prefer it to the big-name browsers. To get a copy, visit the Mozilla organization's home page at `www.mozilla.org`.)

The appName property

While the `appCodeName` property isn't of much use at all, the `appName` property is very useful indeed. If you examine it in a Netscape browser, you get back

"Netscape." If you examine it in Microsoft's browser, you get back "Microsoft Internet Explorer." Here again, this is a simple String object, so you can examine its contents easily:

The appVersion property

This is perhaps the most important property in the `navigator` object. As the name implies, it tells you what the version number is for the browser that your code is executing in. Unfortunately, how you interpret this information depends on which browser you are dealing with. I'll be discussing this process in great detail in the section "Determining the Browser Version." While you might expect this property to be a simple numeric value, it's actually a String object.

The cookieEnabled property

This is a simple Boolean value that lets you determine whether or not cookies are enabled in the browser. This property is new to the latest versions of the major Web browsers, so if you need to check cookie availability in an older browser, don't rely on the existence of this property. (See the `cookiesActive()` function in the cookies.js file for an example of how to check for cookie availability.)

The language and userLanguage properties

These properties can tell you which language a visitor to your site has her Web browser set up to display. Note that the `language` property is only found in Netscape browsers while the `userLanguage` property is only found in Internet Explorer. You can check for the existence of one property or the other simply by comparing it to `null`. (This is similar to the trick used in Session 23 to determine if a frame's contents were loaded.)

```
if (navigator.language != null) {
    // work with Netscape language information
    }
if (navigator.userLanguage != null) {
    // work with Internet Explorer language information
    }
```

The mimeTypes array

This array contains a list of all the MIME types that are known to the client's computer. MIME stands for Multipurpose Internet Mail Extensions. Originally, MIME types were used to identify the types of data that were included in e-mail attachments. This array is closely linked with the plugins array, which is mentioned later in this session. You'll be learning much more about MIME types in Session 29, when you learn how to identify and use browser plug-ins and multimedia.

The platform property

In Session 21, you learned that the navigator.platform property contains a String object that tells you which computer platform the browser is running on. You can use this value to provide platform specific content for your visitors or to direct them to a site devoted to their computer platform. For an example of one way to use this property, see "Deciding Which Style Sheet to Use" in Session 21.

The plugins array

The plugins array contains a list of all of the plug-ins that are installed in the client's Web browser. If you need to display a particular type of multimedia file (like an Acrobat PDF file or a QuickTime Movie) in the Web browser, you can search this array to see if the user has an appropriate plug-in installed. The plugins array is closely linked with the mimeTypes array (mentioned earlier), so you'll be hearing more about both of them in Session 29 when you learn about multimedia.

The userAgent property

Traditionally, this property has simply contained a combination of the appCodeName and appVersion properties, with the two values separated by a forward-slash /. However, the Netscape 6 browser now includes some additional information dealing with its HTML rendering engine (which is named Gecko). (This information is also found in two Netscape 6-specific properties: navigator.product and navigator.productSub. At this point it's unclear how you might use this information, but it's in there if the need should arise.)

Determining the Browser Version

Looking at the properties of the `navigator` object, you might be thinking, "Gosh, it looks like determining the browser version is simple!" Well, it certainly *should* be. But, as I said earlier, each of the browser vendors stores their version information in a slightly different format. So, while it is very simple to determine which browser you are using (via the `appName` property) and which platform your code is running on (via the `platform` property) getting down to the browser version is a little tricky. For example, here is the value of `navigator.appVersion` from Netscape Navigator 6 on the Macintosh.

```
5.0 (Macintosh; en-US)
```

And here is the value of `navigator.appVersion` from Internet Explorer 5 on the Macintosh.

```
4.0 (compatible; MSIE 5.0; Macintosh; I; PPC)
```

Extracting Netscape version information

The Netscape information is fairly straightforward: it's the actual version number of the browser (remember, there never was an official Netscape 5 release, but the internal version for Netscape 6 is actually 5.0), followed in parentheses by platform and language information. So, extracting the version number from this information is actually pretty simple, as shown here:

```
var versionNum = "";
if (navigator.appName == "Netscape") {
    var fParen = navigator.appVersion.indexOf( "(");
    if (fParen != -1) {
        versionNum = navigator.appVersion.substring( 0, fParen);
        versionNum = parseFloat( versionNum, 10);
        }
    else {
        document.write( "Could not determine version number!<br
        />");
        document.write( "The appVersion property contains:<br
        />");
        document.write( navigator.appVersion);
        }
```

```
   }
else {
   document.write( "This is not a Netscape Browser!");
   }
if (versionNum != "") {
   document.write( "You are using version " + versionNum + " of "
      + navigator.appName);
   }
```

As you can see, this is pretty simple. After checking to see that this is indeed a Netscape browser, the code finds the location of the first parenthesis in the appVersion property. This location is then used by the substring() method to extract the actual version number. But, before substring() is called, the code checks to make sure that the first parenthesis was really found. If it wasn't, the code displays an error message telling the user that the version number of the browser could not be obtained. (It's important to check for this because, while rare, it *is* possible to change the information in the appVersion property with browser-customization software. So, it's a good idea to make sure the version information is in the proper format before you base any decisions on that information.)

Extracting Internet Explorer version information

Now that you know how to get the version information from a Netscape browser, it probably seems like a pretty simple task to extract the same information from Internet Explorer. Well, let's take another look at what you actually get from the appVersion property for Internet Explorer 5 on the Macintosh:

```
4.0 (compatible; MSIE 5.0; Macintosh; I; PPC)
```

As you can see here, the version number is 4.0. But, unlike Netscape, Internet Explorer didn't skip a version number so this *should* be version 5.0, right? Right.

What you are seeing here is another example of how Microsoft wanted Internet Explorer to be as compatible with Netscape as possible. So, the first version number in Internet Explorer's appVersion property is the version number of *Netscape* that this version of Internet Explorer is compatible with! In other words, this is telling you that this browser is *compatible* with Netscape version 4.0. How then, do you tell which version of Internet Explorer this is? Well, it's actually pretty easy once you know where to look.

If you'll notice, right in the middle of this appVersion value is the string "MSIE 5.0." *This* is what tells you which version of Internet Explorer you are dealing with. While this information is buried inside the appVersion property, it *always* starts with the characters "MSIE" (which stands for "Microsoft Internet Explorer"), so it's actually pretty easy get:

```
var versionNum = "";
if (navigator.appName == "Microsoft Internet Explorer") {
    var msieFlag = navigator.appVersion.indexOf( "MSIE");
    if (msieFlag != -1) {
        var msieVersionEnd = navigator.appVersion.indexOf( ";",
        msieFlag);
        versionNum = navigator.appVersion.substring( msieFlag + 4,
        msieVersionEnd);
        versionNum = parseFloat( versionNum);
        }
    else {
        document.write( "Could not find version number!<br />");
        document.write( "The appVersion property is:<br />");
        document.write( navigator.appVersion);
        }
    }
else {
    document.write( "This is not Microsoft Internet Explorer!");
    }
if (versionNum != "") {
    document.write( "You are using version " + versionNum + " of "
        + navigator.appName);
    }
```

This is almost exactly the same process as determining a Netscape version number. The only real difference is that you have to pull a string from the middle of the appVersion property rather than from its start.

Requiring a Certain Browser Version

If you create a Web site that uses some of the newer features of JavaScript or Cascading Style Sheets or even HTML, you will need to know when an incompatible browser comes a-calling. The choices here are the same as when you learned about cookie support in Session 16. If the client's browser doesn't support the features your site needs, you can either block them from using the site entirely or you can redirect them to a more appropriate version of your site.

Consider, for example, the site that I've been building throughout this book. While it might seem fairly simple to someone that's been reading along (at least I hope it does), it actually relies quite heavily on many tricks that are only available in the latest versions of the major Web browsers. So, if the site gets visitors who are using older browsers, rather than generate a bunch of errors, the polite thing to do is to tell them that they need to update their browser and provide them with the links to do so. With that in mind, I've created a set of functions that can be used to determine which browser, browser version, and platform my JavaScript code is executing in. These functions can all be found in the browserSnoop.js file which is in the Session26 folder on your CD-ROM. You've actually already seen (at one time or another) the code for all of the functions in this file, so in Table 26-1, you'll find a brief rundown of each function and what it does.

Table 26-1
The Functions Defined in browserSnoop.js

Function Name	Purpose
isNetscape()	Returns true if current browser is Netscape.
isIE()	Returns true if current browser is Internet Explorer.
getNetscapeVersion()	Returns the version of a Netscape browser. (If used with Internet Explorer, it returns the version of Netscape that the browser is compatible with.)
getIEversion()	Returns the version of an Internet Explorer browser.
isMac()	Returns true if the browser is running on a Macintosh.
isWin()	Returns true if the browser is running on a Windows PC.
isLinux()	Returns true if the browser is running on a Linux box.

By using these functions together, you can easily determine what type of browser your JavaScript code is executing in and generate the content that is appropriate. As I said earlier, for the Baby-Palooza site, I want to tell users of older browsers that their browser isn't compatible and give them links to download the latest browsers. So, I've placed this functionality into the index.htm file that's in the Session26 folder on your CD-ROM. This code is a bit long, so open it up in your HTML editor and take a quick look at it. At first this code might look complicated, but if you study it for a bit, you'll see that there really isn't anything to this. A series of simple if statements determines if the current browser is either Netscape version 6+ (by checking for a version number of 5 or greater) or Internet Explorer version 5+. If so, the variable `browserOK` is set to `true`. A final `if` statement uses the value of this variable to decide whether it should write out the `<frameset></frameset>` tags that will create the Web site or a simple "your browser is incompatible" document.

10 Min.
To Go

Creating Code for Specific Browsers

Even if you have the proper version of a browser, that browser still might not be able to support everything that you want it to do. For example, in the last session, I added a highlight outline to the + and - buttons in the shopping cart. I also included a rather cryptic note that, on the Macintosh and with this highlighting code in place, moving the mouse over those buttons might cause errors. The reason for this is, while this code works perfectly in Internet Explorer v5.5 on Windows, it doesn't work in Internet Explorer v5 for the Macintosh. It also doesn't work in Netscape 6! While the errors that are generated aren't fatal, they certainly don't look good.

Fortunately, once you know how to check the browser version and platform, it's incredibly easy to create code that only works in certain browsers. For example, here's the code from the last session that's causing the trouble.

```
// This method highlights an element by turning its border red
function shopCart_doHilightBorder( theID) {
    var theElement = document.getElementById( theID);
    theElement.style.borderColor = "red";
    }
// This method removes the border highlight from an element
function shopCart_doDimBorder( theID) {
    var theElement = document.getElementById( theID);
    theElement.style.borderColor = "white";
    }
```

There actually isn't anything terribly wrong with the code itself. It *does* work when you use it to highlight the border around a text box, but in Netscape 6 and Internet Explorer 5 for the Macintosh, it simply won't work for images. The reason is, these browsers don't supply a style object for Image elements. So, you simply can't set the border color for an image in this way. (With luck, this will be fixed when these browsers become more CSS compliant.) The fix for this is very simple: If the current browser isn't Internet Explorer v5 or later on Windows, don't even

attempt either of these operations. So, you just have to add a simple if statement, like this:

```
// This method highlights an element by turning its border red
function shopCart_doHilightBorder( theID) {
    if (isWin() && isIE()) {
        var theElement = document.getElementById( theID);
        theElement.style.borderColor = "red";
        }
    }
// This method removes the border highlight from an element
function shopCart_doDimBorder( theID) {
    if (isWin() && isIE()) {
        var theElement = document.getElementById( theID);
        theElement.style.borderColor = "white";
        }
    }
```

If you are wondering why I didn't check the browser version, remember that I
checked the this when the user first came to the site. If they didn't have the
appropriate browser version, they would never even see the shopping cart, let
alone get this far!

Requiring JavaScript

At this point, you know how to use JavaScript to require a certain brand and version of browser for your Web site. But, what if JavaScript itself isn't available? Yes,
as ghastly as it seems, there actually are browsers out there that don't support
JavaScript. Worse yet, some JavaScript-capable browsers will let a user turn
JavaScript support completely off!

Fortunately, there's a simple way to handle this situation: the <noscript>
</noscript> tags. Simply place a set of these tags in the first page of your Web
site and any non-JavaScript-capable browsers that load that page will display
whatever is inside the tags. (JavaScript-capable browsers, on the other hand, will
ignore these tags and their contents.) For the Baby-Palooza site, I might want to
include the following:

```
<noscript>
<body>
<h1><img src='../images/sadBaby.jpg' alt='Sad Baby'>
```

```
Welcome to Baby-Palooza!
<img src='../images/sadBaby2.jpg' alt='Sad Baby'></h1>
<span id='badBrowser'>Unfortunately, your browser
is not compatible with the Baby-Palooza Web site.
<br />This site requires either Netscape Navigator
v6+ or Internet Explorer v5+.<br />You can find
these browsers by clicking on one of the following links<br />
<br /><a href='http://www.microsoft.com/windows/ie'>
Get Internet Explorer</a><br />
<a href='http://www.netscape.com/download'>
Get Netscape Navigator</a></span>
</body>
</noscript>
```

Using this code, when a JavaScript-incapable browser, or a browser with JavaScript support turned off, visits my site, the HTML between the `<noscript></noscript>` tags will be displayed telling the user that he needs to upgrade his browser.

Hiding JavaScript from Older Browsers

While it's nice to be able to require that a browser support JavaScript, more often than not, you'll probably find yourself in the situation where you've got a page that's enhanced by JavaScript, but JavaScript isn't essential to the operation of the page. In this case, it's silly to lock a user out of your site simply because the client's browser doesn't support JavaScript. However, if such a user does come to your site, your JavaScript code may well show up in the final output of your page unless you hide it from the browser. This is due to the way that most HTML rendering engines handle tags that they don't support. When an HTML rendering engine encounters a tag it doesn't support, it discards the tag, but it displays the text inside the tag using the default characteristics (font, size, and so forth) for the page.

So, if an older browser encounters a set of `<script></script>` tags, and it doesn't know what they are, it will simply discard the tags, and display the JavaScript inside as if it was regular text, which it is! The solution to this problem is extremely simple: wrap your JavaScript code in a set of HTML comment tags. So, the following block of code:

```
<script language="javascript">
alert( "Welcome to Baby-Palooza!");
</script>
```

Would become this:

```
<script language="javascript">
<!--
alert( "Welcome to Baby-Palooza!");
// -->
</script>
```

When an older HTML rendering engine gets hold of this, it will discard the <script></script> tags and then, thanks to the HTML comment markers, ignore all of the JavaScript code inside. A JavaScript-capable browser, however, is smart enough to know about this trick, so it will ignore the HTML comments and just execute the JavaScript.

Requiring a Particular JavaScript Version

Finally, there's the situation where you need to make sure that the client's browser is running a particular version of JavaScript. Of course, the latest big-name browsers run the very latest version of the JavaScript language, so they include all of the language features that you've seen in this book. Older browsers however, run older versions of JavaScript and those versions are missing such nice things as Arrays (added in JavaScript version 1.1), Image objects (also added in JavaScript version 1.1), and the screen object (added in JavaScript version 1.2).

To require a particular version of JavaScript, you simply specify the version you need in the language attribute of your <script> tag. For example:

```
<script language="javascript1.2">
alert( "Your screen is " + screen.width + "pixels wide.");
</script>
```

Done!

By specifying a JavaScript version in this way you are telling the browser, "If JavaScript version 1.2 or later isn't available in this browser, don't execute this block of code."

REVIEW

In this session, you learned about the navigator object and how to use it along with JavaScript to determine which brand and version of a browser is executing your JavaScript program. You also saw how to use that information to write programs that work around features that may be missing from a particular browser.

You learned how to create an initial page for your site that would check the browser version and, if necessary, present users with a message telling them that they need to upgrade their browsers in order to use your site. You saw how the `<noscript></noscript>` tags can be used to weed out browsers that don't support JavaScript. You also learned how to hide JavaScript code from older browsers by using HTML comment tags. Finally, you learned how the `language=` attribute of the `<script>` tag can be used to tell the browser that a certain version of JavaScript is required to run the code in a particular script block.

QUIZ YOURSELF

1. What does the `navigator.appCodeName` property contain? Why is it somewhat less than useful? (See "The appCodeName property.")

2. How is version information stored in the `navigator.appVersion` property? (See "Determining the Browser Version.")

3. What does the first version number in the `navigator.appVersion` property of an Internet Explorer browser represent? (See "Extracting Internet Explorer version information.")

4. How can you use browser version, brand, and platform information to generate code that works around browser problems? (See "Creating Code for Specific Browsers.")

5. What do the `<noscript></noscript>` tags do? (See "Requiring JavaScript.")

PART

V

Sunday Morning

1. What is a style sheet?

2. What is the purpose of the HTML `<span></span>` tag?

3. Why would you want to use an external style sheet?

4. What method of the `document` object do you use to obtain an element object? What value do you pass to this method?

5. If you assign a value to an element's `style.top` property, and you don't specify a unit of measurement, what unit of measurement will be used?

6. What does the `innerHTML` property of an element represent? What happens if you assign a new value to this property?

7. What does the `style.position` property specify for an element?

8. What does the `top` object represent?

9. When working inside a frame, what does the `parent` object represent?

10. Assuming that an HTML document should only be displayed as part of a set of frames, how can you tell if that HTML document was loaded *without* its frame set?

11. If you open a new window and you only specify its height and width, which toolbars will the window have?

12. How can you close a window that you have created?

13. How can you determine if the contents of a window have been fully loaded?

14. What does the `opener` property tell you about a window?

15. What does the `parseFloat()` function do?

16. Why does JavaScript have difficulty displaying floating-point numbers accurately?

17. How can you make a text box control appear to be just another bit of text on the screen?

18. In the `navigator.appVersion` property, what does the string "MSIE" signify?

19. How do you tell the Web browser that a particular version of JavaScript is required to execute a `<script></script>` block?

20. How can you hide your JavaScript code from older, non-JavaScript-compliant Web browsers?

PART

VI

Sunday Afternoon

Working with Dates, Numbers, and Web Addresses

Session Checklist

✔ Using the Date and Math objects built into JavaScript

✔ Using the history and location objects of the Browser Object Model

**30 Min.
To Go**

A s with any programming languages, some parts of JavaScript are important enough that you need to know about them but not important enough to warrant an entire chapter in a book. So, in this session I'm going to give you a close look at several utility classes and objects. Two of these are part of the JavaScript language, and two are a part of the Browser Object Model. While none of these items is essential for creating JavaScript programs, knowing how to use them can make your life a lot easier.

The Date Class

Perhaps the most useful of these utility items is the Date class that is built into JavaScript. As you learned in Session 16, this class allows you to create objects that hold date and time information. The Date class constructor function can create Date objects in lots of different ways. The easiest is the one you saw in Session 16:

```
var rightNow = new Date();
```

When called this way, the Date constructor will read the system clock in the client's machine and create a Date object using the time and date settings it finds there. You can also create a Date object like this:

```
var numMilliseconds = 0;
var myDate = new Date( numMilliseconds);
```

When you create a Date object this way, the date and time you get represents the number of milliseconds (thousandths of a second) that have passed since 12 a.m., January 1, 1970, Greenwich Mean Time (GMT). However, unless the client is actually in the GMT time zone, the date and time will be adjusted to correspond to the client's time zone.

For example, I live in the Eastern Time Zone of the United States. This is five hours behind GMT. So, when I execute the above code and display the resulting Date object, I see something like this:

```
Wed Dec 31 19:00:00 GMT-0500 1969
```

Which is five hours before midnight, January 1, 1970. This brings up an important point; the millisecond values you use can be positive or negative. Positive values give dates *after* January 1, 1970 GMT, while negative values give dates *before* January 1, 1970 GMT. According to the ECMAScript standard, there are exactly 86,400,000 milliseconds in a day. (Leap seconds are not taken into account.) Date objects can represent any date up to 100,000,000 days before or after midnight, January 1, 1970 GMT.

If you don't know the number of milliseconds that represent your date, you can simply pass the Date constructor a string that specifies your date, like this:

```
var myDate = new Date( "May 5, 2000 21:40:00");
```

The format of this date string is simply "Month Day, Year Hours:Minutes:Seconds". You can omit the "Hours:Minutes:Seconds" portion, but if you do include it, it has to be in 24-hour format.

Finally, you can create a Date object by passing a series of integer numbers that represent the time you want in the new object. For example, an equivalent of the above would be:

```
var myDate = new Date( 2000, 4, 5, 21, 40, 0);
```

In this case, the parameters are:

```
var myDate = new Date( year, month, day, hours, minutes, seconds);
```

It's important to note that, as with just about everything else in JavaScript, several of these values are zero-relative. So, instead of passing 5 for the month of May, I pass a 4. (January is month 0 and December is month 11. There is no month 12. However, for the day of the month, I pass a 5, because there is no 0 day in a month.)

Similarly, hours, minutes, and seconds should be given within the range of 0 to 23 for hours, and 0 to 59 for minutes and seconds. (Because there is no 24th hour in a day and no 60th minute in an hour or 60th second in a minute.)

If you don't want to bother with the hours, minutes, and seconds, you don't have to supply them. So, to represent midnight on May 5, 2000 I could have just coded:

```
var myDate = new Date( 2000, 4, 5);
```

Methods of the Date class

There are over three dozen different methods in the Date class, so rather than bore you to death with all of them, I'm just going to go over the ones that you'll probably find the most useful in your day-to-day programming activities. (You can, of course, find out about all of the Date methods by checking the ECMAScript documentation that's on your CD-ROM.) Furthermore, since most Date methods come in pairs that get and set some value in a Date object, I'll discuss these pairs of methods together.

The getDate() and setDate() methods

These methods get or set the day of the month in a Date object. Let me say that again. These methods get or set the *day of the month* in a Date object. Compare this with the getDay() methods (which is discussed next) and you'll see why I repeated myself here. If you are calling setDate(), you simply pass a value from 1 to 31 that represents the day of the month you want placed in the Date object. When you call the getDate() method, you'll get back a number between 1 and 31.

```
var myDate = new Date( "May 5, 2000 21:40:00");
myDate.setDate( 25);
alert( myDate.getDate());
```

The getDay() method

This method gets the day of the *week* in a Date object. When you call this method, you'll get back a value between 0 (Sunday) and 6 (Saturday).

```
var myDate = new Date( "May 5, 2000 21:40:00");
alert( myDate.getDay());
```

The getFullYear() and setFullYear() methods

These methods let you get and set a full four-digit year value (that is, "1999" as opposed to "99") in a Date object. Note that when you set a Date object's year to a different value, JavaScript will automatically recalculate the day of the week so that the new Date is actually valid. For example, May 5, 2000 was a Friday. But following the execution of this code the day of the week in the myDate object will be Saturday:

```
var myDate = new Date( "May 5, 2000 21:40:00");
myDate.setFullYear( 2001);
```

Yes, the Date object does provide methods that let you set a two-digit year value. However, if the Y2K problem taught us anything, it's that you should *always* use a four-digit year value to avoid ambiguity. So, *please*, always use four-digit years! (Believe me, programmers in 2099 will thank you.)

The getHours() and setHours() methods

These methods get and set the hour value in a Date object. Remember that hours are expressed as values from 0 (midnight) to 23 (11 p.m.).

The getMinutes() and setMinutes() methods

These methods get and set the minutes value in a Date object. Remember that in JavaScript, minutes are expressed as a value from 0 to 59. (Because there is no 60th minute in an hour.)

The getMonth() and setMonth() methods

These methods get and set the month value in a Date object. Remember that in JavaScript, months are expressed as a value from 0 (January) to 11 (December). Note that when you set a Date object's month to a different value, JavaScript will automatically recalculate the day of the week so that the new Date is actually valid. For example, May 5, 2000 was a Friday. But following the execution of this code:

```
var myDate = new Date( "May 5, 2000 21:40:00");
myDate.setMonth( 9);
```

The day of the week in the myDate object will be Thursday.

The getTime() and setTime() methods

**20 Min.
To Go**

As you saw in Session 16 (in the discussion of how to create a cookie expiration date), these methods get and set the time as a number of milliseconds since midnight January 1, 1970. Being able to get a date in this format allows you to easily perform date mathematics. For example, to determine the day my daughter's first birthday will fall on, I could use the following code:

```
var bDate = new Date( "May 5, 2000 21:40:00");
var oneYear = 86400000 * 365;
var bDayMS = bDate.getTime();
bDate.setTime( bDayMS + oneYear);
```

The bDate variable will then contain the date: Sat May 5 21:40:00 EDT 2001

The getTimeZoneOffset() method

This method returns the time difference, in minutes, between the specified Date object and Greenwich Mean Time.

```
var myDate = new Date( "May 5, 2000");
var tzOffset = myDate.getTimezoneOffset();
document.write( "The date is: " + myDate + "<br />");
document.write( "The time zone offset is: " + tzOffset + "
minutes);
```

The toGMTString() method

As you learned in Session 16 (in the discussion of how to create a cookie expiration date), this method will return the contents of a Date object with the time shifted to its equivalent in the Greenwich Mean Time zone. For example, the following code:

```
var myDate = new Date( "May 5, 2000 21:40:00");
alert( myDate.toGMTString());
```

Will produce an alert window showing the following date: Sat, 6 May 2000 01:40:00 UTC

The toLocaleString() method

This method returns the time from a Date object as a formatted string. The format of this string can vary from browser to browser, but you'll usually get the day of the week (completely spelled out, that is, "Saturday" instead of "Sat"), the month (also spelled out), the day of the month and the hours, minutes, and seconds. If you need to display your date in a nice, human-readable format, this is usually the friendliest format that any of the Date methods will give you. If this isn't friendly enough, you can always extract the individual pieces of your date (using the methods discussed above) and build your own date string for display.

The UTC Date methods

Almost all of the remaining Date methods deal with UTC (Universal Coordinated Time). That is to say, they report the time as if the client's computer were located in the Greenwich Mean Time zone. These methods are basically the same as the ones you've just seen, with the addition of the characters "UTC" in their names. For example, the getUTCHours() method will retrieve the hours part of a date as if that date were in the Greenwich Mean Time zone. These methods allow you to standardize all of your time calculations in a single, client-independent time zone if you need to. (For examples of these methods in use, see the UTCmethods.htm file in the Session27 folder on your CD-ROM.)

Using the Date object on your Web site

One of the more common uses of the Date object is to display the time and/or date on a Web site and constantly update it. So, I'll add a date and time display that updates itself once a second to the menu page of the Baby-Palooza Web site. First, I need someplace to actually display the time and date. Since this is going to be a dynamically changing display, it will be easiest to show the information in a text box. So, I need to define a form and a text box, like this:

```
<form name="timeDisplay">
<input type="text" class="noEdit" name="theTime" value="" />
</form>
```

Notice that the class of this text box is noEdit. If you'll remember from Session 25, this is the class I defined that removes the border from a text box and makes sure that the cursor doesn't change when it passes over the text box. So, this text box will appear to just be another bit of text on the page.

Next, I need to define a function that will display and update the time in this text box.

```
function showTime() {
    var rightNow = new Date();
    var tString = rightNow.toLocaleString();
    document.timeDisplay.theTime.value = tString;
    setTimeout( 'showTime()', 1000);
    }
```

This extremely simple function does the trick. It first creates a new Date object that contains the current time (taken from the client's system clock). It then extracts that time information as a formatted string (via the `toLocalString()` method) and places it into the text box I've just created. A final call to the `setTimeout()` method ensures that the `showTime()` function will be called again one second later, which starts the whole process over and updates the time display.

The Math Object

The Math object is a JavaScript object that holds various and sundry mathematical constants and provides access to common mathematical functions. (Note that this is *not* a class! So, you can't create new Math objects. All you can do is use the one Math object that's built into JavaScript. Fortunately, that's all you really need.) Some of these will be familiar from your high school and college math courses, while others will be things you've probably never heard of. Basically, if you need to write JavaScript programs that perform lots of number crunching, you'll be glad that the Math object is available. If not, well, you don't have to use it, but it's good to know that its there just in case you *do* need it one day.

Constant properties of the Math object

The Math object contains the following *constant properties*. These are called *constants* for the simple reason that you can't change them (so they have a constant value). However, you access them just as you would the properties of any other object. (Note that there are more constant properties defined in the Math object. Be sure to check the ECMAScript documentation on your CD-ROM to find out about the others.)

The Math.E property

This is the constant value 2.718281828459045.

The Math.PI property

This is the constant value 3.141592653589793. (that is, π)

The Math.SQRT2 property

This is the constant value 1.4142135623730951. (that is, $\sqrt{2}$)

Methods of the Math object

There are almost twenty different methods in the Math object, very few of which are useful for day-to-day programming. So, I'll just go over the most useful ones here. Be sure to check the ECMAScript documentation on your CD-ROM for details on all of the Math object's methods. Examples of these methods and others can be found in the mathMethods.htm file on your CD-ROM.

The Math.abs() method

This method will return the absolute value of the number you pass to it.

The Math.max() and Math.min() methods

You pass these methods two or more numbers and they return the largest or smallest of those numbers respectively.

The Math.pow() method

You pass this method two numbers. The first number will be raised to the power of the second. For example, the following is the same as 2 * 2 * 2.

```
var result = Math.pow( 2, 3);
```

The Math.random() method

This method takes no parameters and returns a pseudorandom number between 0 and 1.

The Math.round() method

This method rounds the number you pass it to the closest integer value.

The Math.sqrt() method

This method returns the square root of the number you pass to it.

**10 Min.
To Go**

The location Object

In Sessions 8 and 9, you learned about the `window.location` property and the `document.location` property respectively. If you were looking closely, you might have noticed that each of these properties seems to represent the same thing: the Web address of the HTML document that is currently loaded into the Web browser. As you've seen in subsequent sessions, you can actually force the browser to load a new HTML document simply by assigning a new Web address to one of these properties.

While it might seem that these are just simple String objects, each of these location properties is actually a complex object in its own right. While you can use it as a simple redirection tool, the properties and methods of the location object can give you a lot of information about the Web address that is currently loaded into the Web browser.

(While the `window.location` and `document.location` properties hold essentially the same information, the `document.location` property will probably be left behind in favor of the `document.URL` property. So, I'm going to restrict my discussion to `window.location`.)

Properties of the location object

Any of the following properties can be set to a new value. Doing so will usually cause the browser to load the document specified by the new value. However, this is a browser-specific behavior, so, the best way to guarantee that your new document will be loaded is to always build your new Web address as a complete string and then assign it to the `location.href` property.

The hash property

This contains a String object containing the "hash" part of the Web address specified in the `href` property. For example, if the `href` property contains

```
http://www.baby-palooza.com/index.htm#top
```

the `hash` portion is #top.

The host property

This contains a String object containing the host information from the Web address specified in the `href` property. For example, if the `href` property contains

```
http://www.baby-palooza.com
```

the host portion is "www.baby-palooza.com:80".

The hostname property

This contains a String object containing just the host name information from the Web address in the `href` property. For example, if the `href` property contains in this link:

```
http://www.baby-palooza.com
```

The `hostname` portion is "www.baby-palooza.com".

The href property

This contains the complete Web address of the current location. Assigning a new Web address to this property will force the Web browser to load the document at that address.

The pathname property

If the Web address in the `href` property points to a file that's buried in a folder somewhere on the server, this property will contain the path to that file. For example, if this is the `href` property:

```
http://www.baby-palooza.com/strollers/index.htm
```

The `pathname` property would contain the string "strollers/index.htm".

The port property

This is a String object containing the port specified in the `href` property.

```
http://www.baby-palooza.com:80
```

Here, the `port` property would contain the value 80.

The protocol property

This is the protocol (http, ftp, etc.) that was used to load the Web address specified in the `href` property.

The search property

This is the query string specified in the Web address in the `href` property.

```
http://www.baby-palooza.com/search.htm?type=stroller
```

In this example, the `search` property would contain the string `?type=stroller`. Note that the question mark *is* included at the start of the string.

Methods of the location object

If you want to load a new page into the web browser, you *can* just assign a new Web address to the `location.href` property. However, one of the following methods will give you more control over the process.

The reload() method

This method tells the browser to reload the document referenced in the `href` property. This method can take a Boolean parameter, which is named *force*. If the `force` parameter is `true`, the page will be reloaded from the Web server even if an up-to-date copy exists in the browser's cache.

The replace() method

When you call this method, you pass it the Web address of a new document that you want loaded into the Web browser. This new document will be loaded into the Web browser and its Web address will *replace* the Web address of the currently loaded document in the browser's history list. (See the next section for a discussion of the history list.) This can be very handy if you have a series of "invisible" JavaScript pages, each of which triggers the loading of the next until a final page is reached. If each of these interim pages uses the `replace()` method to load the next page, then only the final page (the one the user actually sees), will end up in the history list. So, when the user clicks the Back button in the browser, all of the interim pages will be skipped over and the user will go directly back to the starting page. (A complete example of this can be found in the locationReplaceMethod.htm file on your CD-ROM.)

The history Object

The last object I want to tell you about in this session is the `window.history` object. As the name suggests, this object holds a list of the Web addresses that the user has visited since she started up her browser.

The length property

The `history` object has only one property: `length`. This property tells you how many entries are in the history list.

Methods of the history object

Thus far, the `history` object looks a lot like an Array doesn't it? Well, it is, but it's a rather special Array. Because it contains information about the user's Web surfing habits, it's been decided that JavaScript programs should not be able to actually read any of the Web addresses in the history list. In other words, a statement like `alert( history[0])` will either yield an error or a value of `undefined`. So, the best you can do is use one of the `history` object's methods to move the browser back and forth through the list of pages that have been visited.

The back() method

Calling this method will cause the browser to reload the Web address stored in the previous history list entry, if one exists. (It's just like hitting the browser's Back button.)

The forward() method

Calling this method will cause the browser to load the Web address stored in the next history list entry, if one exists. (It's just like hitting the browser's Forward button.)

The go() method

When you call this method, you pass it a positive or a negative integer. The browser will jump that many places in the history list (forward if the number is positive and backward if the number is negative) and load the Web address stored at that point in the history list.

The history object, frames, and windows

While the history object might not seem that thrilling at first, one very important aspect of it is that every frame and every window you create has its own history object. So, it's entirely possible to create a set of controls that live in one frame and allow you to move backwards and forwards through the history of another frame.

Done!

Another important thing to know is that, in a frames-based Web site, the top object also has a history object that is sort of an amalgam of all the history objects that belong to its frames. So, if the user changes the page in one frame, then changes the page in another frame, those individual changes not only go into each frame's history list, they both go into the top object's master history list. Moving back and forth through this history list will actually change the contents of the appropriate frames and not the top window.

REVIEW

In this session, you learned about several utility objects and classes that are built into the JavaScript language and the Browser Object Model. You saw how the Date class can be used to create Date objects that hold time and date information. You also learned how to perform simple date mathematics to create new dates. You learned about the Math object and its properties and methods. You learned how the location object can be used to move the browser from one HTML document to another and how the properties of this object can give you information about the document that is currently loaded. Finally, you learned how the history object can be used to move back and forth through the list of pages that have been viewed since the browser was started.

QUIZ YOURSELF

---

1. How do you create a Date object that contains the current date and time? (See "The Date Class.")

2. In JavaScript Date objects, what integer value represents Monday? What value represents Saturday? (See "The getDay() method.")

3. What is the difference between the getDay() and getDate() methods? (See "The getDate() and setDate() methods" and "The getDay() method.")

4. How can you use the location object to make the browser load a new HTML document? (See "The href property.")

5. Why aren't JavaScript programs allowed to see the actual contents of the history object? (See "Methods of the history object.")

Communicating with Server-Side Processes

Session Checklist

✔ Preparing data for transmission to a server-side process

✔ Decoding data embedded in a Web address

**30 Min.
To Go**

While JavaScript is a very powerful language, there are some things that it can't do from inside a Web browser. For example, it can't open a connection with a database. It's also not very good at creating charts, graphs, or other graphics. On those occasions when you need to do something that JavaScript simply can't do (or doesn't do very well), you'll probably want to turn the task over to some sort of server-side application.

The Common Gateway Interface

If you've been using the Web for a while now, you've undoubtedly heard of the Common Gateway Interface or CGI. Usually, you'll hear about the CGI in terms of an application — for example, "I had to write a CGI application to collect data from a Web page form and put it in a database." The term *CGI application* is really a bit of a misnomer because it implies that the application is written in some language called CGI. But, the CGI isn't a programming language; it's simply a protocol that client-side programs use to communicate with server-side programs. So, when you hear someone talk about that "CGI application" that they wrote, all they are saying is that they wrote a program that uses the CGI protocol to send/receive data to/from some other process. So, CGI applications can be written in any language that supports the protocol. Perl, C, and Python are all popular languages for creating CGI applications but they are by no means the *only* languages that you can use to create CGI applications.

Understanding the CGI data format

Entire books can be (and have been) written about the CGI. (For all the technical details on CGI, you should visit the CGI specification page at www.w3.org/CGI/.) However, the whole thing really boils down to the way that data is formatted so that it can be transmitted between the client and the server. Basically, data that's formatted for transmission through the CGI looks like this:

```
name1=value1&name2=value2&name3=value3
```

As you can see, this is just a series of name and value pairs that are separated by ampersands. As simple as this appears to be, there are still a couple of rules that you have to follow to properly transmit data through the CGI.

- Spaces are not allowed. Blank spaces and other white space characters are not allowed anywhere in the data that you want to send through the CGI. If you want to send a blank space you must either replace it with a + or send its equivalent hexadecimal code. To transmit other white space characters (like tabs and line feeds) you should send their hexadecimal codes. This of course, leads to the question, "How do I create these hexadecimal codes?" To answer this question, JavaScript provides the escape() function. (Replacing the special characters in a string with their hexadecimal equivalents is usually referred to as *escaping* the string.) You'll be learning about this function and its counterpart, the unescape() function, a bit later in this session.

- Any other special characters, including the ampersand (&) and equal sign (=) should also be transmitted as hexadecimal characters. When you transmit data via the CGI, equal signs are always used to associate a value with a name and ampersands are always treated as separators of name=value pairs. So, if one of your values includes an ampersand or an equal sign, it must be sent as a hexadecimal code, so that the receiving program doesn't misinterpret your data.

As an example of this, assume that you have three fields that you want to transmit through the CGI: firstName, lastName, and address. Further assume that the values of these fields are "John," "Public," and "123 Anyplace Rd." This information could be transmitted through the CGI in either of the following forms:

```
firstName=John&lastName=Public&address=123+Anyplace+Rd.
firstName=John&lastName=Public&address=123%20Anyplace%20Rd.
```

In the first of these, the spaces in the address have been replaced by plus signs (+). In the second, the spaces have been replaced by their equivalent hexadecimal code (20). The percent sign (%) is used to tell the CGI application that the next two characters are a hexadecimal character code that should be transformed back into an actual character before processing further. (This might lead you wonder how you can transmit + and % through the CGI without confusion. I'll be discussing that in just a bit.)

The CGI methods

As I said earlier, the CGI is a protocol that a client and server can use to transmit data between each other. The way that this data is formatted is only one part of this protocol. Another part is how the formatted data actually gets to where it's going. In the CGI protocol, there are two standard methods that are used to transmit data. These methods are known as *post* and *get*. (Note that the CGI protocol doesn't use objects, so these aren't methods in the same sense that toUpperCase() is a method of the String object. They are called methods because they each describe a process for transmitting data. This makes them "methods" in that they describe how to carry out a real-world task, moving data from one place to another, rather than being associated with abstract objects.)

The get method

The get method is the simpler of the two. When data is transmitted in this way, it is formatted as shown above and then simply tacked onto the end of the Web address of the CGI application that the data is being sent to. So, if I wanted to send my firstName and lastName data to an application on the Baby-Palooza Web site via the get method, I would use a Web address that looks like this:

```
http://www.babypalooza.com/cgiapp.exe?firstName=
John&lastName=Public
```

Here, cgiapp.exe is the name of the server-side CGI application that I want to invoke. Everything that comes after the question mark is called *the query string* or *the search string.* (From here on out, I'll be referring to this as the "search string," because that's the way JavaScript refers to it.) When the Web server looks at this, it will see that `cgiapp.exe` is an executable program and not an HTML document. So, it will start this program up and pass to it a parameter that contains the search string that was sent as part of the Web address. It's then up to cgiapp.exe to extract the information it needs from the search string, process it, and return its results to the Web server. The Web server will then take those results (usually a complete HTML document) and send them back to the client.

As you can see, the `get` method is *very* simple to use. However, it does have the drawback that you are limited in how much data you can transmit this way. Web browsers usually have a maximum allowed size for a Web address, so if you want to transmit a lot of data (like the contents of one or more text fields) the `get` method is not the way to go.

The post method

The `post` method is much better suited for transmitting large amounts of data. While the format of the data is exactly the same, the way it's sent is different. When data is transmitted via the `post` method, nothing is added to the end of the Web address. Instead, a special header is sent that tells the Web server how many bytes of data are being transmitted. That actual data is then sent in one big chunk to the Web server. The Web server turns around and passes this same information (the number of bytes and the big chunk of data) to the CGI application. The CGI application can then read the data from a standard input stream (which is similar to the streams you learned about in Session 9) and process it in exactly the same way as if it had gotten the data from the search string.

How CGI Works with HTML and JavaScript

20 Min. To Go

When you create an HTML form, you can use the `method=` attribute to specify which of the two CGI methods (`get` or `post`) that you want the browser to use when it sends the forms data to the Web server. For example, given this form definition:

```
<form method="post" action="cgiapp.exe">
<input type="text" name="fName" />
<input type="text" name="fName" />
<input type="submit" value="submit" />
</form>
```

When this form's Submit button is clicked, its data will be sent to the cgiapp.exe application via the `post` method. If the initial `<form>` tag had looked like this:

```
<form method="get" action="cgiapp.exe">
```

Then the data in this form would be sent via the `get` method. (Many folks don't realize that if you don't specify a method for a form, it will default to the `get` method. This can be very bad news if your form data contains sensitive information like passwords or credit card information. This is because, when the `get` method is used to submit your form data, the browser will attach that data, including any sensitive information, to the end of the Web address that's specified in the `action=` attribute of your form. On the other hand, when you use the `post` method, the data in your form is hidden from casual observers. So, if it's the `post` method you want, be *sure* to specify it when you define your forms!)

Using get and post with HTML

As I mentioned earlier, if you want to send white space or other special characters through the CGI, you need to make sure that those characters have been properly escaped before you send them. If all you are doing is collecting data in a form and then letting the browser send that data when the Submit button is clicked, you don't have anything to worry about. The browser will automatically arrange your data into a CGI-compliant format and escape all of the data that was in the form before it is sent. In other words, if you let it, the browser will automatically handle all of the CGI dirty work for you.

Using the get method with JavaScript

While the browser is perfectly capable of handling simple data submissions, there will probably be times when you need to exercise a bit more control over what gets sent to your server-side process. In those cases, you can actually use JavaScript to build and submit your own CGI-compliant data via the `get` method.

Building and using a search/query string

Using JavaScript to create a `get` method-compliant search string is extremely easy to do and you don't even need to use a form to do it. For example, assume that I need to create a series of links that, when clicked, will invoke a server-side application that generates a sales report. When this application is invoked, it expects to receive two parameters: a year and a quarter for which sales should be summarized. (Note that all of the code for the following example can be found in the files bpReports.htm and qtrSalesSummary.htm, which are in the Session28 folder on your CD-ROM.) First, I have to define the appropriate links, which might look something like this:

```
<a href="javascript:doQtrSummary( 2001, 1)">Q1, 2001</a>
<a href="javascript:doQtrSummary( 2001, 2)">Q2, 2001</a>
<a href="javascript:doQtrSummary( 2001, 3)">Q3, 2001</a>
<a href="javascript:doQtrSummary( 2001, 4)">Q4, 2001</a>
```

In each of these links, I'm calling a JavaScript function named doQtrSummary(). This function will take the parameters I pass to it (a year and a quarter for my report) and build an appropriate search string that I can use to invoke my server-side process. Here's what that function looks like:

```
function doQtrSummary( year, qtr) {
    var sStr = "year=" + year;
    sStr += "&qtr=" + qtr;
    location.href = "qtrSalesSummary.htm" + "?" + sStr;
    }
```

As you can see, there isn't much to this. First, I take the year value and concatenate it with the string year=. This will give me the name=value pair that represents my year parameter. Next, I take this string and concatenate it with the name=value pair that will represent my quarter parameter. Note the ampersand that separates the two name=value pairs. When these first two lines of code finish, I'll have a string that looks like this (assuming that the first link is the one that's clicked): year=2001&qtr=1

All that's left is to append this to the end of the Web address of the server-side CGI application that I want to invoke. This is done in the last line of the function. (Of course, since I don't know what sort of server setup you have, I can't really invoke a conventional CGI application in this example. As a substitute, I'm just invoking another HTML file. However, the way I'm invoking this HTML file is exactly the same way you would invoke any other CGI application.) Notice that, between the Web address of my CGI application and the search string, there is a question mark. This question mark is what separates the actual Web address of your CGI application from the search string that you want to send to it. So, when all of this concatenation is finished, my final Web address will look like this: qtrSalesSummary.htm?year=2001&qtr=1

Once I have this Web address and search string combination built, all I have to do is assign it to the `href` property of the `location` object. As you saw in the last session, this will tell the browser to request this document from the Web server. When the Web server sees this request, it will break off the search string (everything from the question mark on) and pass it to the CGI application that I've requested. It's then up to the CGI application to process the search string and pass its results back to the Web server, which in turn will pass them back to the Web browser.

Escaping the values in a search string

As you can see, building and sending a `get` method request to a CGI application is amazingly simple. However, what I've just shown you is the simplest case. None of the values in this example had any white space or special characters that needed to be escaped before transmitting them through the CGI. So, to make things a bit more interesting, I'll change my function to allow the user to add a title to the report.

```
function doQtrSummary( year, qtr) {
    var title = prompt( "Title for report...", "Sales Summary");
    if (title != null) {
        var sStr = "year=" + year;
        sStr += "&qtr=" + qtr;
        sStr += "&title=" + escape( title);
        location.href = "qtrSalesSummary.htm" + "?" + sStr;
    }
}
```

In this version of my function, a prompt window asks the user to specify a title to use for the report. Since the user can type anything in this prompt window, I need to make sure that any white space or special characters she enters will make it through the CGI properly. So, I take the value that the user typed in and pass it to the `escape()` function. The `escape()` function looks at each character in a string and, if a character is a white space or special character, it replaces that character with its hexadecimal code value, preceded by a percent sign (%). So, for example, the following statement:

```
alert( escape("Hello & Welcome!"));
```

Will open an alert window that displays the following string:

```
Hello%20%26%20Welcome%21
```

In this case, the `escape()` function changed each space character into %20, the ampersand character into %26 and the exclamation point into %21. Unlike the characters that they represent, these character codes can pass safely through the CGI. It's very important to understand that you should only `escape()` individual values in your search string, and *not* your entire search string! Consider this function:

```
function doQtrSummary( year, qtr) {
    var title = prompt( "Title for report...", "Sales Summary");
    if (title != null) {
        var sStr = "year=" + year;
        sStr += "&qtr=" + qtr;
        sStr += "&title=" + title;
        location.href = "qtrSalesSummary.htm?" + escape(sStr);
        }
    }
```

Well, in this version of the function, I'm escaping the entire search string and not just the values that are in it. This would give me a search string that looks something like this:

```
year%3D2001%26qtr%3D1%26title%3DSales%20Summary
```

Instead of the correct string, which is this:

```
year=2001&qtr=1&title=Sales%20Summary
```

Escaping the + character

10 Min. To Go

As I said earlier, when you are building a search string, you must replace any spaces in that string with either a + character or its hexadecimal equivalent (%20). As I write this, it's become less and less common to use the + character to replace spaces. So, many CGI applications simply treat them as + characters if there are hexadecimal equivalents also in the search string. However, many older CGI applications still treat plus signs as spaces and substitute accordingly. Unfortunately, you never know how a CGI application will act until you actually try it (or unless you write it yourself). However, you *can* count on all CGI applications to properly handle hexadecimal equivalents. So, whenever you build a search string, it's always a good idea to escape any plus signs that might be in your data. This can be problem however, because, as it stands right now, the `escape()` function does *not* actually escape plus signs! So, if I execute this statement:

```
alert( escape( "One + One is Two")) ;
```

What will display is this: One%20+%20One%20is%20Two Passing this to a CGI application can lead to trouble if that CGI application doesn't handle plus signs in the way you expect. So, the only real solution is to create a wrapper function for the escape() function that will also escape any plus characters that it finds in a string:

```
function escapePlus( tStr) {
    var escaped = escape( tStr);
    var result = "";
    for (x=0; x<escaped.length; x++) {
        if (escaped.charAt( x) == "+") {
            result += "%2B";
            }
        else {
            result += escaped.charAt( x);
            }
        }
    return result;
    }
```

The first thing this function does is call the escape() function and pass it the string I want escaped. This will escape all of the appropriate characters, except for plus signs. The function then enters a for loop that looks at each character in the escaped version of the string. If a character is a plus sign, the hexadecimal equivalent of a plus sign (%2B) is added to the end of the result string. If the character is not a plus sign, the character is simply copied to the end of the result string. When the loop is finished, the result string is sent back to the caller, giving them a string with all the necessary characters changed into their hexadecimal equivalents.

Retrieving data from a get method request

In my example, the target of my get request is another HTML file. Not many people realize that you can actually pass data to another HTML file using a get method request. Then, in the target file, you can use JavaScript to retrieve that data and act upon it.

In this example, the target of my get method request is the file qtrSalesSummary.htm. When this file loads, the search string that was passed to it will be available in the search property of the location object. So, in the simplest case, I could retrieve this information and display it like this:

```
alert( location.search);
```

What you'll find in the `location.search` property will be the raw data that makes up the `get` method request that was sent to the HTML page. So, assuming that the user clicked on the first quarter link and left the report title alone, the value in `location.search` would be:

```
?year=2001&qtr=1&title=Sales%20Summary
```

Looking at this value, you'll notice that the data is still in its escaped form and that there is a question mark at the beginning of the data. Unfortunately, the question mark will always be there, so before you can process the data you have to get rid of it. (As you'll see however, this isn't too difficult.) Furthermore, since the remaining data is arranged in name=value pairs, processing it is as simple as processing the cookie data that you worked with in Session 16. In fact, it's pretty easy to write a function that will extract any given value out of the search string so that you can easily use it in your JavaScript program. The following code shows such a function from the qtrSalesSummary.htm file.

```
function getParam( paramName) {
    var sStr = location.search.substring( 1);
    var result = "undefined";
    if (sStr != "") {
        var nvPairs = sStr.split( "&");
        for (x=0; x<nvPairs.length; x++) {
            if (nvPairs[ x].indexOf( paramName + "=") != -1) {
                var nvItem = nvPairs[ x].split( "=");
                result = unescape( nvItem[ 1]);
                break;
            }
        }
    }
    return result;
}
```

The first thing this function has to do is retrieve the actual search string from the `location.search` property. Notice that it uses a call to the `substring()` method to extract everything except the question mark at the beginning of the search string. If the search string is not empty, the function then uses the `split()` method to create an array. Each entry in the array holds one name=value pair from the search string. A `for` loop then moves through this array searching for the parameter name that was passed to the function. When it's found, that name=value pair is itself split into a new array. The second element of this array (the value part of the name=value pair) is then passed to the unescape() function and returned to whomever called the function. I'm sure that you can pretty well guess what the unescape() function does. It simply takes a string and searches it for hexadecimal character codes. When it finds one, it replaces it with its equivalent printable character. That's all there is to it!

Using the post method with JavaScript

While using a get method request from JavaScript is fairly simple, using a post method request can be a bit trickier. First of all, there really isn't any way that JavaScript can retrieve data from a post method request. This means that if you want to send data from one HTML page to another, you will have to use the get method. So as far as the post method goes, all this leaves is using JavaScript to build a post method request for transmission to a more conventional CGI application on the Web server.

Actually, you've already seen how to do this. You see, when you validate data, or assign a value to a form control, you are changing the data that will be sent when the user clicks the Submit button for that form or when you call the form's submit() method. So, everything you learned in Sessions 12, 13, and 15 can be used to prepare your data for transmission by the post method. In fact, these same lessons apply to the get method as well. As I mentioned earlier in this session, if you submit a form using the get method, the browser will simply build a search string (just like the one you learned to build earlier in this session — it will even escape the values for you) and tack it on to the end of the Web address that you specified in the action= attribute of your <form> tag.

Done!

REVIEW

In this session, you learned about the Common Gateway Interface (CGI) protocol and how JavaScript can work with it to send data to a server-side process or to another HTML file. You learned how data has to be formatted as a search string to be useful to a CGI application. You learned about the characters that aren't allowed in a search string and how to replace those characters with equivalent hexadecimal codes. You saw how JavaScript can retrieve the contents of a get method request and extract information from it for use in your JavaScript program. Finally, you found out that all the lessons you've learned about validating data in a form and working with a form's controls are really just aspects of creating a valid post or get request that will be sent when a form is submitted.

Quiz Yourself

1. What programming language can you use to write a CGI application? (See "The Common Gateway Interface.")

2. How is data formatted in a CGI-compliant search string? (See "Understanding the CGI data format.")

3. What do the escape() and unescape() functions do? (See "Escaping the values in a search string" and "Retrieving data from a get method request.")

4. What purposes do the ampersand and equals characters serve in the CGI protocol? (See "Understanding the CGI data format.")

5. What is the difference between get and post? (See "The CGI methods.")

Supporting Multimedia

Session Checklist

✔ Detecting and using plug-ins and helper applications

✔ Learning how JavaScript can enhance the `<object>` tag

**30 Min.
To Go**

O ne of the coolest things about today's Web browsers is that they can display a lot of different types of data. However, they don't always do it alone. In fact, when you get right down to it, most Web browsers can only display text (HTML) and basic types of graphics. If you want to display a different type of file or data, you'll probably have to use a browser plug-in or helper application to get the job done.

Understanding Plug-ins and Helpers

A browser "plug-in" is simply a program that works inside the Web browser and allows it to display a type of data that it wouldn't otherwise be able to show. For example, Adobe distributes a free browser plug-in that allows you to view Portable Document Format (PDF) files right in the Web browser without having to start up a separate program.

A *helper application* on the other hand, is a program that is separate from the browser. If the browser doesn't know how to handle a particular type of file, and the browser doesn't have a plug-in available that can handle the data in the file, it will start up an appropriate helper application and tell it to open and display the file.

The nicest thing about plug-ins and helper applications is that, if you structure your HTML code properly, the browser will automatically load the correct plug-in (or run the correct helper) and display your data automatically. While plug-ins and helpers can dramatically increase the power of a Web browser, there is one tiny catch: they have to be installed on the client in order to use them. This is where JavaScript comes in. You can use JavaScript to determine whether or not a client's machine has the plug-in or helper application needed to properly view your particular type of data. If it does, you can dynamically generate the HTML needed to load your data and display it. If it doesn't, you can generate a different batch of HTML that will tell the user that they need a particular plug-in and give them a link to the place where they can go and get it. (This is pretty much exactly the same as the way you handle things when you come across an older or non-JavaScript-capable browser, as discussed in Session 26.) In order to use JavaScript to detect a plug-in or helper application, you have to make use of two special properties of the navigator object: the mimeTypes array and the plugins array.

For some reason Microsoft simply does not support either the mimeTypes **or** plugins **arrays in the current version of Internet Explorer for Windows (This omission is all the more mystifying when you consider that Internet Explorer for the Macintosh *does* support these arrays!) With luck, this will be fixed in the near future. Until then, what you are about to read applies only to Netscape browsers and Internet Explorer for the Macintosh.**

Using the mimeTypes Array

As you learned in Session 26, the navigator object contains all sorts of information about the browser that the client is using to execute your JavaScript program. In addition to this browser information, it also provides information about the MIME types that are known to the client's computer.

What's a MIME (type) good for?

Basically, MIME types were invented so that e-mail programs can look at a file attached to an e-mail message and determine what type of data is in the file. If the user tries to save an attached file, the e-mail program can use the MIME type information to save the file with the correct file type information.

This is a very important capability to have when sending files from one type of computer to another. Windows, for example, tracks file type by using a three-character extension at the end of a file's name. The Macintosh, on the other hand, keeps file type information inside the file itself. So, if you e-mail a text file from a Windows machine to a Macintosh, the e-mail client on the Macintosh will use the MIME type specified for the file to make sure that the file is saved correctly (as a text file) on the Macintosh.

Since MIME types are platform-independent, they quickly became the standard for specifying file types on the Internet. When a Web browser requests a document, one of the first bits of information that the Web server sends back to the browser is the document's MIME type. The browser looks at the MIME type information and uses it to determine how to handle that document.

The first part of a MIME type is a string that specifies the generic type of data that is in the file: for example, "text." This is followed by a forward slash (/), which is followed by a string that specifies the specific type of data that is in the file: for example, "html." So, the complete MIME type for an HTML document would look like this: text/html. When the Web browser receives a document with this MIME type, it knows that it's dealing with an HTML file and reacts accordingly.

 The Internet Assigned Numbers Authority (IANA) maintains the list of currently defined MIME types. You can visit their site at www.iana.org. Once you get there, look in the "Protocol Numbers and Assignment Services" for the MIME types directory. (IANA refers to these as "Media Types.")

What's in the mimeTypes array?

The `mimeTypes` array contains one `mimeType` object for each MIME type that is defined on the client's computer. Each `mimeType` object has four properties:

- `description`: This is a short description of the data that this MIME type represents.

- enabledPlugin: If there is an installed plug-in that handles this type of data, this property will be a reference to that plug-in. (This is actually a reference to an entry in the plugins array. See the upcoming discussion of the plugins array for more information.) If this property is null, then it's very likely that no plug-in is available to handle this type of data. However, this property is not always the best way to determine if a plug-in is available for a certain type of data. To make that determination, you need to check the plugins array.

- suffixes: This is a comma-separated list of the file name suffixes that may be found on files of this MIME type. For example, the suffixes associated with the text/html MIME type are htm and html.

- type: This is the actual MIME type specification string (that is, "text/html").

Getting a list of MIME types

Since the navigator.mimeTypes property is just an array, it's very simple to get a list of the MIME types that are defined on the client's machine. The following listing shows a simple bit of JavaScript and HTML that will generate a nicely formatted table that displays all of the pertinent information from the mimeTypes array. (This code can be found in the mimeTypes.htm file in the Session29 folder on your CD-ROM.)

```html
<table border="1" width="100%">
    <tr>
        <th>MIME Type</th>
        <th>Plug-in Available</th>
        <th>Description</th>
        <th align='left'>File Suffixes</th>
    </tr>
    <script language="javascript">
    for (x = 0; x < navigator.mimeTypes.length; x++) {
        document.write( "<tr>");
        document.write( "<td width='25%'>" +
        navigator.mimeTypes[x].type + " </td>");
        if (navigator.mimeTypes[x].enabledPlugin != null) {
            document.write( "<td width='25%'>" +
            navigator.mimeTypes[x].enabledPlugin.name +
            " </td>");
            }
```

```
        else {
            document.write( "<td width='25%'>Handled by Default
            Plug-in or Helper Application</td>");
            }
        document.write( "<td width='25%'>" +
        navigator.mimeTypes[x].description + " </td>");
        document.write( "<td width='25%'>" +
        navigator.mimeTypes[x].suffixes + " </td>");
        document.write( "</tr>");
        }
</script>
</table>
```

The code in this listing should look very familiar. It's a simple for loop that examines each entry in the mimeTypes array and displays what it finds in a table. The only real trick here is the check to see if an enabledPlugin is available for a MIME type. If one is, the program displays the name property of the plug-in. If not, it displays a short message telling you that this MIME type will be handled either by the Default Plug-in or a helper application. (The Default Plug-in is just what the name implies. If the browser can't find a plug-in specifically intended for a given MIME type, the Default Plug-in will try to handle the data. If it can't, the browser will then search for a helper application to handle the data.)

If you load the mimeTypes.htm file and look at the output, you'll notice that there are some MIME types that look like this: image/x-targa. The x- signifies that this MIME type is not yet a standardized MIME type.

20 Min. To Go

Understanding the plugins Array

Now that you have an understanding of MIME types and how that information is available from JavaScript, I need to tell you about the plugins array. As you saw in the last section, the entries in the plugins array are linked to the mimeTypes array via the enabledPlugin property. Each entry in the plugins array is a plugin object that describes one plug-in that is installed in the client's browser. A plugin object has four properties:

- description: This is a short description that tells you something about the plug-in. This usually includes the name of the plug-in vendor and what the plug-in is supposed to do.

- `filename`: This is the name of the actual file that the plug-in was loaded from. Depending on the platform, this property might contain the complete path to the file or just the file name.

- `length`: This is an integer value that tells you how many different MIME types this plug-in supports. (This is the length of the unnamed array of MIME types that's discussed below.)

- `name`: This is the name of the plug-in.

- unnamed array of MIME types: Finally, each `plugin` object has an array of `mimeType` objects. (These have exactly the same structure as the `mimeType` objects discussed earlier.) Each entry in this array represents one MIME type that the plug-in can display or otherwise supports.

Accessing a plug-in's array of MIME types

The key to working with a `plugin` object is the array of `mimeType` objects that's associated with the plug-in. If you need to know for sure what types of data a plug-in supports, all you have to do is loop through this array and check the MIME type specified in each entry. If the MIME type you need is listed, you can be sure that the plug-in can handle that type of data.

Actually, accessing this list of MIME types isn't too difficult. The biggest trick is simply knowing that it's there. Once you do, you can get at the information inside simply by treating the `plugins` array as a multidimensional array. (Which, in fact, it is!) The next listing shows you a simple program that will display all of the plug-ins that are installed on the client's machine, along with the MIME types that each plug-in supports. (This code can also be found in the plugIns.htm file on your CD-ROM.)

```
<table border="1" width="100%">
    <tr>
        <th>Plug-in Name</th><th>Plug-in File Name</th>
        <th>Mime Types Handled</th><th>Description</th>
    </tr>
    <script language="javascript">
    for (x = 0; x < navigator.plugins.length; x++) {
        document.write( "<tr>");
        document.write( "<td width='25%'>" +
        navigator.plugins[x].name + " </td>");
        document.write( "<td width='25%'>" +
        navigator.plugins[x].filename + " </td>");
```

```
        if (navigator.plugins[x].length > 0) {
            document.write( "<td width='25%'>");
            for (y=0; y < navigator.plugins[x].length; y++) {
                document.write( navigator.plugins[x][y].type +
                "<br />");
                }
            document.write( "</td>");
            }
        else {
            document.write( "<td width='25%'>No MIME Types</td>");
            }
        document.write( "<td width='25%'>" +
        navigator.plugins[x].description + " </td>");
        document.write( "</tr>");
        }
    </script>
</table>
```

Once again, there isn't anything terribly difficult here. This code simply loops through the plugins array and displays the contents of each entry in the array. The only tricky bit is the code that displays the MIME types that a plug-in supports, and even that is fairly simple. The code simply checks the length property of the current plugin object and then loops through each mimeType object that's in the unnamed array. For each entry in this array, the program outputs the actual MIME type information along with a <br /> tag.

Detecting Plug-Ins and Supported MIME Types

Looking at the structure of the mimeType and plugin objects, you might already have some idea of how to go about checking for the existence of a plug-in. There are actually several different ways to do this, so I'll go over them one at a time.

Checking for a plug-in by name

The easiest, and least reliable, way to check for a plug-in is to check for it by name. You can do this because JavaScript uses the name property of each plugin object as an index for each entry in the plugins array. For example, to check for the existence of Apple Computer's QuickTime plug-in, you can simply code an if statement like this one:

```
if (navigator.plugins[ "QuickTime Plug-In"]) {
    // embed QuickTime movie here
    }
else {
    // tell the user to go get the plug-in
    }
```

The trouble with this is that this plug-in name isn't consistent across computer platforms or even from version to version of the plug-in! For example, the name "QuickTime Plug-In" came from version 2.x of the plug-in that is installed on one of my Windows NT computers. Turning to the Macintosh on my desk, I see that the name of the QuickTime plug-in that's installed there is "QuickTime Plug-in 5.0."

A slightly better approach is to loop through the plugins array and check for a telltale part of the plug-in's name. A function that does this is shown below. (Note that this function and several others can be found in the multimedia.js file on your CD-ROM.)

```
function findPluginByPartialName( theName) {
    var foundMatchAt = -1;
    if (navigator.plugins.length > 0) {
        for (x=0; x < navigator.plugins.length; x++) {
            var plugName =
                navigator.plugins[ x].name.toUpperCase();
            if (plugName.indexOf( theName.toUpperCase()) != -1) {
                foundMatchAt = x;
                break;
                }
            }
        }
    return foundMatchAt;
    }
```

If this function finds a match for the partial name that was supplied, it will return the index number into the plugins array where the plug-in was found. This index number can then be used to examine the MIME types associated with the plug-in. The drawback to this approach is that if two plug-ins have very similar names, it's entirely possible that this function might detect the wrong plug-in. While you can check the MIME types to make sure you've got the right plug-in, this is an extra step that really isn't necessary.

Checking for a plug-in by MIME type

By far, the easiest and most reliable way to check for an appropriate plug-in is to simply check each installed plug-in and see if any of them support the MIME type of the data you want to display. As soon as you find a plug-in that supports your data type, you can stop your search and let the browser take care of the rest.

This *does* mean that you might not end up with exactly the plug-in that you want. For example, both QuickTime and Netscape's old LiveAudio plug-in will handle WAV sound files. This means that as long as one of these is installed, you should be able to embed and play a WAV file in the client's Web browser.

Of course, if you *must* have a feature that only one plug-in can provide then you should make sure that the appropriate plug-in is available. But, if that plug-in is not available, you should seriously consider making your data available through an alternate plug-in if one is available. Having said all that, here's a function will check for a plug-in that supports a specific MIME type.

```
function findPluginByMIMEtype( theMIMEtype) {
    var foundMatchAt = -1;
    if (navigator.plugins.length > 0) {
        var numTypes = 0;
        for (x=0; x < navigator.plugins.length; x++) {
            numTypes = navigator.plugins[x].length;
            for (y=0; y < navigator.plugins[x].length; y++) {
                if (navigator.plugins[x][y].type == theMIMEtype) {
                    foundMatchAt = x;
                    break;
                    }
                }
            if (foundMatchAt != -1) {
                break;
                }
            }
        }
    return foundMatchAt;
    }
```

Detecting a helper application

If you can't find a plug-in that supports the type of data you want to display, you might want to check and see if a helper application is available. To do this, simply loop through the `mimeTypes` array and see if the MIME type that describes your data is defined. If it is, the client's machine should have a helper application for that type of data. The following is a function that will check the `mimeTypes` array for a specified MIME type.

```
function findHelperApp( theMIMEtype) {
    var foundMatchAt = -1;
    if (navigator.mimeTypes.length > 0) {
        for (x=0; x < navigator.mimeTypes.length; x++) {
            if (navigator.mimeTypes[x].type == theMIMEtype) {
                foundMatchAt = x;
                break;
                }
            }
        }
    return foundMatchAt;
    }
```

Using Multimedia Files

**10 Min.
To Go**

Now that you know how to detect plug-ins and helper applications, you need to learn how to use this knowledge to actually present multimedia files to your users. Before you look at the code to do this, let me go over the different situations you have to be wary of.

- The absolute best-case scenario you can hope for is that the user will have an appropriate plug-in installed. If so, you can simply generate the JavaScript code or HTML tag (or tags) that will embed the data into your Web page and let the browser take care of the rest.

- If no plug-in is available, the next best situation is that a helper application exists. In this case, you have to trigger the launch of the helper application somehow. You can do this by providing a link to your data file that the user can click. If you want to skip the step of having the user click on a link, you can automate this by assigning the Web address of your data file to the `location.href` property (as seen in Sessions 27 and 28). Either of these will force the browser to launch the helper application, which will then load your data file and process it accordingly.

● Finally, if no plug-in is available, and no helper application is available, you should either tell the user that they need to obtain the plug-in before they can view your site or provide them with an alternate page to view.

As an example of this, take a look at the openPDF.htm file on your CD-ROM. It shows you the code needed to embed an Adobe Acrobat (PDF) file in a Web page. (The PDF file I'm embedding in this example is the ECMAScript documentation file that's also on your CD-ROM.) Looking at this code, you'll notice that, once I've determined that it's safe to load the PDF file (either `plugInAvail` or `helperAvail` is true), I simply assign the Web address of the PDF file to the `location.href` property. The reason for this is because I've found that this is simply the best way to invoke the Acrobat PDF viewer plug-in.

This is an important point: every plug-in is different. Sometimes the same plug-in will behave differently from version to version or from platform to platform. So, the moral is that you need to test extensively with the plug-in you want to use. The techniques shown in this session are just intended to get you to the point where you can tell if a plug-in is available. Actually making that plug-in work will depend on the plug-in itself.

If neither the plug-in nor the helper application can be found, the code displays a simple message telling the user where to go to get the plug-in. It also gives them the chance to click on a link that will try to load the PDF file, just in case the information in the `mimeTypes` and `plugins` arrays was wrong.

Finally, the code checks to see if the current browser is Internet Explorer running on Windows (using a couple of the functions from the browserSnoop.js file in Session 26). Remember, at the start of this session I made note of the fact that the current versions of Internet Explorer for Windows (version 5.x as I write this) don't allow you to do *anything* with either the `mimeTypes` or `plugins` arrays. You can't even find out their lengths! So, if this code is loaded into Internet Explorer v5.x on a Windows machine, it will fail to find either a plug-in or a helper application and simply display the fail-safe text at the end.

However, given the fact that Adobe Acrobat ships with almost every Windows-based computer, it's pretty safe to assume that, if the browser is Internet Explorer on Windows, that the Acrobat Reader plug-in is available. So, if that is the case, I try again to load the PDF file into the browser. If the plug-in or helper is available, the file will load into the browser and the fail-safe text will disappear. Otherwise, the file simply won't load and the fail-safe message will remain on screen.

PDF files are actually a bit odd in that they can easily be displayed in the browser simply by assigning their Web address to the `location.href` property. Usually, once you've determined that a plug-in is available, you'll want to generate an appropriate `<object>` tag to insert your data into the Web page. (In the past, other HTML tags (`<embed>` and `<applet>` in particular) have been used to embed files into a Web page. The `<object>` tag will eventually replace these tags, so that's the tag I'm going to concentrate on here.)

The `<object>` tag has a whole host of attributes you can use, but its basic format is this:

```
<object data="Web address of file" type="MIME type of file">
HTML to parse if file cannot be embedded
</object>
```

When the browser encounters an `<object>` tag, it basically takes the same steps as the code to display a PDF file does. It tries to find a plug-in that supports the specified MIME type. If it finds one, it lets that plug-in display the specified file.

However, if the browser can't find an appropriate plug-in, it won't try to find a helper application for the file. Instead, it will simply parse the HTML that is between the opening and closing `<object></object>` tags. This HTML can be just about anything, including more `<object>` tags. While this does mean that you can nest `<object>` tags to try and embed successively less-impressive types of data in your document, you can't use this technique to launch a helper application if one exists.

Of course, you might think that you could just include a chunk of JavaScript inside your `<object></object>` tags that would check for your helper application and launch it if it exists. Unfortunately, it turns out that any JavaScript inside a set of `<object></object>` tags will be executed regardless of whether or not the object could be loaded.

To make matters worse, the `<object>` tag doesn't support an `onerror` event handler. So, you can't write an event handler that will execute if your object does not load (though the `<object>` tag does support many other event handlers). All of this together means that you have to get a bit sneaky in order to check for a helper application when using the `<object>` tag. The next listing, which tries to display a QuickTime movie, will show you what I mean.

```
<script language="javascript">
function checkHelper() {
    if (findHelperApp( "video/quicktime")) {
        location.href = "baby.mov";
        }
    }
```

```
</script>
<object data="baby.mov" type="video/quicktime"
width="100%" height="100%">
<img src="../images/sadBaby.jpg" onload="checkHelper()" />
You don't seem to have the QuickTime Plug-In. You can go
    <a href="http://www.apple.com/quicktime">here</a> to get it.<br
/>
Or, you can try viewing the movie in a separate window by clicking
<a href="baby.mov">here</a>.
</object>
```

In this example, I've defined an `<object>` tag that attempts to load and play a QuickTime movie. If the QuickTime plug-in is available, the browser will automatically load it and play the movie. If, however, the QuickTime plug-in is *not* available, the HTML code inside the `<object></object>` tags will be parsed and displayed in the browser window.

For the most part, this HTML code is exactly what you've seen before. However, the first line is something new: an `<img>` tag. This tag displays a cute little picture of a sad baby (which is appropriate given that the movie couldn't load). In addition, this `<img>` tag has an `onload` handler. When this sad baby's picture finishes loading, the function `checkHelper()` will be called. This function checks for the existence of a helper application for QuickTime movies and, if it finds one, tells the browser to load the movie immediately. Of course, a sad baby picture might not be appropriate for your site, but you can always use an invisible picture (that is, 1 pixel by 1 pixel or a small square that is the same color as your background) to generate the same effect. It's sneaky, but it works!

Done!

REVIEW

In this session, you learned about browser plug-ins and helper applications and how you can use JavaScript to work with them. You learned what MIME types are and how they are used to specify file type information for files transmitted over the Internet. You learned that the `navigator.mimeTypes` array contains a list of all the different file types that the browser can display, either by itself or with assistance from a helper application. You also learned that the `navigator.plugins` array contains a list of all the installed browser plug-ins along with information on which MIME types that a given plug-in can display. You saw how JavaScript could be used to search these arrays to determine if a particular plug-in is installed or if a helper application is available for a particular MIME type.

Finally, you saw how JavaScript can check for the existence of a helper application when an `<object>` tag fails to load a multimedia file because a plug-in can't be found.

QUIZ YOURSELF

1. What is the difference between a plug-in and a helper application? (See "Understanding Plug-ins and Helpers.")

2. What is a MIME type? (See "Using the mimeTypes Array")

3. What does the first half of a MIME type tell you? What does the second half of a MIME type tell you? (See "What's a MIME (type) good for?")

4. What is the most reliable way to check and see if a plug-in exists to handle a particular MIME type? (See "Checking for a plug-in by MIME type.")

5. How can you use JavaScript and an `<img>` tag to determine if an object has failed to load? (See "Using Multimedia Files.")

Working with Java Applets

Session Checklist

✔ Embedding a Java applet in an HTML document

✔ Learning how JavaScript can communicate with a Java applet

**30 Min.
To Go**

One of the more useful types of objects you can embed in a Web page is a Java applet. Unlike most other types of embeddable objects, Java applets are actually miniapplications. This means that they can do all of the things that a JavaScript program can do, and more! Best of all, depending on which browser the client is using, you can actually control a Java applet using JavaScript.

Everything I'm going to discuss in this chapter *should* work in every one of the major browsers. As I write this however, the only browsers that support JavaScript to Java communication are Internet Explorer 5.x for the PC and Netscape Navigator 4.x. Internet Explorer for the Macintosh doesn't support this type of thing at all. And while Netscape 6 is supposed to support this feature, it seems to be missing from the first release. So, look at this final session as a promise of things to come, or something nice you can do for those users with these browsers.

Adding a Java Applet to Your HTML Document

Most Java development environments will, if you ask them to, automatically generate an HTML document that shows you how to embed your Java applet into an HTML document. However, if you are using Sun's JDK tools to build your Java applet from scratch, you'll need to know how to do this yourself.

The <applet> tag

The ⟨applet⟩ tag is currently the easiest way to add a Java applet to an HTML document. (Note that in the future, the ⟨object⟩ tag will replace the ⟨applet⟩ tag. As of now however, the ⟨object⟩ tag seems to have real trouble when it comes to handling applets.) While the ⟨applet⟩ tag can be fairly complex, you can almost always get by with just a few simple attributes. Usually, an applet tag will look something like this:

```
<applet name="appletName" code="applet.class"
codebase="folderToLookIn">
<param name="param1Name" value="value for first parameter" />
<param name="param2Name" value="value for second parameter" />
HTML to include if browser does not support applets
</applet>
```

As with every other tag I've shown you, the name= attribute specifies the name that JavaScript will use to communicate with the applet. The code= attribute is the name of the Java .class file that will actually be loaded and executed by the browser. (A .class file is the Java equivalent of an .exe file in the Windows environment.) The codebase= attribute tells the browser which folder to look in to find the class file that was specified in the code= attribute. (If the class file is in the same folder as the HTML document the ⟨applet⟩ tag is in, you can omit this attribute.)

If you want to pass parameters to your applet, you can specify a series of ⟨param⟩ tags. Each of these tags will define one parameter that will be passed directly to the applet after it is loaded.

Finally, just in case the client's browser doesn't support Java applets, you can also specify a block of HTML that should be displayed. Usually, this will be a simple message telling the user that they need to use a Java-capable browser to view the applet, but it can be just about anything you want. (Oddly, JavaScript code blocks don't seem to work here. But, as you'll see shortly, you can use the ⟨img⟩ tag trick from Session 29 to trigger a JavaScript function if you need to.)

Communicating with a Java Applet

Once you have a Java applet embedded in your HTML document, your JavaScript code can actually reference that applet and access its `public` methods and properties. ("Public" is the Java equivalent of "global" in JavaScript. You can't access anything in a Java applet unless it was defined as `public` in the applet.)

Basically, the way you do this is just as simple as you might hope it would be. As you'll remember from Session 9, there is an array called `applets` inside the `document` object. As you might expect, this is simply an array of all the Java applets that are defined in the currently loaded HTML document. This means that you can access your applets either by name or via the `applets` array. For example, assuming the first applet in my HTML document is named "myApplet" and it has a public method named `getInfo()`, I could call that method with either of the following JavaScript statements.

```
document.applets[ 0].getInfo();
document.myApplet.getInfo();
```

That's really all there is to it!

You might be thinking that it would be nice if the code in a Java applet could call the JavaScript code in a Web page. Well, yes, it would be! Unfortunately, the only browsers that support this are older versions of Netscape Navigator. Netscape 6 was supposed to support it, but that feature also seems to be broken in the first release.

Working with a banner applet

20 Min. To Go

So, in order to pull all this together, let me show you a complete example. First, I need an applet to work with. When you download the Java Developer's Kit (JDK) from the Java site at `http://java.sun.com`, you'll find that amongst the stuff you get are about two dozen sample programs. So, I decided to take one of those and create a nifty banner for the Baby-Palooza Web site. (Not to worry, the folks at Sun generously allow you to copy, change, and redistribute the sample programs, just as long as you give them proper credit. Like, for example, this fine note.) The applet I started with is called "Nervous Text." This applet takes a string and animates it on the screen as if it had just finished drinking about ten pots of coffee. (In other words, the letters jump around a bit.) The basic `<applet>` tag for this applet looks like this:

```
<applet name="banner" code="NervousText.class"
    width="100%" height="50">
    <param name="text" value="Welcome to Baby-Palooza!" />
</applet>
```

The `text` parameter is simply some string that you want the applet to animate. While this is nice and simple, this applet doesn't allow for any sort of changes *after* the applet is loaded. In other words, once it's loaded, it only animates the string that you initially pass it.

What I wanted was something a bit more flexible. Specifically, I wanted to be able to change the text that was displayed along with the background color of the applet and the color of the text in the applet. So, I had to make a few minor changes to the applet to allow for these features. Now, this isn't a book on Java programming, so I'm not going to go into great detail about these changes. (If you want to see all of the changes, the final source code for the changed applet can be found in the NervousText.java file in the Session30 folder on your CD-ROM.) However, I will go over the change that was needed to reset the text that's displayed by the applet.

Using a public Java method

When the Nervous Text applet is first invoked, it reads the `text` parameter that was passed to it from the HTML file and stores it in a variable named `banner`. This means that, in order to change the text that's displayed by the applet, the value of the `banner` variable has to be changed. So, I added a simple method to do just that:

```
public void setBanner( String newBanner) {
    banner = newBanner;
    resetBanner();
    }
```

As you can see, Java's syntax is remarkably similar to that of JavaScript. The important thing to notice here, however, is that this method is defined as `public`. This means that *anyone* can call it, even the JavaScript interpreter that's running inside the Web browser. So, assuming that my `<applet>` tag is defined as shown earlier, I can call this method using a statement like this:

```
document.banner.setBanner( "Be sure to stock up on baby-wipes!");
```

and the dancing text in my banner will be changed to the string that I passed it.

As I said, I want to be able to change not only the text in my banner, but also the background color and the color of the text. This required the creation of several more `public` methods in the Java applet. But, once they were created, they could be accessed in just the same way.

The nervousBaby.htm file

**10 Min.
To Go**

Open the file nervousBaby.htm in both your HTML editor and web browser. Play with the Applet a bit in the web browser and then follow along in your HTML editor as I discuss what's going on in the paragraphs that follow.

First of all, the `<applet>` tag now includes two new parameters: `bgColor` and `textColor`. These are RGB color values (similar to the ones you learned about in Session 9) that tell the browser what colors to use for the applet's background and text color, respectively. (Note that these parameters should only include the raw color values, without any hexadecimal notation characters — that's to say, you can pass FFFFFF but not 0xFFFFFF.)

There is also a block of HTML text inside the `<applet>` tag that will be displayed if the browser does not support applets. Notice that I'm using the `<img>` tag trick from Session 29 to trigger a JavaScript function if the applet does not load. The function that's triggered then checks to see if the "application/java" MIME type is defined in the client's browser. If it is, it's a pretty good bet that the user has simply turned off Java support in her browser. In that case, the function displays a short message telling the user that if she wants to see the applet, she needs to turn Java support back on.

Next, an `onload` handler attempts to retrieve the applet's default values and display them in the form at the bottom of the page. You'll notice that this handler makes use of another function, `checkAppletStatus()`, that tells it if the applet is loaded or not. Applets can be very large and complex, so it's a good idea to make sure that they are loaded before you try to communicate with them. The process here is exactly the same as you saw in Sessions 23 and 24. The main difference is that I've added a method (`getLoadStatus()`) to this applet that will actually return a `true` when the applet is up and running. (See the NervousText.java file for the details on this method.)

Once it's been determined that the applet is ready to go, the `onload` handler retrieves the banner text, background color, and text color from the applet and places those values in the form for the user to see.

Finally, there's the form at the bottom of the page. This form contains several controls that allow the user to see the values used by the applet and to change those values. Changing a value is accomplished with a simple `onclick` handler that calls the appropriate method in the applet.

Done!

For example, to change the banner text, the user simply types the new text into the form and then clicks the Set Banner Text button. The `onclick` handler for this button extracts the text from the text box and passes it to the applet's `setBanner()` method.

REVIEW

In this session, you learned that controlling a Java applet with JavaScript is really quite simple. The only real requirement is that the Java methods and properties you want to access must be declared as public in the Java applet. Given that, and the proper Web browser, JavaScript can access any public method or property in any applet that is loaded into the HTML document.

QUIZ YOURSELF

1. Where are applets located in the Browser Object Model? (See "Communicating with a Java Applet.")

2. What do the `<param>` tags in the `<applet>` tag represent? (See "The <applet> tag")

3. In order for JavaScript to access a Java method or property, how must that method or property be declared in the Java applet? (See "Communicating with a Java Applet.")

4. How can you tell if an applet is loaded? (See "The nervousBaby.htm file")

5. How can you tell if an applet failed to load? (See "The nervousBaby.htm file")

PART

VI

Sunday Afternoon

1. What statement would you use to create a Date object that contained the date and time January 15, 2001, 9:47:25 a.m.?

2. How can your JavaScript program force the Web browser to reload an HTML document, even if that document is already in the browser's cache?

3. Using the techniques you learned in Session 19, extend the Date class to include two new methods: getDayName() and getMonthName(). The first of these should return the name of the day of the week that's held in the Date object. The second should return the name of the month that's held in the Date object.

4. As noted in Session 25, the Math object does not have a method to round a number to a specified number of digits. Create a new function named roundTo() that will let you round a value to a specified number of digits. This function should take two parameters: a number to round and the number of digits to round to. (Hint: The twoDecimals() function from Session 25 is a good starting point.)

5. How many history objects are there in a frames-based Web site?

6. What is the purpose of the location.replace() method?

7. What is the default CGI method that will be used if a <form> tag does not specify a method= attribute?

8. How can a JavaScript program in an HTML document extract the data from a post method request?

9. If one HTML file sends data to another via a get method request, where will a JavaScript program in the target HTML file be able to find this data?

10. Why must you *escape* the data that you want to send through the CGI?

11. If you need to transmit a large amount of data from an HTML document to a server-side CGI application, which CGI method should you use?

12. What does the `enabledPlugin` property of a `mimeType` object tell you?

13. What does the `length` property of a `plugin` object tell you?

14. What does the `suffixes` property of a `mimeType` object contain?

15. What is the Default Plug-in?

16. When looking at a MIME type, what do the combined characters x- signify?

17. What is (roughly) the Java equivalent of a global function or variable?

18. What does the `code=` attribute of an `<applet>` tag represent?

19. Assuming that an applet named shoppingCart contains a public method named `printCart()` what JavaScript statement would you use to call this method?

20. If this same applet were the fourth applet in your HTML document, how could you call this method via the `applets` array?

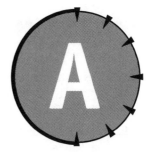

APPENDIX

A

Answers to Part Reviews

Friday Evening Review Answers

1. You can place these tags pretty much wherever you want in your HTML file. By convention, however, they usually end up at the start of an HTML file between the `<head></head>` tags.

2. A function is really just a code block with a name. You can pass it parameters to process and it can return a result.

3. There are only two Boolean values: `true` and `false`.

4. A code block is either a single line of JavaScript code or any number of lines of JavaScript code enclosed in curly braces (`{}`). As far as the JavaScript interpreter is concerned a code block is the logical equivalent of a single line of code.

5. JavaScript variable and function names must start with a dollar sign, underscore, or alphabetic character. After that, they can be any combination of letters, numbers, the underscore, or the dollar sign.

6. Two forward slashes (`//`) anywhere on a line will mark the remainder of that line as a comment. For multiple line comments, include your comments between `/*` and `*/`.

7. This is sort of a trick question. JavaScript code is just plain ASCII text, so you don't have to store it in any special file format.

8. This attribute tells the Web browser which scripting language the script is written in. If you don't specify a value for the `language=` attribute, JavaScript is assumed.

9. Simply use the `return` keyword followed by the value or expression you want to return.

10. Answers will vary. One possible solution is on your CD-ROM.

11. Answers will vary. One possible solution is on your CD-ROM.

12. This is another trick question. A function can have as few or as many parameters as you want. Don't forget however, even a function with no parameters must include a set of parentheses when you define the function and when you call the function.

13. This attribute lets you specify the location of an external file containing JavaScript source code. This code will be loaded and made available to the JavaScript in your HTML file.

14. The first expression sets up the initial state of your loop counter variable. The second expression specifies a test that will be made each time through the loop. If the test evaluates to `false`, execution of the loop will stop. The third expression is executed at the end of each trip through the loop and modifies your counter variable so that the loop will eventually terminate.

15. Global variables are available to any part of your JavaScript program. Local variables are only available in the function where they are defined. Be sure to use the `var` keyword to define local variables.

16. The value in x will be 29. The value in y will be 100. The key to this question is that there is only *one* equal sign in the conditional expression of the second statement. Because of this, y will be assigned a value of 100, the condition will evaluate to `true` (because 100 is not 0 [remember, if its not 0, it's the same as a Boolean `true`]) and so x will be assigned a value of 29.

17. JavaScript variables are loosely typed, so you can assign them any type of data.

18. Answers will vary. One possible solution is on your CD-ROM.

19. Answers will vary. One possible solution is on your CD-ROM.

20. Answers will vary. One possible solution is on your CD-ROM.

Saturday Morning Review Answers

1. The empty string is a string that contains no character data and has a length of zero. However, it is still a string as far as JavaScript is concerned.

2. The contents of `myVar` will be a string object that has one character in it: 9. Why? Well, when you concatenate the number 9 with the empty string, the JavaScript interpreter will convert the 9 into a string and then concatenate that string with the empty string. The resulting string is 9.

3. Answers will vary. One possible solution is on your CD-ROM.

4. Answers will vary. One possible solution is on your CD-ROM.

5. The Browser Object Model is a collection of JavaScript objects that represent the various parts of the Web browser and the HTML document that is loaded into it. The properties and methods of these objects allow your JavaScript program to access and manipulate the Web browser and the HTML document that these objects represent.

6. Answers will vary. One possible solution is on your CD-ROM.

7. In JavaScript, a multidimensional array is merely an array that contains other arrays. So, you would first create your subarrays, and then assign each one to the elements of the main array. The main array would then be considered multidimensional.

8. Answers will vary. One possible solution is on your CD-ROM.

9. To move through the elements of an array with named slots, use the `for . . . in` statement as described in the "Using named array elements" section of Session 6.

10. The `document` object is a property of the `window` object. While the `window` object represents a browser window or frame, the `document` object represents the actual HTML document that is loaded into that window or frame.

11. The `alert()` method is used to display simple messages in a pop-up window. The user can dismiss an alert window by clicking the supplied OK button.

12. A Link object represents an individual set of `<a href="some Web address"></a>` tags. Link objects are kept in the `links` array property of the `document` object.

13. The `document.open()` method opens the `document` object so that you can write new text into it.. You then use `document.write()` or `document.writeln()` calls to send text to the `document` object. When you have finished writing your text, you call `document.close()` to close the `document` and tell the browser to display the text you've written.

14. Answers will vary. One possible solution is on your CD-ROM.

15. The `document.write()` method writes only the text you specify. The `document.writeln()` method follows the text you specify with a new line character.

16. Answers will vary. One possible solution is on your CD-ROM.

17. The `onclick` event represents a mouse click inside an element.

18. When a window or form element is selected and will receive keystrokes, it is said to have the *focus*. An `onfocus` event is fired as soon as a window or form element becomes the focus. When a window or form control loses the focus, it has become *blurred*. An `onblur` event fires whenever a window or form element loses the focus.

19. Answers will vary. One possible solution is on your CD-ROM.

20. When used with an `<img>` tag, an `onload` event tells you that the image has actually finished loading into the Web browser.

Saturday Afternoon Review Answers

1. Answers will vary. One possible solution is on your CD-ROM.

2. The `elements` array holds all of the JavaScript objects that correspond to the controls defined in the form.

3. Calling the `reset()` method of a form is the same as clicking on that form's Reset button. It will fire an `onreset` event for the form and then reset the values in the form to their defaults.

4. The JavaScript `document.forms[2]` represents the JavaScript Form object that corresponds to the third form defined in the HTML document. (Remember, all JavaScript arrays begin numbering with zero, not one.)

5. You can check or uncheck a check box by assigning a `true` or `false` to its `checked` property.

6. Each entry in the `options` array represents a single menu item in the select list.

7. If you pluck the `value` from a password field, you'll actually get back the raw text of the password. It will not be encrypted or otherwise protected in any way.

8. The Submit and Reset buttons for a form have very specific purposes. They either submit or reset a form. You can modify their behavior slightly by writing appropriate `onsubmit` and `onreset` handlers, but you really can't change them much. A generic button, on the other hand, can do just about anything you want. (Including submitting or resetting a form!) All you have to do is write an appropriate `onclick` handler.

9. The `src` property of an Image object holds the Web address of the graphic file that is loaded into the Image object.

10. For `<img>` tags, the `onload` event fires when the graphic file specified in the `src` property has been successfully loaded by the Web browser.

11. The Web browser will fire an `onerror` event for an `<img>` tag if it cannot load the graphic file specified by the `src` property.

12. A JavaScript-based rollover works by taking advantage of two events: `onmouseover` and `onmouseout`. When the `onmouseover` event fires for your `<img>` tag, you switch the `src` property of the image to point to a new graphic that represents the "on" state of the rollover. When the `onmouseout` event fires, you switch the `src` property of the image to point back to the original image.

13. The `parseInt()` function takes a string and converts it into an actual numeric value.

14. Validating your data twice is just another example of good defensive programming.

15. People make mistakes. What? You need another reason?

16. Answers will vary, but the basic concept here is that if the data that comes from your form isn't valid, everything that is based on that data will be flawed. This can mean unfilled orders, bad demographics, and so on. A little up-front data validation can save you a world of heartache later on.

17. A cookie can hold about 4KB of data. This includes the name, the equal sign, and the value that follows it.

18. The `onunload` and `onload` events are ideal times to save and load your cookie values.

19. A cookie's expiration date tells the Web browser when that cookie should be deleted.

20. Answers will vary. One possible solution is on your CD-ROM.

Saturday Evening Review Answers

1. A class is a group of objects, all of which were created by the same constructor function. An instance is an individual object from a class.

2. When used inside a constructor function, the `this` keyword refers to the object that is being created by the constructor function.

3. First decide what type of data your custom class will represent. Second, decide what properties and methods should be included in the class. Finally, write and test the code to implement the class. This includes the constructor function and all of the implementation functions for the methods of the class.

4. You can store any type of JavaScript data in the properties of your objects.

5. A constructor function is still a function, so you can pass as few or as many parameters as you want.

6. Actually, the parameters for methods cannot be shown inside a constructor function. You should only list a method's parameters in the implementation function for the method.

7. Answers will vary, but a method is a function that is tied to a class of objects.

8. A method is a function that belongs to a class of objects. An implementation function is the code that actually carries out the tasks of a method.

9. When used inside a method, the `this` keyword refers to the object for which the method was called. For example, in the statement `myString.toUpperCase()` the value of `this` inside the `toUpperCase()` method would be the `myString` object.

10. This statement is defining a method for the object to be created by the constructor function. The method name is `action` and its implementation function is named `doAction`.

11. You can enhance HTML controls by creating custom JavaScript objects that wrap around standard Browser Object Model objects for those controls. These custom objects can contain new properties and methods that extend the capabilities of the HTML controls.

12. Simply store the original object in a property inside the wrapper object.

13. When you change the prototype for an object, every object based on that prototype gains the new property or method. This even includes objects that already exist.

14. `String.prototype.languageDirection = "leftToRight";`

15. The Object class is a class defined inside the JavaScript interpreter. All the other classes that are defined in the JavaScript language (String, Array, and so forth), and all of the classes you define, are based upon it.

16. Statements passed to the `eval()` function are evaluated and executed immediately.

17. This statement will generate an error. (There is no `documint` object.)

18. By keeping an object's JavaScript variable name inside the object, you can easily create self-referential code from that object. This is invaluable when dynamically creating JavaScript and HTML.

19. The first statement is the one that will succeed. This is because it specifically names the object and method to be called when the timer expires. The second statement will fail because, when the timer expires, the value of `this` will be undefined or completely different than it was when the `setTimeout()` statement was called.

20. Answers will vary. One possible solution is on your CD-ROM.

Sunday Morning Review Answers

1. A style sheet is a list of rules that tells the Web browser how to style the various elements in your HTML document.

2. The `<span></span>` tag is used to mark a chunk of text. You can then attach event handlers and/or styles to that chunk of text without any of the visual side effects that would come from using a different HTML tag.

3. By using an external style sheet, you can place all of your style definitions in one place. Every HTML page in your Web site can then use these definitions by linking in the external style sheet. Then, if you ever need to change a style that's used in your Web site, you simply change the external style sheet and all of your HTML pages will automatically reflect the change.

4. You use the `document.getElementById()` method to obtain an element object. You pass this method the ID of the element you want to retrieve.

5. The default unit of measurement for all of the style properties is pixels (px).

6. The `innerHTML` property represents the actual HTML code (tags and text) that is inside an element. If you change an element's `innerHTML` property, the new value will immediately appear in the browser window.

7. This property lets you tell the browser how you want an element positioned on the page (as opposed to where). A position value of `absolute` tells the browser that you will be providing the exact coordinates (via the `top`, `bottom`, `left`, and `right` properties) of where the element should be positioned.

8. The `top` object represents the actual browser window that is visible on screen. It will contain references to all of the frames that are loaded into the browser, no matter how deeply they are nested.

9. The `parent` object represents the frameset document that loaded the frame.

10. Simply compare the document's `self` object with its `parent` object. If they are the same, the document was loaded into a window by itself and not into a frameset.

11. The window will have no toolbars at all. Remember, if you specify even one feature in the `featuresList` parameter, the features you *don't* specify will all be turned off. So, if you only specify a height and width, all of the other window features will be turned off, which means no toolbars will appear in the new window.

12. Simply call the `window.close()` method for the window you want to close. If your window is in a variable named `myWindow`, you would code: `myWindow.close();`

13. Define a dummy form at the end of the HTML document that will be loaded into your new window. Then, check the `length` of the forms array in the new window. When the length of this array has become equal to the number of forms in your new window, you know that everything in the HTML document has been loaded and is ready for use.

14. If a window was opened by another window, its `opener` property will contain a reference to the window that opened it.

15. The `parseFloat()` function takes a string that contains a floating-point number and turns it into an actual numeric value.

16. This is a bit of a trick question. As I said in Session 25, as far as JavaScript is concerned, the floating-point numbers it's displaying are correct. Indeed, they *are* correct to the precision that is allowed by the way JavaScript represents floating-point numbers internally. Unfortunately, this isn't what we humans expect to see, so in order to display these values for human-consumption, they need to be rounded off using a specially written function.

17. Use a set of style rules to set the border style of the text box to none and the appearance of the cursor (when it's over the text box) to default. The text box should then appear to be just another area of text in the browser window.

18. The string "MSIE" signifies that the number that follows is the Internet Explorer version number for this Web browser.

19. You specify the version of JavaScript that is required inside the language= attribute of the <script> tag. Like this:

```
<script language="javascript1.1">
```

20. Simply enclose your JavaScript code inside a set of HTML comment markers. Like this:

```
<script language="javascript">
<!--
document.write("Hello World!");
// -->
</script>
```

Sunday Afternoon Review Answers

1. var myDate = new Date(2001, 0, 15, 9, 47, 25);
2. By calling the location.reload() method and passing it a parameter of true, you can force the Web browser to reload the HTML document that is currently loaded in the Web browser.
3. Answers will vary. One possible solution is on your CD-ROM.
4. Answers will vary. One possible solution is on your CD-ROM.

5. The answer to this question depends on how many frames there are. Basically, there will be one `history` object for each frame, plus one `history` object for the top object. Each frame's `history` object will hold a list of the pages that have been displayed in that frame. The top object's `history` object will hold a list of all pages displayed in all frames.

6. The `location.replace()` method allows you load a new HTML document and have its Web address replace the Web address of the current document in the history list. This allows you to remove interim documents from the history list for a window or frame.

7. If a `<form>` tag doesn't specify a `method=` attribute, the `get` method will be used by default.

8. This is a trick question. HTML documents don't receive data from `post` method requests.

9. The data sent will be found in the search property of the location object.

10. Certain characters (spaces, ampersands, equal signs, etc.) act as delimiters and/or stops in the CGI protocol. For these characters to pass safely through the CGI, you must replace these characters with their hexadecimal code equivalents.

11. To transmit a large amount of data, you should always use the `post` method. This method transmits the data as a single large chunk and makes it available to the CGI application as an input stream. The `get` method on the other hand, transmits the data as a part of the Web address of the CGI application. This makes it subject to any limitations that Web browsers or Web servers might put on the length of a Web address.

12. The `enabledPlugin` property of a `mimeType` object tells you if a plug-in that can handle this MIME type is installed. If there is, this property will contain a reference to the appropriate plugin object. If not, this property will be null.

13. The length property of a `plugin` object tells you how many MIME types the plug-in supports. An unnamed array of `mimeType` objects that represent these MIME types is a part of every plugin object.

14. The suffix property of a `mimeType` object holds a comma-separated list of the various file name suffixes that are associated with files of this type.

15. The Default Plug-in is a browser plug-in that attempts to handle any MIME type that no other plug-in can handle. If the Default Plug-in can't handle a MIME type, the browser will then attempt to locate and execute a helper application for that MIME type.

16. The characters x- in a MIME type mean that the MIME type is not yet a standard MIME type.

17. In Java, things that you want to be globally accessible must be declared as *public*. This is roughly (very roughly) equivalent to the *global* concept in JavaScript.

18. The code= attribute of the ⟨applet⟩ tag specifies the Java.class file that should be loaded by the browser.

19. You could call this method with the following statement:

```
document.shoppingCart.printCart();
```

20. `document.applets[ 3].printCart();`

B

What's on the CD-ROM

This appendix provides you with information on the contents of the CD-ROM that accompanies this book.

There are seven programs included on this CD:

- Acrobat Reader 4.0
- ECMAScript Standard Documentation
- BBEdit Lite and BBEdit (for Macintosh users)
- A link to Netscape Navigator (for Macintosh and Windows)
- Internet Explorer (for Macintosh and Windows)
- Self-assessment test

Also included are source code examples from the book, a PDF file containing the latest version of the ECMAScript standard, and an electronic, searchable version of the book that can be viewed with Adobe Acrobat Reader.

System Requirements

Make sure that your computer meets the minimum system requirements listed in this section. If your computer doesn't match up to most of these requirements, you may have a problem using the contents of the CD.

For Microsoft Windows 9x, Windows ME, Windows NT, or Windows 2000:

- PC with a Pentium processor running at 120 MHz or faster
- At least 64 MB of RAM

- Ethernet network interface card (NIC) or modem with a speed of at least 28,800 bps
- A CD-ROM drive — double-speed (2x) or faster

For Macintosh:

- An iMac, iBook, or any other G3 processor-based Macintosh
- At least 64MB of RAM
- A CD-ROM drive — double-speed (2x) or faster

You will need at least 150 MB of hard drive space to install all the software from this CD.

Using the CD with Microsoft Windows

To install the items from the CD to your hard drive, follow these steps:

1. Insert the CD into your computer's CD-ROM drive.
2. Open the My Computer icon on your desktop.
3. Right-click on your CD-ROM drive icon and pick the Explore item.
4. At this point, you can install any of the software you wish or you can copy the sample source code files from the CD-ROM to your local hard drive.
5. If you choose to install the third-party software, carefully follow the instructions that you see on the screen after you begin the installation process.

Using the CD with the Mac OS

To install the items from the CD to your hard drive, follow these steps:

1. Insert the CD into your computer's CD-ROM drive.
2. Double-click on the CD-ROM icon that appears on the desktop.
3. At this point, you can install any of the software you wish or you can copy the sample source code files from the CD-ROM to your local hard drive.
4. If you choose to install the third-party software, carefully follow the instructions that you see on the screen after you begin the installation process.

What's on the CD

The CD-ROM contains source code examples, applications, and an electronic version of the book. Following is a summary of the contents of the CD-ROM arranged by category.

Source code

The source code files for each session are each in a separate folder. These folders are named "Session*xx*", where *xx* is the session number. Each folder's contents have been designed to stand alone, so you can just use your browser to open the files directly from any of the session folders. There is also an images folder that contains all of the images that are used by the code in all of the session folders. If you copy the session folders to your hard drive, be sure to copy the images folder as well.

   Some of the questions in the part reviews require you to create JavaScript programs. The answers to these questions can be found in one of the "PartReview*xx*" folders on the CD-ROM. (Where *xx* is the Part Review number.)

Applications

The following applications are on the CD-ROM.

Browsers

A browser is the client software you use to access files on the Internet or to read local HTML files.

- **Internet Explorer:** A Web browser for Windows 9*x* or later and the Macintosh. Freeware. For more information: www.microsoft.com
- **Netscape Navigator:** A Web browser for Windows 9*x* or later and the Macintosh. Freeware. For more information: www.netscape.com

Editors

If you don't already have a good HTML editor, there are a couple of great ones on the CD-ROM.

- **BBEdit Lite & BBEdit Demo:** This is arguably the best text editor for the Macintosh. Two versions are provided: BBEdit Lite is a freeware editor with all the basic features you need. The BBEdit Demo is a restricted-use demonstration of the full BBEdit program. For more information: web.barebones.com

Electronic version of The ECMAScript Standard

The complete text of the ECMAScript standard is on the CD-ROM in Adobe's Portable Document Format (PDF), readable with the Adobe Acrobat Reader (also included). For more information on Adobe Acrobat Reader, go to www.adobe.com.

Electronic version of **JavaScript Weekend Crash Course**

The complete (and searchable) text of this book is on the CD-ROM in Adobe's Portable Document Format (PDF), readable with the Adobe Acrobat Reader (also included).

Self-assessment test

The self-assessment test software helps you evaluate how much you've learned from this Weekend Crash Course. It will also help you identify which sessions you've perfected, and which you may need to revisit.

Troubleshooting

If you have difficulty installing or using the CD-ROM programs, try the following solutions:

- **Turn off any antivirus software that you may have running.** Installers sometimes mimic virus activity and can make your computer incorrectly believe that it is being infected by a virus. (Be sure to turn the antivirus software back on later.)
- **Close all running programs.** The more programs you're running, the less memory is available to other programs. Installers also typically update files and programs; if you keep other programs running, installation may not work properly.

If you still have trouble with the CD, please call the Hungry Minds Customer Service phone number: (800) 762-2974. Outside the United States, call (317) 572-3993. Hungry Minds will provide technical support only for installation and other general quality control items; for technical support on the applications themselves, consult the program's vendor or author.

Index

Continued

E

Continued

Continued

Hungry Minds, Inc.
End-User License Agreement

READ THIS. You should carefully read these terms and conditions before open-ing the software packet(s) included with this book ("Book"). This is a license agreement ("Agreement") between you and Hungry Minds, Inc. ("HMI"). By open-ing the accompanying software packet(s), you acknowledge that you have read and accept the following terms and conditions. If you do not agree and do not want to be bound by such terms and conditions, promptly return the Book and the unopened software packet(s) to the place you obtained them for a full refund.

1. **License Grant.** HMI grants to you (either an individual or entity) a nonexclusive license to use one copy of the enclosed software program(s) (collectively, the "Software") solely for your own personal or business purposes on a single computer (whether a standard computer or a work-station component of a multi-user network). The Software is in use on a computer when it is loaded into temporary memory (RAM) or installed into permanent memory (hard disk, CD-ROM, or other storage device). HMI reserves all rights not expressly granted herein.

2. **Ownership.** HMI is the owner of all right, title, and interest, including copyright, in and to the compilation of the Software recorded on the disk(s) or CD-ROM ("Software Media"). Copyright to the individual programs recorded on the Software Media is owned by the author or other authorized copyright owner of each program. Ownership of the Software and all propri-etary rights relating thereto remain with HMI and its licensers.

3. **Restrictions On Use and Transfer.**

    (a) You may only (i) make one copy of the Software for backup or archival purposes, or (ii) transfer the Software to a single hard disk, provided that you keep the original for backup or archival purposes. You may not (i) rent or lease the Software, (ii) copy or reproduce the Software through a LAN or other network system or through any computer subscriber system or bulletin-board system, or (iii) modify, adapt, or create derivative works based on the Software.

    (b) You may not reverse engineer, decompile, or disassemble the Software. You may transfer the Software and user documentation on a permanent basis, provided that the transferee agrees to accept the terms and conditions of this Agreement and you retain no copies. If the Software is an update or has been updated, any transfer must include the most recent update and all prior versions.

4. **RESTRICTIONS ON USE OF INDIVIDUAL PROGRAMS.** You must follow the individual requirements and restrictions detailed for each individual program in Appendix B of this Book. These limitations are also contained in the individual license agreements recorded on the Software Media. These limitations may include a requirement that after using the program for a specified period of time, the user must pay a registration fee or discontinue use. By opening the Software packet(s), you will be agreeing to abide by the licenses and restrictions for these individual programs that are detailed in Appendix B and on the Software Media. None of the material on this Software Media or listed in this Book may ever be redistributed, in original or modified form, for commercial purposes.

5. **Limited Warranty.**

   (a) HMI warrants that the Software and Software Media are free from defects in materials and workmanship under normal use for a period of sixty (60) days from the date of purchase of this Book. If HMI receives notification within the warranty period of defects in materials or workmanship, HMI will replace the defective Software Media.

   (b) HMI AND THE AUTHOR OF THE BOOK DISCLAIM ALL OTHER WARRANTIES, EXPRESS OR IMPLIED, INCLUDING WITHOUT LIMITATION IMPLIED WARRANTIES OF MERCHANTABILITY AND FITNESS FOR A PARTICULAR PURPOSE, WITH RESPECT TO THE SOFTWARE, THE PROGRAMS, THE SOURCE CODE CONTAINED THEREIN, AND/OR THE TECHNIQUES DESCRIBED IN THIS BOOK. HMI DOES NOT WARRANT THAT THE FUNCTIONS CONTAINED IN THE SOFTWARE WILL MEET YOUR REQUIREMENTS OR THAT THE OPERATION OF THE SOFTWARE WILL BE ERROR FREE.

   (c) This limited warranty gives you specific legal rights, and you may have other rights that vary from jurisdiction to jurisdiction.

6. **Remedies.**

   (a) HMI's entire liability and your exclusive remedy for defects in materials and workmanship shall be limited to replacement of the Software Media, which may be returned to HMI with a copy of your receipt at the following address: Software Media Fulfillment Department, Attn.: *JavaScript Weekend Crash Course*, Hungry Minds, Inc., 10475 Crosspoint Blvd., Indianapolis, IN 46256, or call 1-800-762-2974. Please allow four to six weeks for delivery. This Limited Warranty is void if failure of the Software Media has resulted from accident, abuse, or misapplication. Any replacement Software Media will be warranted for the remainder of the original warranty period or thirty (30) days, whichever is longer.

(b) In no event shall HMI or the author be liable for any damages what-soever (including without limitation damages for loss of business profits, business interruption, loss of business information, or any other pecuniary loss) arising from the use of or inability to use the Book or the Software, even if HMI has been advised of the possibil-ity of such damages.

(c) Because some jurisdictions do not allow the exclusion or limitation of liability for consequential or incidental damages, the above limi-tation or exclusion may not apply to you.

7. **U.S. Government Restricted Rights.** Use, duplication, or disclosure of the Software for or on behalf of the United States of America, its agencies and/or instrumentalities (the "U.S. Government") is subject to restric-tions as stated in paragraph (c)(1)(ii) of the Rights in Technical Data and Computer Software clause of DFARS 252.227-7013, or subparagraphs (c) (1) and (2) of the Commercial Computer Software - Restricted Rights clause at FAR 52.227-19, and in similar clauses in the NASA FAR supple-ment, as applicable.

8. **General.** This Agreement constitutes the entire understanding of the par-ties and revokes and supersedes all prior agreements, oral or written, between them and may not be modified or amended except in a writing signed by both parties hereto that specifically refers to this Agreement. This Agreement shall take precedence over any other documents that may be in conflict herewith. If any one or more provisions contained in this Agreement are held by any court or tribunal to be invalid, illegal, or oth-erwise unenforceable, each and every other provision shall remain in full force and effect.

CD-ROM Installation Instructions

The sample JavaScript programs from each session are contained in a separate folder on the CD-ROM. For example, the programs from Session 1 are contained in the Session01 folder and the programs from Session20 are contained in the Session20 folder. You can load these programs directly into your Web browser from the CD-ROM, or you can copy any of the folders to your hard disk and run the programs from there.

Each of the third-party programs (Netscape Navigator, Internet Explorer, and BBEdit) is contained in their own folders. Simply run the provided setup program and follow the instructions that are provided. See Appendix B for further information.

The directory named Self-Assessment Test contains the installation program Setup_st.exe. With the book's CD-ROM in the drive, open the Self-Assessment Test directory and double-click on the program icon for Setup_st to install the self-assessment software and run the tests. The self-assessment software requires that the CD-ROM remain in the drive while the tests are running.